RELIGION
In Native North America

RELIGION
In Native North America

Edited by Christopher Vecsey

University of Idaho Press   Moscow, Idaho

In honor of Åke Hultkrantz

University of Idaho Press
Moscow, Idaho 83843
© 1990 by the University of Idaho
Design by Karla Fromm
Printed in the United States of America
95 94 93 92   5 4 3 2

Library of Congress Cataloging-in-Publication Data

Religion in native North America / edited by Christopher Vecsey.
    p.   cm.
  Includes bibliographical references.
  ISBN 0-89301-135-5
  1. Indians of North America – Religion and mythology. I. Vecsey,
Christopher.
E98.R3R44 1990
299'.7 – dc20   89-78337
                                                              CIP

CONTENTS

LIST OF ILLUSTRATIONS

Figures

PROLOGUE

Studies of American Indian Religions

Christopher Vecsey

Half a millennium has passed since the Columbian encounter. The peoples native to the Americas and non-natives, mostly from the western extremities of Eurasia, have continued to encounter each other over these five hundred years – one quarter of the time since the days of Jesus – through the circumstances of warfare and sexuality, through economic and biological exchanges, through diplomacy and insult, and through mutual observation.

We have watched each other's manners and fashions, our means of production and our modes of consumption, our eating habits and the habits of our hearts. We have noted one another's variety of colorations and musculatures, and commented on the multiple ways in which we express ourselves in speech, gesture, and art. We have judged one another as individuals, as members of nations, and as racial representatives. How do we build our homes, cure our sick, carry our loads, deliver our children, marry and divorce our spouses, choose our leaders, or dispose of our dead? Indians and non-Indians have asked these, and many other, questions of one another over these centuries.

No question, no observation, has absorbed the peoples of the post-Columbian encounters more than that of each other's religions. From the beginning to this day we have regarded the religious dimensions of one another's lives with fascination, a scrutiny of both attraction and repulsion. Native Americans and Euroamericans in contact with one another have sometimes appropriated, and sometimes disdained, the other's religious forms: expressions of belief regarding a qualitatively superior, powerful, spiritual realm symbolized by aspects of the material world; narratives concerning the coming into being of present existence and its life-and-death matters; the societally sanctioned activities that maintain effective, ritual order and harmony between humans and the universe's other persons; the way of life that carries out and makes sense of these expressions of orientation and signification. For much of our history together, Christians have tried to convince or coerce Indians to give up their religious traditions – their ways of living in a particular orientation to a spiritual realm – and to adopt Christian religious forms. In recent years, but also in the past, Indian religions have drawn non-Indian adherents and effected subtle permutations in the American way of living.

Travelers, traders, marriage partners, missionaries, captives, agents and other non-Indians have written many accounts of Indian religious phenomena over the years. In the past century professional field workers and other scholars trained in academic disciplines such as anthropology and comparative religion have attempted systematic studies of the traditions and transitions of American Indian religion. The following set of essays represents the contemporary state of scholarly understanding regarding the religious dimensions of American Indians' lives a half millennium since the first Columbian meeting.

These essays by eleven scholars from Canada, the United States, England, and Scandinavia focus on a variety of geographical points in North America, from the Inuit of the far north to the Hopis and Navajos of the American Southwest, with some comparative material from Mesoamerica and South America. There are essays about aboriginal world view and ceremony, the aboriginal patterns of Indian religious life, the new formulations and syntheses of ancient native American religiousness. There is also a heightened consciousness in these essays about the very endeavor of studying Indian religions.

The first group of four essays observes religious "tradition" in native North America: the metaphysics of Inuit shamanism; the renewing ritual of the Omaha people; the crucial place of female imagery and iconography not only among the Lakotas but across the continent. The next group of three essays are also about "traditions," but they include an historical dimension that asks how and to what extent aboriginal patterns have persisted since Euroamerican contact: how Navajo individualism has affected participation in Christianity; how Seneca Christians have fashioned a meaningful language for their hymns; how shamanic and Christian images have combined in peyote visions. These articles on American Indian religious "transitions" remind the reader that Christianity and peyotism are "traditional" Indian religions in our present day, possessing now long and meaningful histories among Indian peoples.

If the middle essays concern the Euroamerican impact on Indian religions, the next group examines the charm Indian religiousness has had over some non-Indians. These three articles take a critical look at the twentieth century fascination with Indian religions, and their authors ask what the proper, justifiable methods are of observing and making use of Indian religious forms. The authors attempt to differentiate between the "musers" and "abusers" of American Indian religions.

Åke Hultkrantz has composed the epilogue to this collection of essays, in which he sums up the past decade of scholarship concerning religion in native North America. It is fitting that the Swedish scholar should have the last word in this book, since for the last four decades he has been the world's most prolifically published observer of Indian religions. It is also fitting that with his two doctorates in ethnology and the history of religions, his career mediates whatever differences there might be between the anthropologists and comparative religionists who have written the other essays.

Nevertheless, it is unusual for Professor Hultkrantz to have concluded this collection of essays, since all the other authors wrote their pieces in order to pay homage to Hultkrantz upon his recent retirement as Professor at the Institute of Comparative Religion, University of Stockholm. Some of the authors, Daniel Merkur, Guy H. Cooper, Thomas McElwain and Paul B. Steinmetz, received their doctorates in native North American religions at the University of Stockholm under Hultkrantz's direction. The others are collegial admirers of his contribution to the study of Indian religions. In the editor's view, all of their articles bring honor to Professor Hultkrantz by representing the understanding of Indian religions at its highest caliber. Hence, it is fitting once again that Hultkrantz's epilogue should close the book, since it does honor to himself and to the subject—religion in native North America—to which he has devoted his scholarly life.

I. TRADITIONS

Through the Earth Darkly: The Female Spirit in Native American Religions

Jordan Paper

Feminine spirituality is a major aspect of native American religions, yet little has been written on the subject. Åke Hultkrantz summarized decades of research in a relatively recent essay (1983) that has been criticized in regard to some of the ethnographic sources he cited (Gill 1987, 116–28). This essay is intended to add further evidence, especially nonliterary sources and interpretation, to Hultkrantz's presentation.

Introduction: Accessing Precontact Native American Religion

The cultural context of Western scholarship develops from religions centered on sacred literature: truth is delineated by written text. Accordingly, in the study of oral traditions, reliance is placed on literary descriptions from outside the tradition under study. For those adhering strictly to the logic of traditional Western scholarship, the native American mind (excluding the literate Meso-American civilizations) was effectively blank prior to contact. This perspective assumes that the ideology of oral traditions can be known only from ethnohistorical sources, and further assumes that ethnohistorical sources may be tainted by ethnocentrism. Taking this logic to its extreme, one scholar has recently argued that the normative concept of the female spirit in a number of native American religions is due to Euro-American influence (Gill 1987), even though that influence is non-Western in nature.

3

A second inherent difficulty in the study of precontact native American religions is an assumption, derived from an uncritical understanding of ethnology, that different cultures did not share ideology (e.g., Gill 1982, 35). This assumption arises from early twentieth century ethnology, when individual scholars often devoted their careers to the study of a single culture. In contrast, modern ethnologists examine cultures within larger contexts and tend to find widespread ideological similarities (e.g., Wilbert 1987, 201–2). Although prior to contact with literate cultures there can be no "text-aided" archaeology (Hawkes 1954), modern archaeologists find equivalent ideological homogeneity from their studies of ritual artifacts and symbolism (e.g., Brose 1985, 67).

For the study of the precontact understanding of female spirits, there are further difficulties. All of the early ethnohistorical sources were written by males from a patriarchal culture, many from a misogynist, sixteenth- to seventeenth-century Jesuit subculture (Paper, in press). Early ethnology tended to be equally oblivious to the feminine aspects of religion, both female rituals and female spirits. That approach resulted in a highly skewed understanding, particularly in the case of native American cultures, which have a considerable amount of gender specialization, both economic and ritual.

Furthermore, where there is gender specialization in religion, understanding will not necessarily be shared with someone of the inappropriate gender. Given the male orientation of Western values, female ethnologists, with few exceptions (e.g., Underhill 1979), preferred to concentrate on male culture. Only recently has there developed an awareness of Western scholarship that an exclusively female mode of religiousness, only accessible to female observers, exists within native American religious traditions (e.g., Brown 1985, 8).

South America: The Image of the Female Deity

Among Amazonian cultures unaffected by Western culture prior to this century, the primary spirit for the women of the northern Peruvian Aguaruna is Nugkui (Brown 1985, 50). She is interpreted as the "earth mother [or mothers]" by Harner (1972, 70) and, more narrowly, the "feminine undersoil master of garden soil and pottery clay" by Whitten (1978, 843–45). Nugkui not only controls horticulture, domestic animals and clay for pottery, the foci of the female economy, but she also controls the availability of at least some game animals. She inhabits deep caves as well as garden soil.

The male complement of Nugkui is Etsa, the sun, important to male economic roles. Mediating between Nugkui and Etsa is Tsugki, a powerful female water spirit (or her father). She is the source of shamanistic power, appearing in one of her male or female animal manifestations. Her sexual ambiguity is probably due to individualistic visions. Other spirits, who appear to those seeking visions, are the *ajútap,* ancient warriors who appear in theriomorphic guise or as balls of fire. Among recently converted Aguaruna Christians, Apajuí (Our Father) has become a high god ruling over Nugkui, Tsugki, Etsa and the *ajútap* (Brown 1985, 52–53).

For the area just west of the Aguaruna, early Spanish documents from Peru record several major female deities worshipped by both men and women in the period of initial contact:

It was a common thing among the Indians to adore the fertile earth . . . which they called Pachamama [literally: Earth Mother], offering her *chicha* [corn beer] by spilling it on the ground, as well as coca and other things. (Muria 1590, in Silverblatt 1987, 24)

[From a confession manual] . . . do you adore the clouds and speak to them imploring, "O Mother Sea [Mamacocha], from the end of the world, make it rain and form dew." (Pérez Bocanegra 1631, in Silverblatt 1987, 48)

Pachamama's daughters included crops, e.g., Saramama (Maize) and Axomama (Potatoes), and parts of the Earth: Coyamama (Metal) and Sañumama (Clay).

Of the gold and silver Incan figurines which survived the melting down of vast numbers of images following the Spanish conquest, the most common are small female and male figurines, ranging in height from five to twenty centimeters (fig. 1). Diagnostic features of the female figures include arms folded under the breast and straight hair parted in the middle to the small of the back. One female figurine, found in situ with the mummy of a young girl, was dressed in a mantle and headdress (Emmerick 1965, 50–51). These figurines are quite widespread, from Meso-America to the southern Andes. The female images also encompass a nearly four millennium timespan. The Incan metal female figurines have the same diagnostic features as small pottery figurines (fig. 2) found in large numbers in Valdivia Phase, Period B sites, ca. 2300–2200 B.C.E. (Meggers 1966, 38–41).

Saramama and Axomama were represented by images of corn and potatoes. We know that Pachamama was represented by an image, although there is no recording of its appearance. The common Andean female figurine, found in burials from the coast to the highlands, may very well represent Pachamama.

From a comparative perspective, elaborate burials as found in the Andes often include offerings to the media of the burial. In China, when offerings are made at a grave site, offerings are also made to the deity of the earth, represented by name or image. By a process of elimination, Pachamama is the most likely subject of the Andean female images, although such an identification must remain inconclusive.

Hence, from the present to the beginning of contact, there is evidence in western South America from the Earth Mother as a major deity. Should the ubiquitous female image found in the Andes represent Pachamama, then this understanding is at least four millennia in age.

North America:
The Sign of the Female Deity

Since the French priests in New France were less interested in the Inquisition than the Spanish priests in Peru, manuals of native beliefs for inquisitors were not produced. Indeed, the French Jesuits seemed oblivious to the female aspects of religion, even those who resided among the gynecocratic Iroquoian cultures (Leacock 1978). For these reasons, there is no explicit literary evidence for female spirits at the time of contact. However, there is explicit graphic evidence from the petroglyphic record.

In northeastern Iowa, at the base of a bluff bordering a stream which flows into the Upper Iowa River, there is a small tapering, narrow cave (figs. 3, 4). The sandstone walls of the cave are exclusively covered with a repeatedly engraved petroglyphic image: a vertical ellipse transversed by a vertical line (fig. 5). Similar images of Aurignacian date (ca. 30,000 B.P.) in European caves are generally accepted as representations of vulvae (Sieveking 1979, 76). Although the Iowa engravings cannot be dated or definitely ascribed to a particular culture, by the early historical period, the area was an interface between Siouan and Algonkian-speaking cultures. The images were probably created by speakers of one of these two language families.

At another cultural interface, between Algonkian and Iroquoian-speaking cultures, the same symbol is found in a graphic context that allows for a definite interpretation. The Peterborough Petroglyphs are found on a large, exposed rock slab in southcentral Ontario covered with a large number of petroglyphic representations (see Vastokas and Vastokas 1973). On one side there is a large ithyphalic male figure, and on the other, a large female figure. The latter design centers around a natural oval hole in the rock which forms the vagina of the figure (fig. 6). Elsewhere on the rock, a similar symbol to those engraved on the walls of the Iowa cave is found as a pecked oval about a natural linear fissure (fig. 7). The graphic relationship between the female figure and the sign on the same rock, both using holes in the stone to indicate the vagina, clearly indicates that the sign represents the vulva.

Among Algonkian Ojibwe speakers in northwestern Ontario, following a graphic tradition of indeterminate age exemplified in the Midewiwin birch bark scrolls, the sign for the vagina when rapidly drawn is precisely the same symbol found in the Iowa cave: an ellipse open at the bottom with a transverse vertical line extending past the opening (fig. 8). The Iowa cave in the shape of the human vagina, with walls covered with repeated engraved symbols of the vulva, is subject to but a single interpretation: the cave is a vagina of the earth. Hence, Earth, in the ideational system represented by the cave as symbol, is the life-giving female cosmic creator; Earth is the mother of all life.

The Earth Mother

The theology of the Amazonian Aguaruna described above, in both its essentials and in many details, is also found in North America; for example, among the Ojibwe-speaking Anishnabe. The male complement of Aki, the earth, is Geezis, the sun. The Manitou, the spirits who are the sources of shamanistic power, include Missipisiw (Rogers 1962, D6), the underwater "panther," and theriomorphic spirits, who may also appear as balls of fire (Landes 1968, 30). Following Christian influence, "Grandfather," "Creator," and more recently, "Our Father," have been added as a high god (Paper, 1983).

However, in the ideology of the pan-Indian Sacred Pipe, at least fifteen hundred years in age, female and male symbolism and ritual orientation

Figure 1. Incan gold alloy figurine.

Figure 2. Valdivian pottery figurine.

Figure 3. Iowa cave: entrance.

Figure 4. Iowa cave: interior.

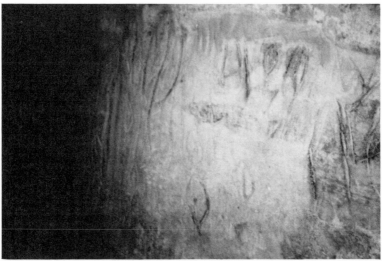

Figure 5. Iowa cave: petroglyphs.

Figure 6. Peterborough Petroglyphs: large female figure.

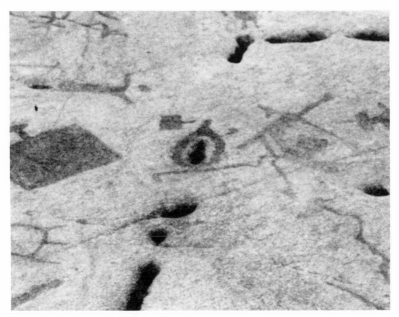

Figure 7. Peterborough Petroglyphs: vulva sign.

Figure 8. Contemporary Ojibwe symbol for vagina.

continue in equal balance (Paper 1988). When smoke offerings are made to numinous beings, they are offered in the directions of the understood cosmos: nadir, zenith, and the four directions. In virtually all ethnographic recordings of this ideology, the nadir is identified as Earth, the primary female numinous entity.

In the contemporary oral traditions of those North American native cultures with which I have some familiarity, Earth is understood as the bringer-forth and sustainer of life. The symbolic anthropomorphization of the earth extends to all its parts. Streams and rivers are understood as the veins and arteries of Earth; water is her life-giving fluid. Sacred herbs, such as sweetgrass, are understood as the hair of Earth; hence, sweetgrass is braided in the northern native American hair style. Since this understanding is in accordance with the ethnographic record, and since this understanding is not Western, it is logical to assume that the understanding is aboriginal.

Further support for assuming this understanding is precontact derives from linguistic analysis. The direct linkage between human females as mothers and Earth as Mother is found in language. In the Algonkian Ojibwe language, the words for Earth and the vagina, respectively *aki* and *akitun*, share the same root. The suffix *tun* signifies movement. Hence, in Ojibwe, either Earth is literally a "still vagina," or the female reproductive organ is literally an "active Earth." It would be illogical to assume that Christian influence introduced a non-Christian concept into the etymological structure of a language.

In emerging from "sweat-lodge" ritual or when smoking the Sacred Pipe, it is common in a number of native North American traditions to state, in translation, "All my relations." All living entities, including spiritual beings, are related. Accordingly, when spirits are spoken to, they are addressed as relatives. As honored and reverenced relatives, the spirits are called "Father" and "Mother," "Grandfather" and "Grandmother," the vocatives varying among cultures. Relational terms and nominatives are not used together in many traditions, such as Ojibwe. It is considered disrespectful to address a spirit with other than the relational term. Hence, Earth when addressed is called "Mother" or "Grandmother."

Transformation is a major aspect of ritual and ideology. It is generally understood that shamanism can involve the transformation of the shaman. Similarly, in shamanic cultures, the spirits can transform themselves. This is well known in regard to culture hero/trickster figures, for example, Nanabush, but not well understood for the primary spiritual figures. In regard to the latter, the principle involved is not transformation per se but rather cosmic linkages and theriomorphic manifestations.

Earth (Sea in some coastal cultures) and Sun in many cultures are paired couples in regard to creation, but Moon (excepting the few cultures in which Moon is male) and Sun are also paired as celestial procreative spirits (as are Evening Star and Morning Star in Pawnee culture). In some myth cycles (e.g., versions of Nanabush), Moon as mother of the Earth can be interpreted. In these traditions, the terminology of Moon as Grandmother and Earth as Mother has a specific logic. Women are equated both to Earth as birthers and nurturers and to Moon in regard to their cyclic flow. Hence, Earth and Moon are also equated from the standpoint of elementary logic.

The major theriomorphic representations of Earth include Bear, Bison, and Turtle; of Moon, Owl. The black bear, particularly her fat, was an essential food source. The bear, of course, is also in many respects more similar to humans than other animals in regard to diet, skeleton, posture, and intelligence. As Earth, the bear dens up and sleeps through the winter. In spring, as Earth wakes to life, the bear emerges from a cave with new life, her cubs. Emerging from Earth, Bear is equated with her. Hence, Bear is not only a source of sustenance, but the major life-giving or healing female spirit.

All the animals which sustain humans, in some respects, are manifestations of Earth. For much of North America, the major animal of sustenance is the bison. The tendency of bison to wallow in dust undoubtedly enhances the symbolism. For the Siouan-speaking Lakota, we have one of the very few ethnographic recordings of the native American oral traditions discussed in this paper:

> The buffalo were given by the Spirit of the Earth to the Indians. The Spirit of the Earth and of the buffalo are the same. . . . An Indian went to a hole in the ground and found the buffalo. They were given to him for his food. He drove some of them up on the earth. From these came all the buffalo. (Short Bull in Walker 1980, 144)

These linkages of Bear and Bison to Earth are graphically represented in a cave near the one previously described, where the late archaeologist, Clark Mallam, found all three symbols interrelated:

One rock shelter, about a mile from the one I visited with you, is also loaded with the vulva designs, but, oddly, its perimeters are bounded by four bison figures. And, deep in the recesses of one fissure, tucked tightly up on the wall of a high ledge, are three bear paws, two on the north and one on the south. If you sit on the narrow ledge and face the entrance it is possible to extend your arms laterally and easily put your hands on the bear paws. (Clark Mallam, letter to the author, August 1985)

In many recreation myths, the earth is rebuilt on the back of a turtle; hence, the name for North America in most traditions, Turtle Island. In some Anishnabe traditions, the graphic sign for *aki* is a turtle. Turtle is the major helping spirit in the Ojibwe "Shaking Tent" ritual (cf. Landes 1968, 48).

Bear, Bison, etc., also have male spiritual aspects. Bear, especially the grizzly bear, and the bull bison symbolize male warrior potency. The gender of spirits is not absolute but relative to the concern of the one summoning or approaching them.

Contact with and later domination by Christian cultures over a period of several hundred years have influenced native religious traditions in a number of ways (Hultkrantz 1980; Paper 1983). The major effect has been the patriarchalization of native cultures. The shift from an egalitarian socioeconomic pattern to a male-dominated one, following the pattern of the dominant culture, has affected religious practice (e.g., Wallace 1969, passim) and ideology (see Tooker 1970, 148–49).

One effect of the patriarchalization over much of North America has been the use of a single vocative, "Grandfathers," for both male and female spirits, in place of the dual "Grandmothers, Grandfathers." (In central British Columbia, among the last areas in North America to come under Christian control, the assumed earlier pattern still continues among elders.) Also, there has been a tendency to adopt the concept of a male "Creator," due to the stress on Genesis in missionary teaching, as a counter to the claim by Christian missionaries that native people are "Godless." This has confused some nonnative scholars into assuming there are no important female spirits.

A second effect of Christian domination was that female rituals became more esoteric than those of males. When the practice of native religion was made illegal in Canada and the United States, female rituals went further underground than the better known mixed gender and male rituals. Female fasting, puberty rituals (except among southern Athapascan-speaking cultures), Full Moon ceremonies, and menstrual rituals are virtually undocumented in the ethnographic literature, yet continue in the present (e.g., Ridington 1983).

The most important effect on spiritual understanding was that female spirits, such as Eve in premodern Christian teachings, became understood as evil. The missionaries insisted that all native religious practices were the work of the devil. These teachings were enhanced by the tendency to turn power destructively inward in oppressed cultures (Paper 1980). However, the fact that the primary healing spirits were female must have also been a factor in the reversal of traditional values. In Anishnabe culture, the use of spiritual power became understood as negative sorcery and was termed "Bearwalking" (for references, see Dewdney 1975, 116–22). Owl, whose feathers were an important symbol on a number of Sacred Pipes prior to the twentieth century (Paper 1988) and who mediated between the living and the dead in the Midewiwin (Hoffman 1891, 171), became understood as a negative symbol of death. The decline of feminine spirituality was paralleled by a rapid decline in the sociopolitical role and status of women.

In summary, in native religious traditions from North to South America, Earth is understood as a numinous being of procreation and nurture. The details of this general understanding vary from culture to culture, subculture to subculture, but the essentials agree. From the Earth Mother's surface grow the plants essential to life and health, from clefts in her body emerge the game animals which share their life with the people, from her veins issue the life-giving fluid of water, from her cycles and those of her celestial and nighttime aspect, Grandmother Moon, come the rhythms of women's bodies. Within Earth's narrow, dark, warm, moist crevices, humans encounter her essence. Earth is the epitome of motherhood.

Women mirror Earth. Their bodies ebb and flow with Earth's and Moon's rhythms. Each month women's spiritual potency increases as their blood flows and merges with Earth, the source of their special power. It is the women, who as Earth, bring forth life from clefts in their bodies; who nurture new life with fluid from their breasts; who gather the herbs and plants and raise the corn and beans essential for life; whose wisdom quietly flows from the stillness of Earth and Moon, so different from male energy, which springs from the lightning flash (Thunderbird/West Wind) and the burning Sun. Within woman's narrow, dark, warm, moist crevice, males encounter her essence.

Women understand Earth from the very nature of their lives. Men must realize Earth indirectly: from the beat of the drum, Earth's heartbeat; from visions of her theriomorphic manifestations, Bear, Owl, Bison, Turtle, etc.; from the food and water she provides that are essential to life; and, most importantly, from women, men's mothers, grandmothers, sisters and wives.

BIBLIOGRAPHY

Brose, David S. 1985. The woodland period. In *Ancient art of the woodland Indians*, ed. D. S. Brose, J. A. Brown, and D. W. Penney. New York: Harry N. Abrams, Inc.

Brown, Michael F. 1985. *Tsewa's gift: Magic and meaning in an Amazonian society*. Washington: Smithsonian Institution Press.

Dewdney, Selwyn. 1975. *The sacred scrolls of the southern Ojibway*. Toronto: University of Toronto Press.

Emmerick, André. 1965. *Sweat of the sun and tears of the moon*. Seattle: University of Washington Press.

Gill, Sam D. 1982. *Native American religions: An introduction*. Belmont, Calif.: Wadsworth Publishing Co.

1987. *Mother earth: An American story*. Chicago: University of Chicago Press.

Harner, Michael J. 1972. *The Jivaro: People of the sacred waterfalls*. New York: Natural History Press.

Hawkes, Christopher. 1954. Archeological theory and method: Some suggestions from the Old World. *American Anthropologist* 56:155–158.

Hoffman, W. J. 1891. The Mide'wiwin or "Grand Medicine Society" of the Ojibwa. *7th Annual Report of the Bureau of Ethnology: 1885–86*:143–300.

Hultkrantz, Åke. 1980. The problem of christian influence on northern Algonkian eschatology. *Studies in Religion* 9:161–184.

1983. The religion of the goddess in North America. In *The book of the goddess*, ed. C. Olson. New York: Crossroad.

Landes, Ruth. 1968. *Ojibwa religion and the Mide'wiwin*. Madison: University of Wisconsin Press.

Leacock, Eleanor. 1978. Women's status in egalitarian society: Implications for social evolution. *Current Anthropology* 19:247–275.

Meggers, Betty J. 1966. *Ecuador*. New York: Frederick A. Praeger.

Murúa, Martín de. 1590. *Historia del origen y geneología real de los Incas*.

Paper, Jordan. 1980. From shaman to mystic in Ojibwa religion. *Studies in Religion* 9:185–200.

1983. The post-contact origin of an American Indian high god: The suppression of feminine spirituality. *American Indian Quarterly* 7,4:1–24.

1988. *Offering smoke: The sacred pipe and native American religion*. Moscow: University of Idaho Press.

In press. The persistence of female deities in patriarchal China. *Journal of Feminist Studies in Religion*.

Pérez Bocanegra, Juan. 1631. *Ritual formulario e institucíon de curas para administrar a los naturales,* in Silverblatt.

Ridington, Robin. 1983. Stories of the vision quest among Dunne-za women. *Atlantis* 9,1:68–78.

Rogers, Edward S. 1962. *The Round Lake Ojibwa.* Toronto: Royal Ontario Museum.

Sieveking, Ann. 1979. *The cave artists.* London: Thames and Hudson.

Silverblatt, Irene. 1987. *Moon, sun, and witches: Gender ideologies and class in Inca and colonial Peru.* Princeton: Princeton University Press.

Tooker, Elizabeth. 1970. *The Iroquois ceremonial of midwinter.* Syracuse: Syracuse University Press.

Underhill, Ruth. 1979. *Papago woman.* New York: Holt, Rinehart and Winston.

Vastokas, Joan M. and Romas K. Vastokas. 1973. *Sacred art of the Algonkians: A study of the Peterborough petroglyphs.* Peterborough, Ont.: Mansard Press.

Walker, James R. 1980. *Lakota belief and ritual.* Ed. R. J. DeMallie and E. A. Jahner. Lincoln: University of Nebraska Press.

Wallace, Anthony F. C. 1969. *The death and rebirth of the Seneca.* New York: Alfred A. Knopf.

Whitten, Norman E., Jr. 1978. Ecological imagery and cultural adaptability: The Canelos Quichua of eastern Ecuador. *American Anthropologist* 80:836–859.

Receiving the Mark of Honor: An Omaha Ritual of Renewal

Robin Ridington

Introduction

One of the five Dhegiha Siouan Tribes, the Omaha were farmers and bison hunters in lands bordering the middle and upper Missouri River during early historic times. Today they occupy a reservation in eastern Nebraska. During their buffalo hunting days, the Omahas practiced an elaborate ceremonial order designed to preserve the unity of both tribe and cosmos (Ridington in press b). One of these ceremonies included ritually tattooing a "Blue Spot" or "Mark of Honor" on the daughter of a man who had counted a hundred special gifts or sacrifices for the benefit of the tribe. The Omahas have continued to adapt their ceremonial life to modern social and economic realities in a form that maintains the essential spirit of a concern or tribal unity and well-being. Despite immense pressures to assimilate into white culture in its entirety, the Omahas continue to be a strong and coherent people. Although the tattooing ceremony no longer takes place, the women who participated in it are still respected and retain the pride and honor bestowed on them (Ridington 1987).

Much of what outsiders know today about traditional Omaha ceremony was recorded by Alice Fletcher and Francis La Flesche during the last decades of the nineteenth century. Francis La Flesche was himself a member of the tribe and participated in many of the ceremonies. They reported their findings in *The Omaha Tribe*, the 27th Annual Report of the Bureau
20

of American Ethnology, published in 1911. Their work is one of the great classic ethnographic accounts of native American tribal life because it provides detailed description of a complex ceremonial order and also because it explains that order in relation to symbolic categories that underlie Omaha thought and experience.

This paper is a recontextualization of information provided by Fletcher and La Flesche in *The Omaha Tribe*. I will describe the order, context, and symbolism of a ceremony in which the daughter of a man being initiated into the *Hon'hewachi* or "Night Dance Society" receives *Xthexe*, the tattooed Mark of Honor. The ceremony is a ritual of renewal and transformation, in which the girl becomes a *Ni'kagahi wau* or "Woman Chief" (Fletcher and La Flesche 1911, 494). In ceremony she becomes a point of focus for the union of male and female cosmic forces.

An image of this cosmic union underlies much of Omaha thought and experience. Their clans are divided into moieties called "Sky People" and "Earth People." The *Huthuga,* the tribe's camp circle during the annual buffalo hunt, brought these two halves together in a union for all to see. "Myths," according to Fletcher and La Flesche, "relate that human beings were born of a union between the Sky People and the Earth People." This union, they say, "was conceived to be necessary to the existence of the tribe." The ceremony for tattooing the Mark of Honor perfectly aligns the girl's body with male and female cosmic forces. The ceremony channels the energy of creation into the life of the tribe, centering the girl who is to become a woman of earth, directly beneath the zenith point, the sky's center and the center of day. It centers her and through her renews the spirit of life. "By the union of Day, the above, and Night, the below," according to Fletcher and La Flesche, "came the human race and by them the race is maintained." "The tattooing," they say, is "an appeal for the perpetuation of all life and of human life in particular" (Fletcher and La Flesche 1911, 507).

The Hon'hewachi Society

Fletcher and La Flesche give the literal meaning of Hon'hewachi as "in the night-dance." A man obtains membership in this society or "order of honorary chieftainship" by giving away a hundred or more gifts or actions known as *Wathin'ethe*. Fletcher and La Flesche translate *Wathin'ethe* literally as *wa* (thing having power), *thin* (nothing), *the* (to make or to cause). They say that the symbolic meaning of the name implies that the

Wathin'ethe are sacred gifts or sacrifices "for which there is no material
return but through which honor is received." These acts or gifts must
"have relation to the welfare of the tribe by promoting internal order
and peace, by providing for the chiefs and keepers, by assuring friendly
relations with other tribes." They are sacred "acts and gifts which do not
directly add to the comfort and wealth of the actor or donor, but which
have relation to the welfare of the tribe" (Fletcher and La Flesche 1911,
202–3). Actions of the Hon'hewachi can be seen to move with a rhythm
the Omahas associate with a personal emotion and mythic reality that
reveals the order of the cosmos. In particular, a man entering the
Hon'hewachi Society gives away so that the union of male and female
principles may be felt throughout the tribe. Members of the Hon'hewachi
are called Hon'ithaethe, "those blessed by the night" (Fortune 1932, 148).

According to Fletcher and La Flesche, the true meaning of the name
Hon'hewachi is deeply rooted in Omaha philosophy and cosmology.
"Wachi," they say, "does not mean 'dance' in our sense of the word but
dramatic rhythmic movements for the expression of personal emotion or
experience, or for the presentation of mythical teachings." In colloquial
Omaha usage, wachi also refers to the physical act of love, "rhythmic
movements of the night" (Koontz personal communication). "Hone'he,"
Fletcher and La Flesche add, "refers to creative acts, for through the mysterious power of Wakon'da [the creative principle in Siouan cosmology]
night brought forth day." "Night was therefore the mother of day, and the
latter was the emblem of all visible activities and manifestations of life"
(Fletcher and La Flesche 1911, 493–94).

Fletcher and La Flesche say that to the Omaha ear, the rhythm of
Hon'hewachi songs is a distinctive signature of the Society's particular
emotions of revelation and compassion, just as the Hethu'shka and Wa'wan
songs are respectively distinctive of actions in defense of the tribe and of
the intertribal alliances symbolized by the Wa'wan or Pipe Ceremony. The
activities of teh Hon'hewachi Society and the rhythm of their songs evoke
an emotion the Omaha people associate with the complementary nature
of night and day. The Hon'hewachi initiate would compose a song "which
had to conform to the rhythmic standard of the initial Hon'hewachi song."
The song should reflect the initiate's personal experience of "a dream or
vision that came in answer to his supplication" (Fletcher and La Flesche
1911, 502–3).

Hon'hewachi rites carry with them the idea of "bringing into prominence to be seen by all the people as something distinctive" (Fletcher and

La Flesche 1911, 219). They carry with them an invocation of powers revealed by "Night, the great mother force," the helping compassion and pity of the night force. "The feminine cosmic force," Fletcher and La Flesche report, "was typified not only by night but by the heavenly bodies seen by night." Its complement is the masculine cosmic force, "symbolized by day and by the sun" (Fletcher and La Flesche 1911, 494). The day force is typified not only by day but by the sun, a heavenly body seen by day. A daughter of the Night Dance Society initiate receives this body's heavenly power in ceremony for the benefit of the tribe. Although tattooing the Mark of Honor is a ritual within the overall Night Dance Society initiation ceremony, it also provides an opportunity for people to visualize and enact the symbolic and ceremonial union of the complementary male and female forces that give life to the tribe.

The Omaha tribe is made up of moieties call Hon'gashenu or the Earth People and Inshta'thunda or the Sky People, associated respectively with female and male cosmic principles. On the annual buffalo hunt, the Omaha tribe formed a camp circle called the *Huthuga* in which the Inshta'thunda camped to the north and the Hon'gashenu to the south. The Huthuga was open to the east. "Through it, the people went forth in quest of game, and through it they returned with their supply of food, as one enters the door of one's home" (Fletcher and La Flesche 1911, 138). The tribe as a whole views itself as a union of complementary opposites that is like sunlight streaming through trees onto an earth that is "mottled as by shadows." Hon'hewachi songs and rites focus attention on the cosmic union of these male and female principles. They dramatize the creative acts through which the Omahas realize themselves as a people and through which "night brought forth day" (Fletcher and La Flesche 1911, 494). They bring these acts into prominence to be seen by all the people as something distinctive. Hon'hewachi rites include tattooing *Xthexe,* the Mark of Honor, on the unmarried daughter of an initiate (Fletcher and La Flesche 1911, 502).

Waxthe'xe – The Sacred Pole of the Omaha Tribe

The name *Xthexe,* the Mark of Honor, means "mottled as by shadows" (Fletcher and La Flesche 1911, 219). The name *Waxthe'xe* refers to the Sacred Pole by which the Omaha represented themselves as a people during much of the nineteenth century. The Pole's name Waxthe'xe implies, "the power to bestow honor or distinction" (Fletcher and La Flesche 1911, 494). The name also "signifies that the power to give the right to possess this 'mark of honor' was vested in the Pole" (Fletcher and La Flesche 1911, 219). The name Waxthe'xe was also given to "the ancient pole of cedar [which] according to tradition and myth, was allied to ceremonies connected with Thunder and with the creation of the human race" (Fletcher and La Flesche 1911, 494). The name Waxthe'xe represents the power to bestow honor or distinction, the same power by which an initiate to the Hon'hewachi society has the Mark of Honor tattooed upon his daughter. Fletcher and La Flesche translate Waxthe'xe literally as, Wa, "power, the power of motion, of life," and Xthexe, "mottled as by shadows." The word Xthexe, according to Fletcher and La Flesche, "has also the idea of bringing into prominence to be seen by all the people as something distinctive" (Fletcher and La Flesche 1911, 219).

The Pole and its rites were kept by a member of the Honga or Leader Clan during the tribe's days as buffalo hunters. Today, the story of its origin is widely known among members of the other clans. The last keeper of the Pole, Shudenachi (Yellow Smoke), gave the Pole's story over to the keeping of Alice Fletcher and Francis La Flesche who published it in *The Omaha Tribe* (Ridington in press a). The story tells of a chief's son who discovers the Pole under the influence of the "night force." He finds a mysterious luminous tree at night beneath the "motionless star" or pole star. Fletcher and La Flesche remind us that, "the feminine cosmic force was typified not only by night but by the heavenly bodies seen by night" (Fletcher and La Flesche 1911, 494). The luminous tree appeared to the chief's son in a place of power beneath the center of the night sky and the compassion of the night force in the same way that Hon'hewachi songs are revealed to an initiate into the "Night Dance Society." In the story, the young man's father tells his son that the luminous tree is where the Thunders come to rest at night. From this tree the young man, his father, and the tribal elders, cut Waxthe'xe, the Sacred Pole of the Omaha tribe.

Xthexe – The Mark of Honor

Xthexe is also the name given to the Mark of Honor tattooed on a girl whose father qualifies for membership in the Hon'hewachi Society. The Mark of Honor consists of cosmic symbols tattooed in blue on the forehead and throat of the Hon'hewachi initiate's daughter. The "blue spot" on her forehead represents the sun. The star sign at her throat "is emblematic of the night, the great mother force," according to Fletcher and La Flesche. "Its four points," they say, represent "the life-giving winds into the midst of which the child was sent through the ceremony of Turning the Child" (Fletcher and La Flesche 1911, 505). These two cosmic signs represent the complementary principles of night and day that are fundamental to Omaha thought and experience.

Membership in the Hon'hewachi represents a man's "recognition of Night, of the feminine force or principle" (Fletcher and La Flesche 1911, 507). Every member of the Hon'hewachi Society must compose a song in the Hon'hewachi rhythm. The song must express the initiate's personal experience, and frequently it refers to "a dream or vision that came in answer to his supplication" (Fletcher and La Flesche 1911, 503). Initiation into the Hon'hewachi Society represents a man's contact with "dramatic rhythmic movements for the expression of personal emotion or experience." It places him in position "for the presentation of mythical teachings" (Fletcher and La Flesche 1911, 393) and recognizes that he has been blessed by the night. The Hon'hewachi songs, ceremonies, and symbols "refer to the creative cosmic forces typified by night and day, the earth and the sky" (Fletcher and La Flesche 1911, 495). They empower him to present mythic teachings to the tribe, representing "the fundamental ideas on which the tribal organization rested" (Fletcher and La Flesche 1911, 495).

The Hon'hewachi Feasts

The ritual of tattooing the Mark of Honor is part of a four-day set of ceremonies initiating a girl's father into the Hon'hewachi Society. In their speeches, society members address their fellows as Hon'ithaethe, those blessed by the night (Fortune 1932, 148). The ceremonies begin with Watha'wa, the Feast of the Count, in which the initiate recounts from memory the hundred or more gifts or sacrifices he has made over a period of years. During the feasting he must also give away the entire contents of his lodge. At the climax of the ceremonies he gives his daughter to the life-giving power of the sun.

The gifts and sacrifices of the initiate's count are brought to mind by a bundle of willow sticks he has been accumulating over the years. Each stick represents one of his *Wathin'ethe* gifts. Chiefs from each of the two sides of the *Huthuga,* the Hon'gashenu (Earth People) and Inshta'thunda (Sky People), sit at the back of the lodge. They are *Ni'kagahi U'shu,* chiefs who have counted the largest number of Wathin'ethe. They face east toward the entrance of the lodge and the rising of the sun, the round sun. The chiefs represent the female and male principles that combine to make up the tribe as a whole. Each chief (*U'zhu*) is called a "chief to the left" because of the direction in which he passes the bundle.

First the Hon'gashenu U'zhu takes the bundle and passes it to his left in the direction of the sun's travel. He passes it to his complement, the *Inshta'thunda U'zhu.* The bundle moves from hand to hand around the circle of Hon'ithaetha, those blessed by the night. They are seated according to the rank of their Wathin'ethe gifts. When the bundle has completed its circle and returned to the Hon'gashenu U'zhu, the herald carries it back to the initiate sitting at the eastern entrance of the lodge. The initiate must then begin to "count" his hundred gifts entirely from memory and without error or hesitation. Fletcher and La Flesche report that, "it was a severe tax on a man's memory, for these gifts often extended over a period of ten or twenty years" (Fletcher and La Flesche 1911, 498).

The Feast of the Count is followed by the Feast of the Hon'hewachi. On the evening before the tattooing, chiefs of the tribe and the Hon'ithaethe assemble to receive the record of the initiate's count. They sing a song in recognition of the candidate's steps toward initiation. The rhythm of this song is a model for all other songs in the Hon'hewachi rhythm, indicating that the Hon'ithaethe accept the initiate's count of one hundred Wathin'ethe gifts. Many of these gifts are the products of women's labor, and because of this they represent the female cosmic principle. The song's words sum up the purpose that brings the society's members together, meaning literally:

See you
As the result or Outcome of a decision
Coming
They
To look into – to consider – to judge
Coming for that purpose
They. (Fletcher and La Flesche 1911, 502)

As the chiefs and Hon'ithaethe sing the final stanzas of the "judgment song," the initiate's daughter, the young woman who will receive the Mark of Honor, enters and dances before them. She will send her children into the midst of the winds and with the other "woman chiefs" will dance at meetings of the Hon'hewachi. She will carry Xthexe, "mottled as by shadows," among her people when she is an old woman. Her dance before the Hon'hewachi members, Fletcher and La Flesche tell us, "dramatized the awakening of the feminine element – an awakening everywhere necessary for a fulfillment in tangible form of the life-giving power" (Fletcher and La Flesche 1911, 502).

The girl wears a tunic embroidered with porcupine quills. Her hair is parted in the middle, pulled back across her forehead, and braided behind the ears into thick buns that rest upon her shoulders. Three young woman who have already received the Mark of Honor dance with her, singing Hon'hewachi songs. Fletcher and La Flesche point out that the song to which the girl dances in preparation for receiving the Mark of Honor "gives the rhythmic model after which all songs that pertain to the Hon'hewachi were fashioned. It therefore represented, they say, "the fundamental rhythm that expressed the musical feeling concerning those ideas or beliefs for which the Hon'hewachi stood" (Fletcher and La Flesche 1911, 502).

The Tattooing

The chiefs and Hon'ithaethe spend the night preceding the tattooing in the lodge of the girl's father. They continue to be his guests until the tattooing is completed. On the morning following the Feast of the Hon'hewachi, the sun, the round sun, emerges from a point on the eastern horizon behind the spot where the girl's father stood to recite his count. It begins to move toward the zenith point, the same direction the bundle of willow sticks took in its circle around the hands of the Hon'ithaethe. The sun moves toward the moment when the tattooing will be consecrated.

The initiate's daughter begins her preparation to receive the sun, the round sun. Early in the morning, servers of the ceremony set up scaffolds on either side of the entrance to the initiate's lodge. On these they suspend the articles given as fees to validate the ritual. These articles must include a hundred knives and a hundred awls that are required as emblems of male and female activities and in honor of the hundred count the initiate has accomplished in the Feast of the Count. It is honor of the hundred count that the initiate has accomplished the Feast of the Count.

The tattooing begins later in the morning when the sun is already high enough to bring heat and to shorten shadow. Two women already bearing the Mark or Honor prepare food for the assembled guests. The lodge has been emptied of all the initiate's possessions during the preceding days of feasting, with only the final gifts remaining on the scaffolds that frame its entrance to the east. Only the girl remains to be given away to the life-giving power of the round sun. Servers of the ceremony then thrust the hundred knives and hundred awls into the ground on either side of the morning fire. The time for the presentation of mythical teachings is approaching.

Behind the hearth at the place of honor, servers of the ceremony lay out "a bed of the costliest robes." They place a pillow toward the east, the direction of the sun's first appearance. The initiate and his guests take their morning meal in the lodge that has been prepared for the work of tattooing. The girl takes her meal with her family in a lodge adjoining the one in which the ceremony is to take place. Then the Hon'ithaethe and women who have received the Mark of Honor sing a song to the girl. Its words are:

> They are coming for you
> They are coming for you
> Because it is time. (Lee and La Vigna 1985)

The morning meals have been completed. Servers of the ceremony escort the girl into the lodge of her father, laying her with great care and dignity upon the fine robes on the bed of honor. She faces West "for, being emblematic of life, she had to move as if moving with the sun" (Fletcher and La Flesche 1911, 503). She wears "a skin tunic embroidered with porcupine quills" (Fletcher and La Flesche 1911, 502). When she has taken her place of honor with the chiefs and members of the Hon'hewachi Society, two heralds stand at the entrance of the lodge. The sun, Mithon, the round sun, moves in his slow and certain circle closer to the zenith point. The heralds call the names of those who are to sing during the tattooing. They give voice to the war honors achieved by the men who are to sing. Some of these men are already in the lodge as the herald recognizes them, while others enter following his salutation.

A ring of silence encircles the lodge and extends outward into the places where people are living. They respect the blessing of the night that has come among them and the silence into which the sun, the round sun,

will speak. They keep children, dogs, and horses at a distance. The
Hon'ithaethe speak among themselves in gentle voices. The lodge has
become a holy place at the center of the cosmos, a place of waiting for the
presentation of mythic teachings. One of the Hon'ithaethe, those blessed
by the night, has been chosen perhaps by right of inheritance, to perform
the tattooing. He must be able to suck the blood and charcoal pigment
from the girl's freshly tattooed skin without harm. He must also be blessed
and protected with power by a vision of a serpent whose flashing eyes
and moving cry, in Omaha symbolism, is the noise of "teeming life and
'moves' over the earth" (Fletcher and La Flesche 1911, 506).

Servers of the ceremony prepare charcoal pigment in a wooden bowl.
The tattooing chief outlines the sun circle and the star with a flattened
stick dipped in a charcoal solution, or in later times, India ink. He takes
up a tightly bound bundle of flint points to which rattlesnake rattles are
fastened. Later these implements are replaced with needles and small
bells. The girl lies on her bed of honor in absolute silence. She must make
no noise throughout the ceremony. "If she should do so," Fletcher and La
Flesche say, "it was considered as evidence that she had been unchaste. If
the healing process was rapid, it was considered a good omen" (Fletcher
and La Flesche 1911, 506).

Silence surrounds the lodge. The Earth People and Sky People who
make up the tribe keep their distance in respect for the sacrifice that is
taking place for their well-being. The chiefs and Hon'ithaethe begin to
chant the sun song:

Mithon shui the tha
Mithon shui the tha
Mithon shui the tha
Mithon shui the tha
Mithon gathu ti thon de shui the tha
Mithon shui the tha
Mithon shui the tha

These words mean literally:

The sun the round sun
Comes – speaks – says
The sun the round sun
Comes – speaks – says

The sun the round sun
Comes – speaks – says
The sun the round sun
Comes – speaks – says
The sun the round sun
Yonder point
When it comes – speaks – says
The sun the round sun
Comes – speaks – says

"This ancient song," according to Fletcher and La Flesche, "refers to the sun rising to the zenith, to the highest point; when it reaches that point it speaks" (Fletcher and La Flesche 1911, 504).

The tattooing chief begins to prick the sun sign into the skin of the girl's forehead. Against the rhythm of the Hon'hewachi song evoking the power of the sun at its zenith point, the girl can hear the dry rhythmic percussion of the rattles of the flint that pierces her skin and draws her blood. She endures and waits in perfect silence. Above the lodge of her father the sun, Mithon, the round sun, moves silently toward his zenith point, the moment of their meeting. When the sun reaches that point, "it speaks, as its symbol descends upon the maid with the promise of life-giving power" (Fletcher and La Flesche 1911, 504).

The dry sound of rattling stops. The girl's forehead is hot with a circle of her own blood, hot with the promise of the Hon'hewachi song and the anticipation of the round sun's movement to the zenith point. The momentary silence that surrounds her anticipates the sun, the round sun as it comes, speaks, says. Her silence reaches out to receive the life-giving power of his voice as he reaches the highest point.

The tattooing chief bathes her forehead with a cooling charcoal solution. The rattling begins again. The rhythm of the Hon'hewachi again surrounds her. The chief's bundled flint fangs inject the pigment beneath her skin. They complete the sun sign as the Hon'hewachi song comes to an end. Both the song and the sign promise life-giving power when the moment arrives for the sun to descend upon her.

The tattooing chief moves toward the young woman. His lips move toward where she is hot with the round sun sign and her own hot blood. Protected from harm by the blessing of his serpent vision, he sucks the mixed blood and charcoal from the freshly tattooed surface of her skin. With his action, the sun sign is ready for the teeming cry of the living creatures. Her sign is ready to receive the sun, the round sun, as he moves like living wind in the trees.

There is a pause in the ceremony. The girl can feel the sun sign press-ing into her skin at the center of her forehead. The people will know her by this sign when she is an old woman and will honor her for it always. She can hear the sound of her own breathing, moving in a rhythm like wind in the trees. She knows that in time she will send her children "into the midst of the winds" in the ceremony of "turning the child." In silence, the Hon'hewachi rhythm continues to surround her. Her father, the chiefs, the women who serve her in ceremony, the Hon'ithaethe, are suffused with the rhythm of the great mother force. Filled with her emotion and an "awakening of the feminine element," they are ready to experience the mythic teachings of *Hon'he*, the "creative acts" by which, "through the mysterious power of *Wakon'da*, night brought forth day" (Fletcher and La Flesche 1911, 494).

The shadow cast by the initiation lodge creeps up as the sun arches toward midday. The tattooing chief picks up his flint bundle. Its rattles shake the girl's silence like the flickering tongues of heat lightning and distant thunder that penetrate the mystery of a sultry summer night sky. The rattling sound reminds her of serpent power, "the teeming life that 'moves' over the earth" (Fletcher and La Flesche 1911, 506). It reminds her that the name of the Sky People, Inshta'thunda, means "flashing eyes," and that the Sky People "in union with the Earth People, gave birth to the human race" (Fletcher and La Flesche 1911, 135; 185). The sky powers bring forth life by descending upon the earth in the form of lightning, thunder, and rain.

The time has come for the Hon'ithaethe, those blessed by the night, to think about the night sky and its promise of day to come. The singers give voice to the rhythm of the night dance:

Honthin the tha
Honthin the tha
Honthin the tha

Umba ia tho
Umba ia tho
Umba ia tho

The song's words mean:

Night moving
Going
Night moving
Going
Night moving
Going

Day is coming
Day is coming
Day is coming

Fletcher and La Flesche translate the meaning of these words as, "Night moves, it passes, and the day is coming" (Fletcher and La Flesche 1911, 505).

As the singers chant these words in the Hon'hewachi rhythm, the tattooing chief resumes his rhythmic penetration of the girl's skin with his bundle of flints. The rattles shake in response to his motions. The rattling sound blends with the words of the song, penetrating the girl's consciousness as well as her skin. The figure that takes form in hot bright blood upon her throat is a four-pointed star.

"The star," according to Fletcher and La Flesche, "is emblematic of the night, the great mother force. . . . Its four points represent," they say, "the life-giving winds into the midst of which the child was sent through the ceremony of Turning the Child" (Fletcher and La Flesche 1911, 505). The star also evokes the pole star beneath which a chief's son discovered the luminous tree that was to become Waxthe'xe, the Sacred Pole. The Hon'itaethe know that, "The name of the Pole, Waxthe'xe, signifies that the power to give the right to possess this 'mark of honor' was vested in the Pole" (Fletcher and La Flesche 1911, 219). According to the sacred legend of the Pole, "the Thunder Birds come and go upon this tree, making a trail of fire that leaves four paths on the burnt grass that stretch toward the Four Winds" (Fletcher and La Flesche 1911, 218). Membership in the Hon'hewachi comes to a man who has been "pitied (compassionately helped) by night. . . . The feminine cosmic force was typified not only by night but by the heavenly bodies seen by night, as the masculine cosmic force was symbolized by day and the sun" (Fletcher and La Flesche 1911, 494).

The shadow of the initiation lodge has nearly vanished. Mithon, the round sun, has nearly reached the zenith point in line with the day and night signs of the girl's body. As the moment of alignment draws near, the Hon'ithaethe sing a song of completion whose words are:

Gathin xue tha
Gathin xue tha
Eda tonda ha xue tha
Gathin xue tha
Gathin xue tha
Hio

The words mean literally:

Yonder unseen is one moving
Noise
Yonder unseen is one moving
Noise

For that reason
Over the earth
Noise
Hio – The cry of the living creatures

The sound of the flint's rattles pauses. The tattooing chief bathes the girl's star sign with soothing charcoal. Then he picks up the bundle of flints for the last time. He pricks the pigment into her skin with a final dry rattling of the serpent-tailed flint fangs. He removes the remaining blood and charcoal by sucking with his mouth. The designs are now part of the girl's body. They have become centers of the universe that will honor the Omaha Tribe throughout her life as an old woman.

The sun moves directly into line with the girl's body. Its rays fall upon the girl through the smoke hole's shaft of light. She receives the sun's light as "the cry of the living creatures," the serpent-like noise of teeming life moving over the earth, the noise of the Sky People come to join the People of Earth. The energy of their union passes through the girl's body and into the earth. It passes through the sun sign and the star sign. It passes through the girl's young womb and into the ancient and constantly fertile womb of the Earth.

"By the union of Day, the above, and Night, the below," Fletcher and La Flesche tell us, "came the human race and by them the race is maintained. The tattooing [is] an appeal for the perpetuation of all life and of human life in particular" (Fletcher and La Flesche 1911, 507). Women bearing the Mark of Honor are still alive among the Omaha people even as I write. The spirit of Xthexe, mottled as by shadows, continues to unite the Sky and Earth People into a single tribe. The creative rhythm of the Hon'hewachi is still very much alive among the Omaha people in the presentation of mythical teachings.

BIBLIOGRAPHY

Barnes, R. H. 1984. *Two Crows denies it: A history of controversy in Omaha sociology.* Lincoln: University of Nebraska Press.

Dorsey, James Owen. 1884. *Omaha sociology.* BAE 3rd Annual Report. Washington: Government Printing Office.

1980. *The Cegiha language.* Contributions to North American ethnology, vol. 6. Washington: U.S. Geographical and Geological Survey of the Rocky Mountain Region.

Fletcher, Alice Cunningham. 1885. Lands in severalty to Indians: Illustrated by experiences with the Omaha tribe. *Proceedings of the American Association for the Advancement of Science* 33:654–55.

1888. Glimpses of child-life among the Omaha tribe of Indians. *Journal of American Folk-Lore* 2:115–23.

1892. Hae-Thu-Ska society of the Omaha tribe. *Journal of American Folk-Lore* 5:135–44.

1893. A study of Omaha Indian music. *Archaeological and ethnological papers of the Peabody Museum* 1(5).

1894. Love songs among the Omaha Indians. *Memoirs of the International Congress of Anthropology,* ed. Staniland Wake, 153–57. Chicago: The Schulte Publishing Company.

ms a. *Glimpses of Omaha life.* Lecture notes, Washington: National Anthropological Archives 4558, Box 19, Item 65–2.

ms b. *The Omaha tribe with special reference to the position, work and influence of Indian women.* Lecture notes, Washington: National Anthropological Archives 4558, Box 19, Item 65–3.

Fletcher, Alice C. and Francis La Flesche. 1911. *The Omaha tribe.* Washington: Bureau of American Ethnology 27th Annual Report.

Fortune, Reo F. 1932. *Omaha Secret Societies.* New York: Columbia University Press.

Green, Norma Kidd. 1969. *Iron Eye's Family: The Children of Joseph La Flesche.* Lincoln: Johnson Publishing Co.

Koontz, John. (personal communication)

La Flesche, Francis. 1963. *The Middle Five: Indian Schoolboys of the Omaha Tribe.* Madison: University of Wisconsin Press.

Lee, Dorothy Sara and Maria La Vigna. 1985. *Omaha Indian music: Historical recordings from the Fletcher/La Flesche collection*. Washington: American Folklife Center, Library of Congress.

Liberty, Margot. 1976. Native American "Informants": The contribution of Francis La Flesche. In *American anthropology: The early years*, ed. John V. Murra, 99–110. St. Paul: West Publishing Co.

———. 1978. Francis La Flesche, Omaha, 1857–1932. In *American Indian intellectuals*, ed. Margot Liberty, 45–60. St. Paul: West Publishing Co.

Lurie, Nancy Oestreich. 1966. Women in early American anthropology. In *Pioneers of American anthropology: The uses of biography*, ed. June Helm, 29–82. Seattle: University of Washington Press.

Mark, Joan. 1980. Four anthropologists. In *An American science in its early years*. New York: Science History Publications.

———. 1982a. Francis La Flesche. In *An American science in its early years*. New York: Science History Publications.

———. 1982b. Francis La Flesche. In *American Indian as anthropologist*. Isis 73 (269):497–510.

Mead, Margaret. 1932. *The changing culture of an Indian tribe*. New York: Columbia University Press.

———. 1965. Consequences of racial guilt. Introduction to 2nd Edition, *The changing culture of an Indian tribe*.

Prucha, F. P. 1984. *The Great Father: The United States government and the American Indians*. Lincoln: University of Nebraska Press.

Ridington, Robin. In press a. Mottled as by shadows: A sacred symbol of the Omaha tribe. In *Voices of the first America: Text and context in the New World*. New Scholar.

———. In press b. Omaha images of renewal. *History of Religions*.

———. 1987. Omaha survival: A vanishing Indian tribe that would not vanish. *American Indian Quarterly* 11(1):37–51.

Tibbles, Thomas Henry. 1957. *Buckskin and blanket days*. Garden City: Doubleday.

Welsch, Roger L. 1981. *Omaha tribal myths and trickster tales*. Chicago: Sage Books.

Wilson, Dorothy C. 1974. *Bright Eyes: The story of Susette La Flesche, an Omaha Indian*. New York: McGraw-Hill.

Mistress, Mother, Visionary Spirit: The Lakota Culture Heroine

Marla N. Powers

Introduction

My point of departure is Åke Hultkrantz's characterization of the Lakota metaphysical figure called today White Buffalo Calf Woman as "mistress of the buffalo, related to Mother Earth, a culture heroine . . . and . . . visionary spirit" (Hultkrantz 1983:210). Despite recent criticisms of this categorization of goddesses in general,[1] none of which incidentally applies to the Lakota goddess, I would like to focus this brief contribution on the various ways this important female personage has been described and analyzed in both oral tradition and historical treatment. I am not so much concerned about the many transformations that Hultkrantz has attributed to her as I am about the reasons why she has represented these transformations. As I will show, the multivariate, sometimes contradictory, attributes of the White Buffalo Calf Woman underscore the high value that Lakota males and females place on the role of women at each stage of their life. In so doing, these attributes emphasize the nature and the function of the Sacred Pipe, the major symbol of traditional Lakota religion, which, according to Lakota tradition, White Buffalo Calf Woman brought to the people for the first time.

Perhaps the most overlooked function of the White Buffalo Calf Woman is that she is what Hultkrantz calls a "culture heroine." Hultkrantz argues that she fulfills this role because the Lakota do not have a typical culture hero such as those found in other American Indian tribes. Although it

36

could be argued that in Lakota mythology the trickster and culture hero are merged, particularly in the guise of Inktomi, I am in agreement with the idea that the White Buffalo Calf Woman introduced the Lakota people to all of their religious traditions.[2] However, it was Inktomi and other deities associated with the origin myths who actually taught the Buffalo People, who migrated to the earth's surface and to whom the White Buffalo Calf Woman is incontrovertibly related, how to hunt, cook, make clothing, and build their shelters even though he abandoned them after doing so. Although a trickster and culture hero may be merged, this does not negate the important function of the culture heroine, and in many ways is simply another way of expressing the complementarity between the sexes even at a mythological level. Stated another way, the Lakota have a cosmological system in which both males and females participate in constructing the universe for the first time, just as they do in reality, by sharing responsibilities equally among the sexes forever.

It has long been accepted that the White Buffalo Calf Woman who brought the Sacred Pipe to the Lakota is at once a cosmological figure and an historic one. She appeared to the Lakota in rather recent times according to numerous Winter Counts kept by different individuals in various bands.[3] It is also an established tenet of Lakota tradition that she represents much more than this historic figure and is ranked highly under other transformed guises in the Lakota pantheon. A careful study of the mythology demonstrates quite convincingly that she is the most important personage in the Lakota cosmology. At once related to the prime movers of time and space during the creation of the universe, she is as well the major culture figure related to humans or Buffalo People who come from a previous subterranean existence.[4] But what makes the White Buffalo Calf Woman a sacred person is not that the actions and attributes in her many transformations are well known and clearly defined among the Lakota medicine men and other keepers of the tradition. She emerges as a sacred person precisely because there is so little agreement about who she was and what she did through the course of history and cosmological time. Thus the White Buffalo Calf Woman is indeed worthy of Hultkrantz's appellation of "goddess" because she displays the characteristic nature of other females and males that are similarly classified as goddesses and gods. She most strongly displays all the attributes of mystery and awesomeness normally associated with other "high" religions.[5]

I recognize that Hultkrantz's notion of the North American Indian goddess has been challenged,[6] but I would like to say that these criticisms almost totally ignore what Indian people have to say about their female deities. In fact, calling the White Buffalo Calf Woman, among others, a goddess, Hultkrantz does a great service to American Indians by releasing them from the racist category of "primitive" religion which other historians of religion have invented for the sake of their own culture's edification. Those who would use, for example, leaky theories derived from poor historical scholarship as well as fatuous anthropological pronouncements probably suffer from what every good scholar fears: an absence of anything of substance to say about a subject, particularly a subject that is at the very foundation of the beliefs and philosophies of the people whose religious systems he or she studies.

A further problem is that, except for the concepts of "higher" gods and goddesses that have been introduced to Indian people through missionaries, there never has been any concrete evidence that the Lakota, and perhaps others, believe in the notion of "god" in the Euroamerican sense. If they do not believe in gods, then they do not believe in goddesses. Although I understand that Indian people are often bedazzled by the language used by historians of religion, anthropologists, and others who study American Indian religions, they often and justifiably feel excluded from a continuous dialogue that concerns their most cherished beliefs, frequently spoken in a language that no one can understand outside the disciplines in question. On the other hand, it is a greater disservice not to include American Indian religions with others that are practiced elsewhere in the world or at different times, particularly from the comparison of religion analyzed, dissected, examined, hierarchized, and generally, if not thoroughly identified almost exclusively on the basis of this classificatory device. Hence, in my opinion, it is better to begin to understand important cosmological figures in American Indian religions by applying the same categories, in this case "goddess," to those counterparts appearing in the so-called "higher" religions of the world.

This comparison, of course, has as its major goal the ability to discover universals in religion and thus in all human life. But ironically, comparative studies that lead to universal claims are all based on disparate particularizations. Universality, then, becomes a sum total of the specific religious concepts that have been discovered and analyzed. Frequently, these particularizations are selected in advance to meet the research interests of an individual scholar. This is why I say that by considering American Indian deities on equal footing with others found throughout the world, and by classifying them by the same terms as are the others, American

Indian religions are provided a better service, are better represented, and
are thus more likely to be respected for the function they serve. In this
case, the White Buffalo Calf Woman should be considered a full-fledged
goddess.

The Name of the Goddess

To begin examining the often contradictory aspects of this Lakota goddess, it is perhaps worth looking at the very name by which she is known.
It would seem that the most important female deity in the Lakota pantheon would easily be identifiable by name, but this is not the case. She is
most frequently addressed as White Buffalo *Calf* Woman or White Buffalo
Cow Woman in English, distinctions which I think are significant and
which I will address below. But, in addition to these common names, she
is referred to in many more ways.[7] For example, if we examine the literature on the goddess in the native language or listen to the legend in
Lakota, we find that she is most frequently referred to as a *calf*. The most
consistent appellation in Lakota is *Ptehincala Cannunpa Win* or 'Buffalo
Calf Pipe Woman'. More recently, the most consistent variant of her name
is *Ptehincalasan Win* or 'White Buffalo Calf Woman.'[8] If we look for a
moment at the derivation of these names we find that the term *ptehincala*
is the traditional term for a buffalo calf, a contraction of *pte* 'buffalo cow'
and *cincala* 'offspring,' which includes human offspring. There is no question that the first part of her name should be rendered as buffalo calf and
not buffalo cow which would simply be *pte*. If we look at the last part of
her name, *Win,* which is a female name-marker, there is also no doubt
that her name should be rendered 'woman'. However, in numerous contemporary translations and English renditions she is frequently referred to
not only as woman but as 'maiden'.[9] Although I think that these distinctions are important to Lakota, the confusion is in the selection of appropriate translations which are frequently changed to satisfy the stylistic
needs of various authors, Lakota and non-Lakota alike. Interestingly, in
some native texts she is never mentioned by name at all, although her
attributes frequently are. For example, she has been called The Beautiful
One and Beautiful Lady which seem fair enough given that in the native
Lakota she is called beautiful (*owang wašte*), or is described in such a way
that she resembles a strikingly handsome woman. She always has long
flowing hair, and frequently, when it blows in the breeze, smells of
sweetgrass.[10]

It should also be noted that the ending in the name *Win* is the typical name-ending indicating that the person is female. There is nothing unusual about this ending and it is applied to all female names whether they are sacred or secular. Today, the ending is sometimes translated "Mrs." but that is because Lakota women now take the names of their husbands, whereas in early times their names were unique. In contemporary use *Wanbli Wašte* means 'Good Eagle' and *Wanbli Wašte Win* 'Miss' or 'Mrs. Good Eagle', but in everyday translation, *Win* is not glossed.

Thus, in the strict sense this goddess could be simply called White Calf, but she is not. Additionally, it is not clear at what time the adjective *white* was added to her name. The term *san* 'white' refers to a greyish-white which is applied generally to markings on animals. *San* may be contrasted with *ska* which also means 'white' but indicates a higher degree of intensity. The addition of the adjective may have come about by people identifying a relationship between the white buffalo, a sacred animal among the Lakotas and others (hence Hultkrantz's "mistress of the buffalo"), or it may have been added to suggest a characteristic of the goddess to non-Indians, white being equated with purity, another attribute of the goddess made quite clear in all the stories.

The Legend

Although it appears in variations, the basic legend is told as follows:

There is a famine in camp and two hunters are sent out to scout for buffalo. They see an object in the distance, and as it comes closer they see that it is a woman carrying an object. One of the hunters wishes to have sex with her; the other advises him not to because she is mysterious. Not heeding the advice, the first hunter approaches her and he is immediately covered by a mist. When the mist rises he has been transformed into a pile of bones through which snakes are crawling. The woman then advises the second hunter to return to camp to tell the chief to erect a council lodge; she will come later with something very important for them. Later she arrives with the sacred pipe and teaches the Lakota the Seven Sacred Rites. She then leaves, but before disappearing over the hill, she turns into a white buffalo calf.[11]

On this point, the sexual status of the White Buffalo Calf Woman is usually not a topic of discussion among the Lakota or scholars, and it would be unfair to read into it any more than can be justified on theoretical grounds. Hassrick is the only one to impart to the female personage an "Oedipal" explanation of the legend implying that the White Buffalo Calf Woman is somehow a mother figure whom one of her errant sons has tried to seduce.[12]

Without acquiescing to once-voguish but obsolete Freudianisms, there is ample evidence that the Lakota are quite capable of seeing various metaphors in their own mythology and of understanding their implications. Lakota mythology is replete with references to temptation, of good versus evil, of pure versus impure, that is, of what is acceptable as opposed to unacceptable behavior in Lakota society. After all, the greatest perpetrator of social trangressions including sexual ones is the trickster Inktomi, who goes to war with his mother-in-law and marries his own daughter.[13]

In fact, purity versus impurity, and one might argue, motherhood versus "mistresshood," are exemplified in the attempted rape of the White Buffalo Calf Woman in all variants of the legend. The perpetrator is reduced to a pile of bones, while a second man, himself pure, carries the message of the sacred woman back to the camp.

I doubt that the average Lakota listening to this legend would have any doubts about the propriety of a hunter ravaging a mysterious and beautiful woman. I would also doubt that the picture of the White Buffalo Calf Woman is painted the way it is to give the illusion that she is anything but sexually appealing. After all, in the older versions she appears nude; in later versions she is clothed in almost every fashion of the day including a beaded belt and headband. In several renditions she is dressed in red, while in others she is in white, both symbolic of purity and sexuality not only in Lakota culture but in our own.

It does not require much imagination in Lakota or non-Lakota culture to understand the implications of two men viewing a naked, or at least fashionably-dressed, beautiful woman, carrying an unidentified object which will later become the major symbol of the Lakota religion, the Sacred Calf pipe. Presumably, both men see her and envision her differently, one as a harbinger of sacrality, the other as a potential object of his sexual desires – not uncommon choices for male storytellers in those cultures in which the female is either reified or denigrated. Good clearly wins over evil when the lascivious hunter approaches the White Buffalo Calf Woman, who in some variations actually entices him, and who, despite the pleading of his virtuous comrade, is immediately engulfed in a mist which clears leaving a heap of bones on the ground through which snakes or

worms crawl. These crawly things are appropriate symbols in Lakota
culture not only of death but of defilement, appropriate rewards for one
who not only denigrates women but who at the same time desecrates
the pipe and with it the whole of Lakota religion. Indeed the message is
clear.

I might add that there is a general agreement in all the collected versions of this myth with respect to the *dramatis personae* and motives in
the above version. However, the details vary greatly, particularly concerning the woman's dress, and whether or not she enticed the first hunter to
come to her before enveloping him in a mist. Also at variance are the
details of her departure, some believing that she turned into several buffalo calves.[14] Others make no mention of this transformation at all, simply
stating that she turned into a white buffalo calf. There is only one explanation as to why the pipe is called the Calf Pipe, to wit, that if she is
Buffalo Cow, then the pipe is her calf. But in every case she is clearly not
a cow but a calf. Moreover, the reverse of the argument that she is called
the Buffalo Calf woman because the pipe is called the Calf Pipe would
make as much sense.[15]

Of particular importance, I think, is that neither the *personae* in the
legend change – the sacred woman, two hunters, and the chief – nor does
the episode in which the lascivious hunter approaches the sacred woman
and is enveloped in mist. Although all the legends consider the woman
beautiful, there is disagreement over whether she was dressed or naked.
In either case, there is no question that from a male point of view the
woman was sexually desirable by one hunter, but not by the other. More
simply put, the White Buffalo Calf Woman appears as a woman who is
both sacred and sexual, and immature as a calf and mature as a cow. One
the other hand, as Hultkrantz has pointed out, she is related to Mother
Earth and is mistress of the buffalo, who is master of the game. Here I
would agree that she is related to Mother Earth but not necessarily a transformation of her. In the earlier creation stories Mother Earth is established
when the Four Winds and other *personae* are sent to form the earth by
establishing the four directions. Later, in mythical time, the daughter of
the Sun and the Moon, *Wohpe* or 'Falling Star' falls to the earth and later
lives in the lodge of the South Wind. Old Lakota believe that Wohpe and
White Buffalo Calf Woman are the same.

She appears twice in the major text that relates Wohpe to White Buffalo
Calf Woman, once in Walker's early work (Walker 1917) and once in a
posthumous work (Walker 1980). In these texts, Walker interviewed an

Oglala by the name of Finger on March 25, 1914, who stated that "the
Earth and the Beautiful Woman are the same" (Walker 1917:154-55).
This is the only equation between Woȟpe, White Buffalo Calf Woman
(here the Beautiful Woman) and Mother Earth. Finger also identifies the
role of Woȟpe. In the interview he asks, "Has a Lakota ever seen Woȟpe?
Yes. When she gave the pipe to the Lakota. She was in their camp for
many days" (Walker 1917:155). Furthermore, Finger states that "When I
pray I smoke the pipe and burn the sweetgrass and Woȟpe carries my
prayer to the Wakan Tanka (Walker 1917:155).

From a symbolic point of view, the color of the South Wind is white.
Though I am not suggesting that her name includes the adjective *white*
because of her relationship with the South Wind, it is important to consider this relationship as part of the overall symbolic process. A female
goddess, whom the Lakotas see as the transformation of Woȟpe to White
Buffalo Calf Woman in one myth, lives with the South Wind, the indis-
putable symbol of masculinity in Lakota culture. With him she raises
Yumni, the fifth wind, who has a dubious birthright, and who has no
direction of his own and never grows up.[16] Woȟpe also has a sacred side,
however, because even though she lives with the South Wind, she never
gives birth to any children. Both Woȟpe and the White Buffalo Calf Woman
are also similar because they are implicitly virgins. This is why contemporary Lakotas are quite willing to describe their female goddess meta-
phorically as an analogue of the Virgin Mary to non- Indians.

Elsewhere I have indicated the importance that virginity plays in Lakota
culture, and that virginity itself is synonymous with prepubescence.[17]
Thus, the Lakota *witanšna*, meaning 'virgin' or woman who is single, in a
continuing state of celibacy, is permitted to handle sacred objects and to
touch and carry the Sun dance pole. Similarly, menopausal woman participate in the same types of ritual behavior because they also are considered sacred. Frequently, the older women are in charge of herbal medicines, as well as instructing the younger women about menstruation, sex,
and child-rearing.

One of the major ceremonies of the Lakota is the Išna awicalowanpi,
'they sing over her first menses', the Buffalo or White Buffalo Ceremony in
English, which initiates the transition of a prepubescent female into a
stage of life marked by reproduction. She is removed from an asexual
world and reincorporated into her world as a fully reproductive sexual
female. Implicit in the name of the ceremony is the relationship between
the pubescent female and the buffalo.

This relationship between woman and buffalo is not drawn from the scientific imagination of the symbolist scholar, but from the Lakotas themselves who fully understand the significance between the birth and nurturing of the people. Stated more formulaically, in the White Buffalo Ceremony it is the buffalo that serves as a mediating factor between virginity and fecundity, just as the White Buffalo Calf Woman serves as a mediating factor between starvation and plentitude. Because a virgin is chaste, she becomes the clearest manifestation of the symbol that underscores the Lakota belief that improper sexual behavior with a close relative will cause the buffalo to disappear. But in the myth and in the puberty ceremony, the virgin is for a moment transformed into a mature buffalo cow in an intensified ritual drama. In the ceremony, held before the child's family, a medicine man actually takes on the character of a buffalo bull in the rutting season sidling up to the girl, lowing, and generally behaving as a kind of buffalo suitor. This mimetic behavior is not by accident. Not only the cultural, but the biological imperatives could not be dramatized more poignantly. When the ritual dance has ended, with the song of buffalo lowing in the west, a characteristic symbol of the mating buffalo, the girl has now been transformed into a woman. Her menstrual bundle is discarded discretely so that it will not fall under the evil influence of the Coyote, and she is instructed to place her legs together to one side and sit like a woman.

But, returning to the myth, if one of the attributes of the White Buffalo Calf Woman is that of a virgin, that is, an asexual female, she is unlike the virgins of other religious lore such as the Virgin Mary. It is perhaps appropriate to make this analogy since today both Lakotas and non-Lakotas are under pressure to compare the nature of the White Buffalo Calf Woman to the Virgin Mary. Although missionaries are likely to understand this comparison as a prefiguration of the Christ figure in traditional Lakota religion, I personally regard this comparison as a means of equating the goddess of one religion with the goddess of another, and as such the comparison really serves to demonstrate that the Lakota venerate and respect the White Buffalo Calf Woman as Catholics do the Virgin Mary.

However, unlike the Virgin Mary, the White Buffalo Calf Woman does not give birth to a child. As Leach has explained virgin birth in other parts of the world,[18] the belief is not so much an ignorance of the consequences of sexual intercourse or the denial of paternity as it is a means of underscoring the sacrality of, in this case, the offspring, Jesus. But the White Buffalo Calf Woman is another sort of virgin. She symbolizes the transition between the sacredness of the child and the sexuality of a woman. The Lakota saying, *Wakanheja kin wakanpelo* or 'children are sacred', is an important tenet of Lakota belief.

In the myth, the White Buffalo Calf Woman clearly demonstrates that she is simultaneously child and woman. Because her mission, the one incontrovertible fact in the legend, is to bring the sacred pipe to the people, then the ambiguity of her dual nature and the mystery of her appearance and disappearance are purposeful in that they serve to underscore the sacrality of the pipe. It is after all, no ordinary pipe; it is the *cannunpa wakan,* the Sacred Pipe, and as such represents the major symbol of Lakota belief, ritual, thought, and knowledge for the first time and for all times. Therefore, it is no wonder that the legend is imbued with contradictions, wonders, and inconsistencies. These aspects of the myth are the most powerful and the most religious.

Historical references to the White Buffalo Calf Woman as indicated in several Winter Counts leave us with the same sense of ambiguity and awe. She appears at different places, different times within a generally short span of time, and to different people. Some even believe that she continues to appear on earth and was seen as recently as 1974 accompanied by another woman which was interpreted as a dangerous sign.[19]

The danger may very well stem from a prevailing Lakota belief associated with duality and temptation. The legend of the White Buffalo Calf Woman is in many ways characteristic of a genre of Lakota myth in which two persons, or two aspects of the same person, visit an individual, who is required to make a choice between the two. The general conclusion to these myths is that they represent a choice between good and evil. But, more importantly, what they have in common is that the choice between right or wrong is first of all voluntary, and secondly, testable in the near future. The wrong choice will certainly result shortly in the death of a child, or some other terrible misfortune that confronts the visionary or his or her family.

Most frequently this dual pair of tempters or temptresses are women. They may be seen in the form of *Anukite,* the Double Face Woman who also variously appears as the Black-Tail and White-Tail Deer, who have the power to seduce men, drive them insane or force them to make frivolous choices about their future.[20]

From the point of view of general scholarship, I could not agree more that personages such as the White Buffalo Calf Woman, Woȟpe, Mother Earth, Anukite, and other females associated with benevolent and malevolent acts, should be equated with female counterparts of other cultures. They are as much goddesses as those normally associated almost exclusively with monotheistic religions. Thus, by regarding the Lakota females as goddesses, as Hultkrantz has done, we are able to compare them favorably with similar personages of other religions, great or small, which in fact is the common task of history, social science, and the humanities.

I do not agree, however, that goddesses can be equated with particular kinds of traditions, such as agricultural traditions, and that these traditions themselves can be dated so as to demonstrate that some goddesses are older than others. My own understanding of the female goddess in her many forms as virgin, mistress, mother, sister, and daughter is that these persons represent real-life females in their many-faceted shapes and forms in empirical reality. I suspect the same to be true of gods. But if there is any difference in the way gods and goddesses are treated in myth and ritual, the great variance in goddesses is probably because the relationship between parent and child is always skewed toward the female side. The long dependency of the child on the mother makes the female-child bond much stronger than the male-child relationship. The argument that Mother Earth or other goddess figures are universal should be considered equally on biological grounds as on historical ones.

The female is transformed in mythology because she is transformed in reality. She is mistress and mother to other females and to males, but males can never fulfill the same kinds of roles toward other males and females. The biological primacy of the female-child relationship must be considered in any attempt to understand the universality of the goddess in her varied forms.

As Hultkrantz has indicated, White Buffalo Cow Woman is indeed mistress of the buffalo. She is related to Mother Earth. She is a visionary spirit and, most importantly, she is a culture heroine. The many transformations and manifestations of this important goddess, and the sometimes confusing and contradictory ways in which she is symbolically represented, add to the mystery, the authority, and the legitimacy of the Sacred Pipe, which she alone has borne to the Lakota people.

NOTES

1. In a recent book by Gill (1987).

2. Most of this may be found in Walker (1917).

3. For the best description of the Calf Pipe, which includes references to the appearance of the White Buffalo Calf Woman in the Winter Counts, see Smith

(1967). For a lengthy reconstruction of the legend see my *Oglala Women in Myth, Ritual and Reality* (1986).

4. Again the primary source is Walker (1917).

5. I do not personally subscribe to distinguishing between "high" and "low" religions, but because it is part of the way historians of religion classify belief systems, I use their term in quotation marks here.

6. Gill's attacks seem to be aimed at Hultkrantz more than any other scholar.

7. Other names by which she is known in the more popular books would include "White Buffalo Cow Woman" and "White Buffalo Maiden" (Brown 1953); "White Buffalo Maiden" (Densmore 1918); "The Beautiful One", "White Buffalo Maiden" and "Buffalo Maiden" (Hassrick 1964); "Ptesan Winyan 'White Buffalo Woman' " (LaPointe 1976); "Calf Pipe Woman," "White Buffalo Calf Maiden" (Mails 1979); "Beautiful Lady" (Riegert 1975); "White Buffalo Maiden" (Smith 1967); "Ptehincala Cannunpa Win 'Buffalo Calf Woman' " (Sword n.d.).

8. For example, see Bean *et al.* (1976).

9. As indicated above in n. 7.

10. This attribute is mentioned in Buechel (1978).

11. In Black Elk's version (Brown 1953) she turns into four colors. The order in which the buffalo calves appear in Black Elk's account vary with the usual order: West, North, East, South. Black Elk indicates the order through the colors described: North, East, South, West in which case she lastly appears as a black buffalo calf rather than a white buffalo calf. For an exegesis see Powers (1977).

12. In Hassrick (1964).

13. For these trickster stories see Deloria (1932).

14. As mentioned above, Black Elk is the only one to my knowledge. However, the number four figures prominently in other variations of the legend including one in which the buffalo is transformed from calf to old cow (in LaPointe 1976).

15. This statement may be found in G. A. Dorsey (1906). Interestingly, in this oft-cited article, Dorsey does not name the White Buffalo Calf Woman but assumes that, because she turned into a buffalo, "the people call it the 'calf pipe' . . . " (Dorsey 1906:329).

16. See Powers (1977) for an analysis of the characteristics of the South Wind and his relationship to Woȟpe.

17. In a discussion of menstruation and reproduction (Powers 1980) my main point is that these females are significant because they are not reproductive.

18. The classic argument on virgin birth may be found in Leach (1969).

19. The reference to the recent sighting of the White Buffalo Calf Woman is by Fools Crow in Mails (1979).

20. References to temptresses may be found in Powers (1977) and Powers (1986).

BIBLIOGRAPHY

Brown, Joseph Epes. 1953. *The sacred pipe.* Norman: University of Oklahoma Press.

Buechel, S. J., Eugene. 1978. *Lakota tales and texts,* ed. Paul Manhart, S. J. Pine Ridge, South Dakota: Red Cloud Indian School.

Deloria, Ella C. 1932. *Dakota texts.* New York: G. E. Stechert and Company.

Densmore, Frances. 1918. *Teton Sioux music.* Bureau of American Ethnology Bulletin 61. Washington, D.C.: Smithsonian Institution.

Dorsey, G. A. 1906. Legend of the Teton Sioux medicine pipe. *Journal of American Folk-Lore* 19:326–29.

Gill, Sam D. 1987. *Mother earth: An American story.* Chicago: University of Chicago Press.

Hassrick, Royal B. 1964. *The Sioux: Life and customs of a warrior society.* Norman: University of Oklahoma Press.

Hultkrantz, Åke. 1983. The religion of the goddess in North America. In *The book of the goddess,* ed. Carl Olson. New York: Crossroad.

LaPointe, James. 1976. *Legends of the Lakota.* San Francisco: The Indian Historian Press.

Leach, Edmund. 1969. *Genesis as myth and other essays.* London: Jonathan Cape.

Mails, Thomas E. 1979. *Fools Crow.* Garden City: Doubleday and Company.

Powers, Marla N. 1980. Menstruation and reproduction: An Oglala case. *Signs* 6:54–65.

———. 1986. *Oglala women in myth, ritual and reality.* Chicago: University of Chicago Press.

Powers, William K. 1977. *Oglala religion.* Lincoln: University of Nebraska Press.

Riegert, Wilbur A. 1975. *Quest for the pipe of the Sioux.* Rapid City, South Dakota: Printing, Inc.

Smith, John L. 1967. A short history of the sacred calf pipe of the Teton Dakota. *Museum News* 28(7–8):1–37.

Sword, D. George. n.d. Calf Pipe. Ms. on deposit with the American Museum of Natural History, New York, N.Y.

Walker, J. R. 1917. The Sun Dance and other ceremonies of the Oglala division of the Teton Dakota. *Anthropological Papers* of the American Museum of Natural History 16(2):53–221.

———. 1980. *Lakota belief and ritual,* eds. Demallie and E. Jahner. Lincoln: University of Nebraska Press.

Metaphysical Idealism in Inuit Shamanism

Daniel Merkur

To refer to their shamans, the Inuit, formerly known as the Eskimo, used the terms *angekoq, kalalik,* and *tunghalik.* Each means "one who has a spirit" (Merkur 1985a, 41). Inuit shamans' spirits were drawn almost exclusively from a class of metaphysical beings termed *tornaq* (plural, *tornat*) or a dialectical variant thereof. Most spirits were human or animal ghosts that had been prevented from journeying to afterlife realms and had, consequently, turned malignant, while few were wholly mythic beings. Spirits were ordinarily invisible, but might appear either to lay people or, in any of several forms, to shamans. They were inherently malevolent and dangerous, and all manner of misfortune, accident, disease, and death was ascribed to them. Generally feared and despised, spirits were warded off, exorcised, and assaulted, but never venerated. Under two circumstances, however, they could be controlled: spirits could be made to serve people through amulets, or, as the Inuit held, shamans could gain control of spirits, to command them as servants or helpers. (For more detailed accounts of Inuit spirits, see Merkur 1985a; 1985b.)

Most of what the ethnographic literature records as the power of shamans – and this is true of comparative shamanism, and not Inuit shamanism alone – was actually the power of the helping spirits that shamans had at their disposal. What has not generally been recognized, however, is that shamans controlled spirits, transforming malevolent beings into helpers, by exercising another kind of magical power. As the ultimate basis of shamanic power, this transformation was a closely guarded secret

that was, however, also found in simpler forms as a practice of Inuit lay
people.

The Magical Power of Words
and Thoughts

Magic songs, spells, or words were generally discussed in Alaska as a
type of song, but distinctively termed *erinaliut* in Canada (Rasmussen
1929, 157; 1932, 113; Mowat 1975, 237) and *serrat* in Greenland (Rink
1875, 51; Holm 1911, 87; Rasmussen 1908, 140; 1938, 172). Some were
sung, others chanted, still others spoken. They made animals approach
hunters, altered the weather, accomplished healing, etc. (Birket-Smith 1924,
445–46; 1953, 32, 118-19; Boas 1901, 153; 1907, 506; Bogoras 1907,
359; de Coccola and King 1954, 236–37; Freuchen 1961, 277–78; Giddings 1961, 149; Hawkes 1916, 124, 162; Holm 1911, 87–88; Holtved
1967, 176–77; Lantis 1946, 205–7, 240; Malaurie 1982, 217–18; Mowat
1975, 237–38; Nansen 1893, 290–92; Rasmussen 1908, 140–45; 1921,
31; 1927, 136–38; 1929, 157–68, 234; 1931, 13–15, 208–12, 278–93:
1932, 41, 113–18; 1938, 172; Rink 1875, 51–52; Schultz-Lorentzen 1928,
241; Spencer 1959, 277–81; Stefansson 1921, 411–14; 1913, 180–81).

The Copper Inuit had a unique variant. They understood magic spells
of the hunt to function through thought, rather than through the spoken
word (Rasmussen 1932, 116). Verbal ideas might also forestall the malice
of another person. "Without his hearing it, one makes magic songs so that
there may be calm in his mind, to make his thoughts pleasant" (Rasmussen 1932, 113). Indeed, thought might entirely replace spoken words.
During his fieldwork, Stefansson (1913, 295) was repeatedly asked to
" 'think away' sickness from them and 'think them' plenty of game and
good fortune." In connection with weather magic, Jenness found that direct,
colloquial expressions of wishes might take the place of traditional verbal
formulations.

> Most interesting is their peculiar belief in the projection of human
> will. . . . During a storm the natives often cry out, "Be fine, it is very
> unpleasant when the weather is bad, be fine;" or again, "We can't seal
> when the weather is stormy, be fine!" . . . It was not the spirit world
> that the[y] . . . had in mind when they made these appeals, for once

when I added, "Hearken and obey," they all burst out laughing; rather they seemed to hold that the very expression of one's thought, the mere utterance of a wish, in some dim and obscure manner worked for its fulfillment. (Jenness 1922, 229)

A related view of language occurs in Inuit myths (Rasmussen 1931, 208–13; 1929, 252–56). For example, Raven and other protagonists once casually expressed a desire for light which resulted in its origin (Boas 1901, 306; Jenness 1926, 78; Lucier 1958, 92; Rasmussen 1929; 253; 1930, 81-82; 1931, 208; 1932, 217). Myths of the origin of death similarly ascribed creative force to the verbal pronouncement of a casual desire that death exist (Birket-Smith 1924, 442; Nansen 1893, 272–75; Rasmussen 1929, 92; 1932, 62; Rink 1875, 41; Thalbitzer 1921, 406–7).

The magic power of words was also a fundamental premise of Inuit shamanism. It was through the mental direction of his or her thoughts that a shaman controlled helping spirits. A Polar Inuit shaman boasted, "My helping spirits know my thoughts and will, and they help me when I give commands" (Rasmussen 1908, 148). An East Greenland shaman described shamans' acquisitions of helping spirits in similar terms when he said, "They find them after careful search, calling them forth only by the use of thought, with the *angakut's* [shaman's] special prayers" (Thalbitzer 1921, 479).

When the Inuit were asked, they said that the magical power of words was intrinsic (Holm 1911, 87–8; Jenness 1922, 229; Malaurie 1982, 218; Rasmussen 1927, 140; 1931, 13, 211; Rink 1875, 51). What did they mean by this claim?

Indwellers and Metaphysical Idealism

Like the Lapps (Bäckman 1975) and Siberians (Louise Bäckman, personal communication, 1985), Inuit shamans maintained a strict distinction between the helping spirits that they commanded and the guardian spirits that were the shamans' patrons. Guardian spirits were drawn from the class of metaphysical beings that the Inuit termed *inua* (plural, *inue*) or dialectical variants (Merkur 1985a, 232–40). An excellent account of the Aleut and Alaskan Inuit concept was offered by Marsh, who translated *inua* etymologically as "person (of the preceding noun)."

When the object disappears or is destroyed, its "person" ceases to exist. Thus, the "person" of a fire vanishes when the fire goes out. . . .

"Persons" are not in their nature immortal beings, but it is obvious that
the "person" of a cliff, lake, or island, will have from a practical standpoint a permanent existence. Likewise the "person" of something such
as grass is not in reality the "person" of a given patch of grass or of a
given year's growth of grass, but is in fact what we could describe as
the "person" of the idea of grass, and this likewise from a practical
standpoint has a perpetual existence. . . .

In the beliefs of the entire Eskimo-Aleut region of Alaska there are,
besides the "persons" of places and objects, also the "persons" of animals and all other non-human creatures. These "persons" of animals
are spirit-beings distinct and apart from the souls of animals. The
"persons" of animals are envisaged (and also depicted) as humans,
while the [free-]souls take the form of their respective species. And
whereas the souls of animals are the spiritual counterparts of individual creatures, the "persons" of animals are as a matter of fact the spiritual projection of the idea of each type. Thus they are the "persons" of
groups or species. The "person" of the walrus, for example, is not the
"person" of one specific walrus, but the "person" of the type walrus; in
fact, of the ideal walrus. Hence the "persons" of animals have a perpetual existence. Furthermore, since the "person" of any given species of
animal is in actuality the "person" of the ideal animal of that species,
this animal "person" stands in relation to all the individuals of that
species or band as a headman of a human household or community to
his fellow members. Therefore this animal "person" is thought to control the activities of all the members of his band or species. (Marsh
1954, 24)

We gain a deeper appreciation of the concept of an *inua* from remarks
that Gubser heard among the Nunamiut Inuit in the northern Alaskan
interior.

An *inua* is not the personality or even a characteristic of an object
although an *inua* itself may have a personality. The spirit of an object
may be thought of . . . in the case of inanimate objects, [as] the essential existing force of that object. Without a spirit, an object might still
occupy space and have weight, but it would have no meaning, it would
have no . . . real existence. When an object is invested with an *inua,* it
is a part of nature of which we are aware. (Gubser 1965, 199)

The concept of an *inua* presupposes a distinction between matter and idea. As pure matter, the substance of an object "might still occupy space and have weight," but physical substance does not of itself constitute any existent phenomenon. "It would have no meaning . . . no . . . real existence." Every real phenomenon has also its characteristic nature, activity, or function, its "essential existing force," that makes it "a part of nature of which we are aware." An *inua* is thus the differential factor that transforms matter, considered in the abstract, into a discrete phenomenon. Because an *inua* is not the personality or even a characteristic of an object," it is apparently transcendent of, rather than inherent in, matter – an idealistic, as distinct from an empirical, viewpoint. Moreover, because it is metaphysical, rather than physical, an *inua* "may have a personality."

A strikingly similar concept was recorded by Williamson among the Iglulik Inuit, thousands of miles to the east on the western shores of Hudson Bay.

> The Eskimo believed that the emitting of a word evoked an image, which was an actual reality. No one could say that an image once evoked, by being spoken, was not a reality, though a mental one. The language is a complex of mental images, but both the physical objects, and the words used to evoke them – are, in Eskimo thinking, equally real. The name of an individual is more than a label, it is the name whereby a person's separate social existence is evoked, it is the symbolization of his personality, it is his very essence, and the spiritual and functional means whereby he is identified and related with the rest of his society and his physical and metaphysical environment.
>
> In that a word is an image and a name is a word, and in that an image-word-name is also therefore a soul, the Eskimo believed that the animals and birds too have a soul, though not an individual soul, but rather a group soul. One word-name is used to identify all creatures of one species. (Williamson 1974, 23-24)

Williamson's discussion of the epistemic function of group souls is closely consistent with the *inua* concept documented by Gubser. Words evoke images and, as names, constitute group souls that make the work intelligible to human thought. Gubser's informant instead held that *inua* make the world intelligible as such.

Of course, because few people in any culture are given to philosophic inquiry, most of the ethnographic evidence on the *inua* concept is considerably less articulate. To summarize data that I have reviewed closely elsewhere (Merkur 1985b, 108–16), the term *inua* is best translated as "indweller" and understood as an idea that indwelled and imparted individual character to a phenomenon. It had, employed, and most essentially, was a power. As the idea of the phenomenon, the indweller informed the phenomenon even as it transcended the phenomenon's substance. Because it both was an idea and had active power to implement the idea in substance, an indweller was actively engaged in thinking. An indweller's thought was both structural, imparting the idea of what it was to the phenomena in which it indwelled, and man-like or anthropopsychic, involving cognitions, emotions, and motivations.

An invisible personal being, an indweller was specific in location to the phenomena that it informed. They were completely autonomous and disinterested in the Inuit who could hurt themselves by abusing indwellers, or derive benefits by according with them. In both events, the indwellers were what they were, with neither positive nor negative ambitions toward the Inuit. Because indwellers were anthropopsychic, however, they were accessible to social intercourse. In principle, all phenomena were informed by indwellers, but, in practice, it was only the indwellers of phenomena that underwent periodic change – the game animals, the weather, the sea, etc. – who received sacrifice, propitiation, and reconciliation. The Inuit hoped to persuade these indwellers to act in a manner beneficial to people.

The Inuit concept of indwellers, the gods and godlings of Inuit religion, brings us closer to an understanding of the magical, creative power of language, but a gap remains to be closed. Verbal ideas ordinarily have the power to create and to reinforce culturally shared world views, but they do not have the power of indwellers actually to create and to control physical phenomena. For human speech and thought to have magical power, the collaboration of one or more indwellers is required.

Sila and Shamanic Power

Inuit shamans tended to be very secretive about the basis of their power, but their occasional remarks on the topic were consistent with what Rasmussen was told at Icy Cape in northern Alaska.

The shaman does not get the power from the animal [spirit], but from a mysterious "power" in the air; at the same time as it is near to them, it is so infinitely remote that it cannot be described. It is a power in the air, in the land, in the sea, far away and around them. Only a shaman knows about this power; he is the medium. He works on the mind and thoughts as much as he can. (Rasmussen 1952, 133)

Although Rasmussen's informant declined to name the source of his power, his reference to "a mysterious 'power' in the air," was a transparent reference to the god known as Sila, a belief common to the shamans of other Inuit groups. Although Inuit shamans knew that their power consisted of a mastery of their own thought, they did not credit themselves with the power's origin. The power was theirs to exercise, but they acquired it from indwellers – and most frequently Sila (Merkur 1985a, 235–37).

Inuit beliefs about Sila require a brief preface. Åke Hultkrantz (1953, 55–60) established that the Inuit traditionally believed that every person and animal possessed two types of souls (cf. Merkur 1985b, 93–107). The shadow, or free-soul, might leave the body in dreams and ecstatic visions; it was also subject to attack by evil spirits and, after death, became a ghost and reincarnated. The second type of soul was called the breath-soul which imparted life, warmth, breath, and waking consciousness to the living body. At death, a breath-soul became a name-soul and functioned as the tutelary guardian of the children that shared its name. Name-souls inculcated rational intelligence within children's breath-souls by furnishing the children with indwellers.

Due to its composition of breath, the breath-soul was integrally related to Sila or, more technically, *silap inua*, the indweller in Sila. As a common noun, the word *sila* has an extensive range of meanings: the world, the universe; nature, the natural order; common sense, reason; consciousness; the air, the wind(s), the weather; the place or space outside, the open sky (Petersen 1966–67, 262). The key to an understanding of the god Sila was explained to Williamson when he was among the Iglulik.

Sila is the life-giving element, which enfolds all the world and invests all living organisms, and without which there can be no life. *Sila* is the word for air, without air there is no life; air is in all people and all creatures; anything deprived of air ceases to live. In that air therefore gives life and without air there is no life, the Eskimos believed that they are part of the Life-Giving Spirit, that each individual is animated by the Life-Giving Spirit, and that the part of his soul, that part which is the essence of all things living, is part of the ultimate deity *Sila.* . . .

Every individual is said to have as part of his soul the life force, the
life-giving spirit, which is part of the whole animating force *Silap inua.*
This is of course something which never dies, air and the life-giving
force go on indefinitely, and so then does the soul of man. When the
air passes out of the body at the moment of physical death, it is simply
the passing of the soul back into its original matrix. (Williamson 1974,
22–3)

Inuit most frequently remarked on Sila's identity with the air, command
of the weather, cosmic scope, and activity as a vivifying power. Sila possessed the attributes of the human breath-soul on a cosmic scale because
Sila was at once the cosmic body, "the world, the universe," and its vivifying breath, "the air, the wind(s), the weather." As the cosmic breath-
soul, Sila encompassed "consciousness," inclusive of "common sense, reason."
The latter manifested dynamically in the world as "nature, the natural
order."

In the context of cultic rituals, the Inuit tended to approach Sila as a
provider of bodily health and strength and as the controller of the sun,
the winds, and storms (Merkur 1983). In the context of religious experience, however, Sila was more important as the intelligence structuring and
imparting order to the cosmos. Not only was Sila the breath-soul of the
cosmos, but this consciousness was accessible to human consciousness.
For example, the creative inspirations of songs were highly prized, eagerly
sought, and very frequently experienced by the Inuit. Inspiration was
considered a religious experience, as the following lines from a Caribou
Inuit song attest.

I call forth the song . . .
I draw a deep breath . . .
My breast breathes heavily
As I call forth the song.
I hear of distant villages
And their miserable catch
And draw a deep breath . . .
As I call forth the song
−From above. (Rasmussen 1930a, 71)

Breath provided the singer with inspiration because his breath-soul participated in the cosmic breath-soul that was Sila. Inspiration by an indi-

vidual breath-soul was always ultimately an inspiration by Sila. A sacred event, inspiration was often held in reverence and sought ceremonially (Rasmussen 1931, 321; 1952, 102; Schultz-Lorentzen 1928, 261).

Sila also required the traditional observances, watched that they were kept, and punished when they were not, in the beliefs of the Asiatic, Point Hope, Copper, Caribou, Polar, and perhaps the West Greenland Inuit (de Coccola and King 1954, 198; Malaurie 1982, 213, 218; Menovscikov 1968, 446–48; Rasmussen 1930, 49–50; 1932, 22–23, 31, 36; 1952, 271–72; Weyer 1932, 390–91). These beliefs do not imply that Sila anciently instituted the customs, for the Inuit had no such myths, and further remarks encourage a different interpretation. The Nunivak Islanders, Copper, and Caribou Inuit knew Sila's voice. It was heard sometimes loudly, but sometimes as a whisper (de Coccola and King 1954, 198; Rasmussen 1927, 385–86; 1930, 46–47, 51; 1932, 193). Sila apparently spoke the words of moral inspiration that Westerners term conscience. A third type of inspiration was explicitly remarked only among the Caribou Inuit. When Sila spoke invisibly to shamans, they received advice and prophecies (Rasmussen 1930, 46–47, 51).

The participation of the breath-soul in the cosmic consciousness of Sila was not restricted to the god's provision of inspirations. The relationship also placed Sila's many powers at the individual's disposal. What an individual thought and willed, Sila thought and willed perforce. By any standard, it was a case of the little toe wiggling the whole body. It was only the occasional, exceptionally endowed breath-soul that had the power to direct Sila's actions. Within these limits, however, Sila's intermediacy of magic was taken for granted. The Copper, Netsilik, and Iglulik, who maintained that magic words had intrinsic power, also asserted that the souls of animals understood and obeyed the words (de Coccola and King 1956, 237; Rasmussen 1929, 157; 1931, 278). The West Greenlanders considered deceased relatives to be involved in words' magical efficacy (Rink 1875, 52). In both cases, Sila functioned as a connecting medium – in Birket-Smith's view (1924, 435), a "mystic, supernatural power" – through which the breath-souls of animals and deceased relatives could be contacted.

Idealism and Shamanic Séances

The Inuit system of theurgy is remarkable for its philosophic depth and coherence. Ethnographic data rarely permit comparable demonstrations.

Few oral cultures are as well-documented as the Inuit, and few shamans
have been so unsecretive. On the other hand, with an ethnographic record
only a few centuries deep in time, external influence is certainly possible.
And so the question must be asked: How did Inuit shamans come by this
system?

Consider a séance that Rasmussen observed among the Copper Inuit.
The shaman sought to end a blizzard by mollifying Arnakapshaluk, goddess of the sea and its creatures. The séance commenced with various
preparations that need not detain us here.

> At last the shaman announced that Arnakapshaluk was approaching,
> and that all the men in the *qagsje* [feast hut] should hold on to him.
> They immediately threw themselves upon him, for now the Sea Woman
> had beset him, that is to say her soul had taken up its residence in his
> body, and she now spoke in a deep voice through the shaman. As a
> rule, she would tell them that the bad hunting was the result of some
> taboo having been broken, and that the constantly bad weather was
> due to people's indifference to the traditions of their ancestors. Scarcely
> had she launched these accusations when the women in their fear
> began to confess the breaches of taboo they had committed, the men
> meanwhile fighting desperately with Arnakapshaluk, who had quite
> taken possession of the shaman's body. He writhed in pain, struck out
> with his fists and moaned incessantly. They kept a firm hold on him. . . .
> Then, as soon as women and men had confessed all, the shaman cried
> in a loud voice that Arnakapshaluk's lamp was once more turned the
> right way up – indicating that as long as bad hunting lasted the lamp
> always stood bottom upwards, extinguished and dark. Shortly after-
> wards the shaman who was still fighting with the Sea Woman, shouted
> that now her hair was smooth and clean again: for as long as all sins
> are not confessed her hair is usually in the wildest disorder. Only
> when everything has been put in order again does Arnakapshaluk return
> to her house by the same route she has come. (Rasmussen 1932, 24–26)

In this séance, the Sea Woman was conjured into the feast hut where she
took possession of the shaman's body. The shaman, aware that he was
possessed, struggled with the Sea Woman for control of his body.

In the moments when the Sea Woman controlled him completely, the
shaman was oblivious to his physical environment and beheld dream-like
visions. In the intermittent periods when he regained partial control of his

body and sense perception, he verbally reported the contents of his visions to his audience. His visions conformed to a stereotypical religious scenario in which he beheld both himself and the goddess in her sea-bottom home. She was enraged because human sins had taken form as filth that fouled her hair. Since she was unwilling to be helped by the shaman, he was obliged to overpower her before he could restore order to her hut and cleanse her hair (Rasmussen 1932, 24). With this general scenario known to his audience, the shaman announced only those details that indicated his success: the corrected position of the Sea Woman's lamp and the cleansing of her hair.

Rasmussen, who recorded the séance, failed to note a remarkable curiosity. During the séance, both the Sea Woman and the shaman were both in the feast house on top of the offshore sea ice and in her house on the sea bottom. We do not know whether the Inuit audience noticed this anomaly and if so, how they understood it. However, the shaman's actions clearly indicate that he thought it irrelevant whether, in any moment, he and the Sea Woman were in the feast house or on the sea-bottom. Both locations were part of a continuous struggle – she to control his body in the feast house, and he to dominate her spirit on the sea bottom.

Much the same logical problem may be detected in Rasmussen's report of a shamanic séance among the Iglulik Inuit on the western coast of northern Hudson Bay.

I was just then making preparations for a sledge journey . . . and the purpose of his séance . . . was to ensure a free passage for our party, with plenty of game and no misfortunes on the road. He would ask the advice of the Giant Bear, Tulorialik: when that particular spirit deigned to occupy his body, he, Unaleq, could transform himself into a bear or a walrus at will, and he was able to render great service to his fellow men by virtue of the powers thus acquired. . . .

All was in darkness, we could only wait for what was to come. For a long time not a sound was heard, but the waiting only increased our anticipation. At last we heard a scraping of heavy claws and a deep growling. "Here it comes" whispered Tuglik [the shaman's wife and assistant], and all held their breath. But nothing happened, except the same scraping and growling mingled with deep, frightened groans; then came a fierce growl, followed by a wild shriek, and at the same moment, Tuglik dashed forward . . . and began talking to the spirits. She spoke in their own particular spirit language. . . . The spirits spoke now in deep chest notes, now in a high treble. We could hear, in between the words, sounds like those of trickling water, the rushing of wind, a stormy sea, the snuffling of walrus, the growling of bear. These, however, were not produced with any superlative art, for we could distinguish all through the peculiar lisp of the old shaman acting ventriloquist. This sitting lasted about an hour, and when all was quiet once more, Tuglik informed us that her husband, in the shape of the fabulous bear, had been out exploring the route we were to follow on our long journey. All obstacles had been swept aside, accident, sickness and death were rendered powerless, and we should all return in safety to out house the following summer. All this had been communicated in the special language of the spirits, which Tuglik translated for us. (Rasmussen 1929, 38–39)

At the beginning of the séance, a "long time" passed without apparent event while the shaman entered the trance. Dramatic enactment announced the arrival of the bear-spirit to the audience. The bear was reluctant. It growled. Then suddenly at the moment the shaman assimilated the spirit to himself, the bear-spirit gave one wild shriek as it merged with the shaman's free-soul, lending the shaman its powers. His wife knew the meaning of the event and immediately rushed forward. Because the shaman now had the abilities of the bear-spirit, he could understand and speak only in the esoteric language of the spirits. His wife, acting as assistant, appears to have spoken only briefly. For about an hour the shaman carried on alone, envisioning his disembodied soul journeying in the form of the bear-spirit. Simultaneously, this master of shamanic trance had the presence of mind to employ ventriloquism in order to produce audible effects appropriate to those that he heard during his visionary journey. Rasmussen was too preoccupied with the man's lisp to recognize the magnificence of the shaman's ability to mediate the contents of his vision. The shaman's consciousness was fully engaged in his soul's flight within the environment depicted in his visions. Though completely oblivious to his own bodily and external sensory perceptions, he had the presence of mind to auto-suggest ventriloquisms.

How did shamans understand experiences in which their free-souls were seemingly in two places at the same time? Shamans' beliefs in soul dualism have provided no explanation. The Sea Woman, unique among Inuit deities as both an indweller and a spirit, possessed the Copper shaman's body by occupying his free-soul, the bodily site of all spirit-intrusion, yet it was his free-soul that he beheld on the sea-bottom. Similarly, the Iglulik shaman's free-soul, which had journeyed abroad in flight, was nevertheless able to direct his body's activity.

The séances may be explained, I suggest, by reference to shamanic belief in metaphysical idealism. In the Copper séance, the shaman envisioned the Sea Woman in her sea-bottom home, but he believed her to be an invisible, anthropopsychic idea. What he saw could not be the Sea Woman. It had to be a vision that manifested the idea of her in pictorial form. A parallel interpretation will explain the Iglulik séance. In both cases, the shamans never left the séance hut, either from our perspective or from theirs. They knew that their visions were experiences occurring within the bodily seats of their souls.

At least, so I interpret. What I will maintain, however, is that shamanic séance practice provided incentive for the development of metaphysical idealism. There is no need to attribute the Inuit philosophic achievement to a diffusion of metaphysical idealism from a technologically more advanced culture, such as ancient India or classical Greece. Because shamans remain intellectually alert and active during their trances – where spirit mediums, for example, are passive and amnesic – they required a complex doctrine to explain their séance experiences. For the most part, soul dualism was a sufficient paradigm. The distinction between the free-soul and the bodily breath-soul, however, did not adequately explain a few, comparatively rare varieties a shamanic experience. The desire to solve these logical puzzles may have encouraged some shamans to develop explanatory doctrines, and it is metaphysical idealism that we know them to have possessed.

Bibliography

Bäckman, Louise. 1975. *Sajva: Forestallningar om hjalp-och skyddsvasenn i heliga fjall bland samerna.* Stockholm: Almqvist and Wiksell. [English summary, 140–50].

Birket-Smith, Kaj. 1924. Ethnography of the Egedesmind District, *Meddelelser om Gronland* 66.

1953. *The Chugach Eskimo.* Copenhagen: Nationalmuseets.

Boas, Franz. 1901. The Eskimo of Baffin Land and Hudson Bay. *American Museum of Natural History Bulletin* 15/1.

1907. Second report on the Eskimo of Baffin Land and Hudson Bay. *American Museum of Natural History Bulletin* 15/2.

Bogoras, Waldemar. 1907. *The Chukchee.* Leiden: E. J. Brill and New York: G. E. Stechert.

de Coccola, Raymond and Paul King. 1954. *Ayorama.* Toronto: Oxford University Press.

Freuchen, Peter. 1961. *Book of the Eskimos*. Cleveland: World Publishing.

Giddings, James L. 1961. *Kobuk River people*. College: University of Alaska.

Gubser, Nicholas J. 1965. *The Nunamiut Eskimos: Hunters of caribou*. New Haven: Yale University Press.

Hawkes, Ernest W. 1916. *The Labrador Eskimo*. Ottawa: Government Printing Bureau. Rpt. New York: Johnson Reprint, 1970.

Holm, Gustav. 1911. Ethnological sketch of the Angmagsalik Eskimo. *Meddelelser om Gronland* 39/1.

Holtved, Erik. 1967. Contribution to polar Eskimo ethnography. *Meddeleser om Gronland* 182/2.

Hultkrantz, Åke. 1953. *Conceptions of the soul among North American Indians: A study in religious ethnology*. Stockholm: Ethnographical Museum of Sweden.

Jenness, Diamond. 1922. *The life of the Copper Eskimos*. Rpt. New York: Johnson Reprint.

———. 1926. *Myths and traditions from northern Alaska, the Mackenzie Delta, and Coronation Gulf*. Ottawa: F. A. Acland.

Lantis, Margaret. 1946. The social culture of the Nunivak Eskimo. *Transactions of the American Philosophical Society* 35/3.

Lucier, Charles. 1958. Noatgmiut Eskimo myths, *Anthropological Papers of the University of Alaska* 6/2. 89–111.

Malaurie, Jean. 1982. *The last kings of Thule: With the polar Eskimos, as they face their destiny*. New York: E. P. Dutton.

Marsh, Gordon H. 1954. A comparative survey of Eskimo-Aleut religion. *Anthropological Papers of the University of Alaska* 3/1, 21–36.

Menovscikov, G. A. 1968. Popular conceptions, religious beliefs and rites of the asiatic Eskimos, in *Popular beliefs and folklore tradition in Siberia*, Vilmose Dioszegi, ed., Bloomington: Indiana University, and The Hague: Mouton.

Merkur, Daniel. 1983. Breath-soul and Wind Owner: The many and the one in Inuit religion, *American Indian Quarterly* 7, 23–39.

———. 1985a. *Becoming half-hidden: Shamanism and initiation among the Inuit*. Stockholm: Almqvist and Wiksell.

———. 1985b. Souls, spirits, and indwellers in nature: Metaphysical dualism in Inuit religion. *Temenos* 21, 91–126.

Mowat, Farley. 1975. *The people of the deer*, 2nd ed. Rpt. Toronto: McClelland and Stewart-Bantam, 1980.

Nansen, Fridtjof. 1893. *Eskimo life*. London: Longmans, Green.

Petersen, Robert. 1966–67. Burial-forms and death cult among the Eskimos. *Folk* 8–9, 259–80.

Rasmussen, Knud. 1908. *The people of the polar North: A record*. London: Kegan Paul, Trench, Trubner and Co.

———. 1921. *Greenland by the Polar Sea: The story of the Thule expedition from Melville Bay to Cape Morris Jesup*. New York: Frederick A. Stokes.

———. 1927. *Across arctic America: Narrative of the fifth Thule expedition*. Rpt. New York: Greenwood Press, 1969.

1929. *Intellectual culture of the Iglulik Eskimos.* Rpt. New York: AMS Press, 1976.

1930. *Observations on the intellectual culture of the Caribou Eskimos.* Rpt. New York: AMS Press, 1976.

1931. *The Netsilik Eskimos: Social life and spiritual culture.* Rpt. New York: AMS Press, 1976.

1932. *Intellectual culture of the Copper Eskimos.* Rpt. New York: AMS Press, 1976.

1938. Knud Rasmussen's posthumous notes on the life and doings of the East Greenlanders in olden times, ed. H. Ostermann, *Meddelelser om Gronland* 109/1.

1952. *The Alaskan Eskimos: As described in the posthumous notes of Dr. Knud Rasmussen,* ed. H. Ostermann. Rpt. New York: AMS Press, 1976.

Rink, Henrik. 1875. *Tales and traditions of the Eskimo.* Rpt. Montreal: McGill-Queens University Press, 1974.

Schultz-Lorentzen, C. W. 1928. Intellectural culture of the Greenlanders, in *Greenland,* M. Vahl, G. C. Amdrup, L. Bobe, and Ad. S. Jensen, eds., Vol. 2. Copenhagen: C. A. Reitzel, and London: Humphrey Milford.

Spencer, Robert F. 1959. *The north Alaskan Eskimo: A study in ecology and society.* Rpt. New York: Dover Publications, 1976.

Stefansson, Vilhjalmur. 1913. *My life with the Eskimo.* New York: Macmillan.

1921. *The friendly Arctic: The story of five years in polar regions.* New York: Macmillan.

Thalbitzer, William. 1921. The Ammassalik Eskimo: contributions to the ethnology of the East Greenland natives. III. Language and folklore, *Meddelelser om Gronland* 40/3.

1926. The cultic deities of the Inuit (Eskimo), *International Congress of Americanists* 22/2, 367–93.

Weyer, Edward Moffat. 1932. *The Eskimos: Their environment and folkways.* Rpt. n.p.: Archon Books, 1969.

Williamson, Robert G. 1974. *Eskimo underground: Socio-cultural change in the central Canadian Arctic.* Uppsala: Almqvist and Wiksell.

II. Transitions

Individualism and Integration in Navajo Religion

Guy H. Cooper

Within the enormous diversity of religious belief and expression in native North America, it is possible to determine two broad types of religious configuration or emphasis – that of the hunters and that of the horticulturists. Most recently, Hultkrantz (1987, 14) highlighted the main features of these two types, the hunting, oriented toward animal ceremonialism, personal quests for power, shamanism and annual ceremonies of cosmic rejuvenation, and the horticultural, oriented toward rain and fertility ceremonies, priestly ritual, medicine societies and calendrical rites. In general, hunting societies are strongly oriented toward individualism and horticultural ones toward collectivism. Hultkrantz has pointed to the different structuring within religious beliefs and practices that these two orientations produce. With regard to the Shoshoni, an example of a hunting, individualistic culture, he states:

> Because religious ideas are so flexible and the organization of the world view is so loose, a number of belief complexes are formed that pull together and unify otherwise separate beliefs and practices. For example, individual beliefs form links, like links of a chain, and these connect an association of beliefs into a larger complex. (Hultkrantz 1987, 129)

Horticultural societies, on the other hand, emphasize traditional bodies of religious knowledge and practice, collectivism and cooperation, in keeping with sedentary living patterns and the collective nature of agriculture. The problems facing each type result from these emphases: individuality requires mechanisms of integration into a cultural whole, whereas collectivism must allow space for individual expression. Individualism is an economic and social necessity in hunting tribes, since hunting relies on individual skills and initiative, and occasionally meager food sources necessitate the dispersal of small groups. This individualism is encouraged by the guardian spirit complex, whereby individuals seek a personal link with the sacred to aid them in their personal lives. This relationship with the sacred can at times attain the level of an almost individual religion (Benedict 1923). Individual status rests of individual personality and capacities; personal qualities, not hereditary positions, determine one's prestige, and the consensus of others sustains one's position. For example, a medicine man's position is dependent on his success in carrying out his tasks.

Communal living patterns, on the other hand, rely more on hereditary positions and possession of esoteric knowledge. Status depends on position, as well as personal characteristics, in keeping with communal agricultural activities and a communal, sedentary lifestyle. Here the individualism of hunting tribes is frowned upon as potentially dangerous to the good of the entire tribe.

Many societies within native North America blend these two orientations, and a study of Navajo patterns in this regard would be useful in assessing how individualistic patterns are integrated in Navajo culture. The processes whereby individual beliefs and practices are integrated into a unified culture should also suggest how resilient a culture is to external pressures and how successful it may be in preserving a distinct religious and cultural identity.

The historical dimension is important in this regard. Navajo culture, like all cultures, has a distinct history, and more is known of Navajo history than of many other native American peoples. The Navajos arrived as hunter/gatherers in the Southwest some time in the fifteenth century and their religious system at this time involved hunting ritual and shamanism. Their seminomadic lifestyle changed, however, under the influence of various Pueblo peoples in the seventeenth century. The adoption of the Pueblos' horticultural religion and mythology changed these living patterns. Economically, the adoption of sheep herding led to a decline in the importance of hunting, accompanied by adoption of agricultural techniques and raiding of Spanish and Pueblo settlements. The Navajo developed the use of elaborate religious ceremonials for the curing of illness under the leadership of independent medicine men or "singers" and established a mythology centered around an agricultural Emergence motif (Cooper 1984). The Navajo are unique in that no other native American tribe has traditionally derived a major income from the herding of domesticated animals or devoted their religious practices almost exclusively to the curing of individual illness. The Emergence mythology and ceremonial practices are what we know as "traditional" Navajo religion.[1]

While there has been a move away from shamans and the personal religious experience of the individual, typical of hunting societies, toward more priestly medicine men, learned knowledge, and well-defined, structured ceremonials, scholars have noted the individualistic base of Navajo culture. Ceremonials are for the cure of an individual under the guidance of individual singers, but there are no medicine societies. The diagnosis of illness is in the hands of inspirational diagnosticians, who seem to be bearers of the earlier shamanic traditions (Cooper 1984, 66–67). The general belief in the importance of individual religious knowledge, as well as the survival of earlier hunting ritual and mythology, is separate from mainstream cosmology and ceremonialism, which is in the hands of certain individuals (Luckert 1975). The widespread belief in witchcraft also highlights the importance of individual action, and many scholars have observed that the Navajos are certainly more individualistic than the Pueblos, who emphasize community.

Hill, referring to traditional Navajo culture stated:

Speaking in a strictly political sense, a Navaho tribe does not exist. Such cohesiveness as occurs in a national sense is due to a common linguistic and cultural heritage, to the occupation of a defined territory, and to a common designation for themselves *dine* "people" as against all others. The Navaho have never functioned as a unit in a concerted action. Never have all of them been brought, even temporarily, under the leadership of a single or individual group for a common purpose. (Hill 1940, 23)

Despite this strong individualism, Navajo mythology and religious practice display a remarkable coherence, allowing for minor individual variations, and it seems worthwhile to examine the ways in which individuals have traditionally been integrated into this coherent and unified central body of religious belief and practice. The Navajo live in small groups scattered over a 25,000-square-mile reservation and are not unified by the large scale tribal gatherings, such as the annual Sun Dance that one finds, for example, on the Plains.

The two most basic integrative mechanisms among the Navajo are their language and their clan system. Navajo language has remained the predominant language of most Navajos, and the Navajo have consistently refused to learn other people's languages, even though the Navajos have always been extensively involved in trading. English is the only foreign language that has become extensively adopted by the Navajo, and that only since World War Two.[2] Their own language has been one of the most unifying forces among the Navajo, and as Witherspoon has demonstrated (Witherspoon 1977), language relates to perceptions and constructions of reality. Conceptions of the creative and transforming power of language are firmly embedded in Navajo religion. The acquisition of language, therefore, already places the individual in a shared reality. The clan system involves aspects of reciprocity and responsibilities which allow social linkages across the reservation.

The traditional Navajo home, the hogan, is where the religious and social worlds meet. Traditionally, there are two forms of hogan, the conical and the round roof. The conical type, now found in few areas of the reservation, was the first construction in the present world as described in detail in the Creation Myth, the home of First Man. The Holy People sang into being the inner forms of the natural phenomena which constitute the present world. Thus, the hogan is not only the first, original center of the world, but from it radiates the creation of the entire world. Traditionally, ceremonials should be held only in the conical hogan, but its construction leaves limited room. In the myth the Holy People blow the walls further apart to allow more room for large numbers of people. Humans do the same by constructing a round roof hogan, now the most common, which accommodates the large dry-paintings of the ceremonials, as well as more people. The myth describes the original construction of the first hogan and provides strict rules governing their building and orientation (Wyman 1970, 10–16). The Hogan songs describe the hogan as the microcosm of the universe, embodying vital parts of the world in its construction. The Navajo, therefore, inhabit the center of the world, a place where the religious base of life forms the basis of their economic and social activities. Haile described the hogan as follows:

This place home is to be the center of every blessing in life: happy births, the home of one's children, the center where good health, property, increase in crops and livestock originate, where old age, the goal in life, will visit regularly. In a word, the hogan spells a long life of happiness. (Wyman 1970, 10)

The construction of a new hogan necessitates a performance of Blessing Way ceremonial, which incorporates the mythology and knowledge regarding hogans, as well as concerns for long life, happiness, and the fundamentals of Navajo cosmology. Blessing Way songs and rituals are performed at the beginning of any ceremonial, which must always take place in a hogan, to consecrate and purify the hogan. The hogan is thus a major religious and social integrating force among the Navajo. As Wyman states:

Through Blessing Way the Navajo have become hogan dwellers. Blessing Way's hogan songs which it alone has kept alive makes it responsible for the existence of the place home and the dwellers there. Moreover, this ideology has unified all hogan dwellers into a distinctive tribe, differentiating them from the neighboring house-dwellers, the Pueblo Indians, or from tipi- dwellers like the Jicarilla Apache. (Wyman 1970, 16)

Accompanying this central point in a Navajo's life are conceptions of the four sacred mountains and the mountain soil bundle. The four sacred mountains, forming the boundaries of the Navajo world, are primary orientation points for any Navajo, for whom knowing where one is is of prime importance. The myths are full of the travels of hero figures over Navajo territory and provide extensive geographical information. The physical terrain of the Navajo Reservation is an outer manifestation of the sacred world, and in keeping with all native American tribes, the land is imbued with the sacred. Navajos are therefore concerned about orienting themselves in space relative to the four cardinal mountains. Indeed, being lost is akin to being ill. The Mountain soil bundle is a medicine bundle containing soil from the four sacred mountains and is linked to the medicine bundle of First Man, from whom all creation springs. A mountain soil bundle is customarily held by the head of each clan and can also be held by individuals. It is thus a visible and potent link to the boundaries and protectors of the Navajo universe (Wyman 1970, 16–24). Thus, every Navajo traditionally inhabits a dwelling which establishes him or her directly

at the sacred source of the Navajo world and integrates him or her into the
common cosmology of the Navajo tribe.

The traditional living pattern of small communities of between ten and
forty families falls under the leadership of a chosen headman:

> Factors governing the choice included exemplary character, oratorical
> ability, personal magnetism, and proven ability to serve in both the
> practical and religious aspects of the culture. It was a foregone conclu-
> sion that the chosen individual would be a practitioner and it was
> necessary that he control at least the Blessing Way ceremony. (Hill
> 1940, 25)

Each community, therefore, would have a leader who was knowledgeable
in the central ceremonial, Blessing Way, and would thus consolidate knowledge of the central tenets of Navajo cosmology.

Personal knowledge of religious matters is, of course, variable. Navajos
regard religious knowledge as a form of power and a kind of possession,
and thus every individual would regard it as beneficial to possess some
religious knowledge, however slight. Knowledge could be used for one's
own benefit, and in keeping with general Navajo tenets, would not be
given away without some form of recompense (Opler 1968). This is by
no means unusual. The Navajo culture is an oral culture, and the telling of
myths is a customary part of any traditional Navajo upbringing.

The extent to which individuals participate in ceremonial activity is, of
course, of great importance in assessing the degree to which they are
exposed directly to the sacred powers of the Navajo world. An individual
can participate at the level of singer, curer, assistant, patient, or spectator.
A singer knows one or more distinct ceremonial,[3] whereas curers know
parts of the ceremonials, but do not have the same status as proper singers. An assistant helps in the carrying out of a ceremonial, often acting as
an apprentice to a singer, or working on the dry-paintings under the
singer's direction. There is a graduated range of sacred specialists. Another
major figure is the diagnostician, often female, whose abilities come from
a particular gift, rather than from training. Her knowledge of ceremonials
is more limited (Kluckhohn 1939, 66–71; Morgan 1931). Singers clearly
are the most knowledgeable about Navajo cosmology and myth, but it
should be noted that, in a very large number of distinct ceremonials, it is
rare to find a singer who knows more than two or three ceremonials.
Singers are apprenticed to individual teachers for many years. These teach-

ers pass on their distinct knowledge, leading to minor variations in the practice of the ceremonials. Even though there is considerable overlap, each ceremonial has a particular relationship to a group of sacred beings relevant to the particular illness (Wyman 1983, 538–39). The number of specialists among the Navajo is almost impossible to determine. Kluckhohn, in a survey of one particular Navajo community in the 1930s, found that twenty out of sixty-nine adult men in the community conducted ceremonials, but only three could be considered singers (Kluckhohn 1938, 361–62).

Most Navajo have experience of ceremonials as patients or participants. Ceremonials cure individuals by identifying the patient with the original patient of that particular ceremonial, and by summoning the powers associated with it, they bring the patient into a state of harmony with these powers. In Navajo terms, the "inner form" or "wind soul" of the patient is brought into a harmonious relationship with the "inner forms" of the various powers involved in a particular ceremonial through songs, dry-paintings and various ritual procedures (Witherspoon 1977; Gill 1979; Wyman 1983). The patient has direct contact, albeit in symbolic form (Sandner 1979), with the Holy People of Navajo cosmology in a ritual context where mythic and present time meet. In this context a Navajo will have direct experience of the basic tenets of Navajo cosmology in its most dramatic and meaningful way. In a 1930s study Kluckhohn found a fairly high degree of participation in ceremonials in a sample period of six months. Two singers committed an average of five days out of fourteen to ceremonial activity with 148 ceremonials being carried out in the same time in a community of about 400 people who spent an average of twenty percent of their annual income on ceremonials. Kluckhohn notes:

> Adult men in the community tend, on the average (at least during this portion of the year), to devote one-fourth to one-third of their productive time to ceremonials; adult women one-fifth to one-sixth. The figure for men would probably have been higher in the not very distant past, for a large number of younger men would almost certainly have been engaged in systematically learning the ceremonials. (Kluckhohn 1938, 364)

Kluckhohn's study is also noteworthy for its attention to nonceremonial religious activity, that is, religious acts which occur outside ceremonials. These range from songs designed for individual protection or luck to prayers and songs employed at crop-planting, marriages, sweat-lodges, and so forth (Kluckhohn 1938, 365–66). Traditionally, then, Navajo individuals are integrated into a common tradition of cosmology, religious belief, and practice by the degree of their religious knowledge, their participation in ceremonials, and the small communities in which they live under the guidance of religious specialists.

Initiation occurs as a ceremonial, with an individual as a specialist or as a patient initiated fully into the specifics of a particular ceremonial. Traditionally, both an apprentice and a patient must have a particular ceremony "sung over" him or her four times. The Navajo view, in keeping with the widespread significance of the number four, is that this signifies completeness and is believed to render the singer or patient immune from any further problems with a particular set of Holy People. Regarding more general initiation, boys were probably initiated into hunting and war rituals, although there is no record of this, and there is no general initiation of boys in Navajo culture. Girls are accorded a ceremonial of the *Kinaalda,* a puberty ceremonial belonging to the Blessing Way group, at first menses. The *Kinaalda* stresses the importance of women and fertility in Navajo culture, during which the girl is identified with Changing Woman, the most prominent female Holy Person in Navajo cosmology. The girl's puberty ceremony, shared with other Apache groups, suggests that it is in essence a very old and original part of Navajo culture (Frisbie 1967).

General initiation occurs in the Night Way or Night Chant ceremonial. The Night Chant is a long ceremonial lasting nine days and nights and is central to the group of ceremonials which have masked deities, or *ye'ii,* present during most of the procedures. On the fifth night of this ceremonial, the masked *ye'ii,* under the leadership of Talking God, "the Grand father of the *ye'ii*" as the Navajo refer to him, lead the candidates for initiation into the hogan. Talking God applies meal to various parts of their bodies and strikes them with yucca leaves. Following this, the candidates bow their heads and cover their faces as the men impersonating the masked deities take off their masks and place them on a buffalo robe. The candidates are then bidden to look up and see the impersonators (Matthews 1901).

This is an initiation into the secrets of the *ye'ii* or masked dancers and traditionally occurred for all Navajos, male and female. Apart from being the only general initiation, it is noteworthy for the striking resemblances it has to the Hopi tribe's initiations into the kachina cult. During a performance of the Powamu ceremony, all children are brought into the ceremonial chamber, the kiva, and ceremonially whipped with yucca leaves by masked kachinas, who later teach the children their secrets (Voth 1901). Similarities in the use of corn, yucca leaves, and the role played by *ye'ii* and kachinas in the lives of children suggest that the Navajo ceremony has been influenced by the Hopi ceremony (Matthews 1901, 355; Sekaquaptewa 1976, 36–39). Initiation into the cult could, therefore, be seen as initiation into a discrete segment of Navajo religious life, one that derived from Hopi (and indeed wider Pueblo) practices, were it not for the fact that the *ye'ii* are integrated into basic Navajo cosmology. Although the *ye'ii* only appear in a restricted number of ceremonials and are not typical of Navajo ceremonial practices in general, they are nonetheless of great importance in Navajo cosmology. Talking God, in particular, is a leading figure in the creation of the world, the discoverer of Changing Woman, and a hunting and agricultural deity (Cooper 1984, 42–43). He is the most prominent male deity among the Navajo, prominent not only in Emergence cosmology, but prominent also in earlier hunting mythology and ritual. Therefore, initiation into the *ye'ii* cult must be seen as initiation into a central part of Navajo religion. Furthermore, the Night Chant, unlike most Navajo ceremonials, is a long ceremonial which attracts the attendance of large numbers of Navajos. The cost of the ceremonial, requiring a large number of kin to help with expenses, and its benefits which extend beyond the cure of one individual, draw many people at large, who see it as a communal ceremonial (Matthews 1901, 353). All Navajo ceremonials have generally beneficial effects over and above the cure of one individual, but the Night Chant, with its initiation of large numbers of Navajo and the attraction of the public dancing of the *ye'ii*, has the hallmarks of a communal ceremony benefiting all, as well as a communal experience of sacred powers.

The social and economic aspects of the Night Chant and other major ceremonials, such as the Enemy Way, cannot be overlooked. Such occasions provide a means for large numbers of Navajos to congregate. As Hill has demonstrated, however, ritual, economic, and social aspects of life are not separated, but are linked in the minds of Navajos (Hill 1938).

In traditional Navajo culture, therefore, various mechanisms exist to integrate the individual into a common religious tradition and shared cosmology. This traditional pattern, however, must be placed in the historical context of the development of the Navajo tribe. As I have discussed elsewhere (Cooper 1984), traditional Navajo religion and culture is a particular historical state resulting from historical circumstances and their cultural and individual responses. Navajos arrived in the Southwest in small

bands with hunting ritual, myth, and shamanism as important aspects of their religious lives. Individualism is part and parcel of Navajo culture. Hunting, and later raiding, were activities relying on individual prowess and initiative. The two were also related on a ritual level. Hunting ritual formed the basis for war ritual and techniques, both developing logically from hunting. As we have seen, there were leaders of local community groups, as well as war leaders. As Hill states:

> The choice of war leader or leaders was entirely dependent on ritual attainment. Anyone who had acquired the knowledge of one or more of the War Ways, upon which the success of any punitive venture was thought to depend, was eligible as a leader. (Hill 1940)

There are, therefore, two distinct ritual and political patterns. Peace leaders represent Blessing Way, fertility, harmony, and central Navajo cosmology; War leaders represent killing and ritual based on hunting traditions. Hunting ritual was regarded as separate, even opposite, to the main concerns of Navajo religion (Hill 1938, 98–99). When successful, such techniques and practices were socially sanctioned. However, these raiding techniques led to the incarceration of the tribe in 1864, and afterwards such practices were associated with witchcraft and socially decried (Hill 1940, 24). Navajo religion, through its interlinking ceremonial practices, succeeded in ousting shamanism, pushing hunting and war rituals to the fringe, thereby consolidating a central body of knowledge and practice.

These patterns refer to a particular stage in Navajo history, which began to change in this century after major events such as the sheep cull of the 1930s and the Second World War. They resulted in some disaffection with the ability of traditional practices to deal with this type of trauma and saw the rise of the peyote cult on the reservation. The Second World War exposed a large number of Navajos to the outside world. Extensive contact with whites and the pervasive effects of white culture through education, medicine, wage labor, and so forth had a significant impact on Navajo culture and traditional religious practices.

Individualism has, of course, persisted throughout Navajo cultural history in the ways I have outlined, in hunting ritual and mythology, which lie outside mainstream Navajo religious practices (Luckert 1975), in individual variation of belief, in individual choice of diagnostician and singer, and in the continuation of traditional widespread living patterns. There are differences even between relatively close communities. One informant noted linguistic and sex role differences between two communities living only a few miles apart. Individual singers and curers acquire reputations which attract patients from far afield (Cooper 1978). Individualism is also recognized within ceremonialism. Spencer, in an exhaustive analysis of Navajo Chant Way myths, shows that the myths sanctioning each ceremonial depend on their genesis on the self-assertive acts of individual hero figures:

> Characteristic is the persistence, obstinacy and even defiance with which he pursues his course. Not only his family but also the supernaturals become objects of this defiance. He offends against his family by gambling away their property or he ventures in disobedience of their instructions. More often it is the authority of supernaturals that is flouted by reckless violation of ritual taboos. These actions are directed against forces that seem to be felt as constricting. (Spencer 1957, 37)

Within the ceremonial system ritual knowledge is acquired by individualism, even by defiance of norms, and thus individualism has both negative aspects with, for example, the hero falling ill, and beneficial or ceremonial aspects.

The events of this century, however, have tended to affect the traditional patterns of integration which I have outlined above. Before looking at these changes, however, it must be noted that, with the U.S. government's imposition of a tribal council, the Navajo have attained a level of political cohesion they had previously lacked (Shepardson 1983). Members of the tribal council are elected from different "chapters" of the reservation, showing a clearly integrative awareness of the "Navajo nation." On the other hand, pressures imposed by Anglo culture have affected traditional areas of integration. Hogans are still retained for ceremonial activity, but there is a tendency toward western style housing with its conveniences. Many Navajos who live off the reservation or on school compounds rely on access to the hogans of their kin. Thus, at this level, the traditional mode of living has been disrupted for many Navajos. The use of the language is still strong. It has been incorporated into the school curriculum and seems in little danger of declining.

A major change has been the decline in the number of ceremonials still known and practiced on the reservation. Numerous informants stated that many ceremonials would become extinct because there were no young men to learn them and that many of the elderly men who did know them had died. Despite efforts to arrest this decline, such as the School for Medicine Men at Rough Rock (see Bergman 1973), the number of traditional ceremonials practiced will decrease. Learning a traditional ceremonial is a long and financially burdensome affair which does not carry the same high reward and status as it did in the past (Harman 1964).

Blessing Way has always been the major integrating ceremonial of the Navajo because it embodies the central facets of Navajo cosmology and through its practice maintains and reinforces this cosmology. Many Navajos regard it as the original Navajo ceremonial that was developed from the girls' puberty ceremonial, the Kinaalda, an original part of Navajo culture (Frisbie 1967, 9). The Blessing Way functions as a blueprint for all other ceremonials in traditional Navajo religion as they all include prayers and songs from it. A decline in other ceremonials might not affect the basics of Navajo religion if Blessing Way maintained its presence in Navajo life. Information on its current practice would be very useful. My own impression in 1978 was that Blessing Way was still very widely practiced. The Blessing Way singer I met was in high demand and in the process of teaching it to his own daughter (Cooper 1978).

Performance of the major ceremonials, such as Enemy Way and the Night Way, continue to attract large numbers of Navajos. Some informants stated that the Enemy Way ceremonials tended to attract many young men socially because it involves girls selecting men as dance partners and is often marred by drunkenness (Cooper 1978). Nonetheless, as Witherspoon has pointed out, the Navajos emphasize the distinctly Navajo elements in its performance and spend, in his estimate, around one million dollars per year on its practice (Witherspoon 1975). This suggests that it is still a major integrating force in Navajo culture, even though the social rather than religious aspects seem to be of importance, at least to many young people. The Night Way ceremonials are also widely practiced. Although the number of Navajos now initiated into the secrets of the ye'ii is unknown and one suspects it to be much less than previously thought, the sight of large numbers of Navajos crowding around the line of masked figures making their final dance toward the rising sun on the last night of the ceremonial indicated to me that the presence of the sacred in the form of the masked ye'ii has great meaning for Navajos today (Cooper 1978).

The peyote cult and Christianity are two alternative forms of religious practice on the reservation, indicative of the strength of individual choice by Navajos. Peyotism grew rapidly and without much opposition following the sheep cull in the 1930s. I have discussed this elsewhere (Cooper 1984, 101–5) and here will only point to the Navajo's individual search for alternatives to traditional ceremonialism at a time when the Navajos, particularly the poorer ones, felt powerless in opposing the sheep cull. Other problem areas in Navajo culture, such as witchcraft, seemed to many Navajos to be better served by peyotism than by traditional practices. Peyote rituals are short and cheap compared to traditional ceremonials, and they fit in with the fast pace of life demanded by Anglo living patterns, wage labor, and off-reservation living. Western modes of living are strongly competitive and individualistic, and have thus encouraged the individualism present in Navajo culture. Peyotism has grown through the determination of individuals to participate, despite opposition and its being seen as "non-Navajo", with recent signs that peyotism is becoming more integrated into the culture (Wyman 1983, 536).

Christianity varies in its impact, with many denominations having little disruptive effect. Some fundamentalist sects, however, have encouraged their members to avoid traditional practices, imposing great stress on kinship obligations and interpersonal relationships.

Individualism has thus become more prominent as historical circumstances have affected traditional cultural patterns. But Navajo cultural patterns have always consisted of a tension and a balance between individualism and integration. Culturally, the Navajo are renowned for their capacity to adapt elements from other cultures and at the same time maintain a distinctly Navajo identity. The issue is the means by which this balance is maintained, without resulting in fragmentation, and the effect on the Navajo religion. Traditional ceremonialism displays elements of individualism and integration. Each ceremonial is a distinct entity, concerned with particular sacred powers, under the direction of an individual singer. Luckert referred to them as self-contained mini-religions, each having its own distinct history and soteriology (Luckert 1979, 7), and yet they are integrated, not into a coherent "system", but by their links, common themes, and structures, like the links of the chain referred to above by Hultkrantz.

Individuals themselves integrate different elements within their culture. Navajos are rarely exclusive in their approaches to the solutions to their problems, and individuals will often combine traditional ceremonialism, peyotism, Christianity, and Western medicine in their search for a successful resolution. This is a strength rather than a weakness in Navajo culture and attests to the importance of individualism as a contributing factor in the identity and the resilience of the culture. Individuals have

kept alive certain traditions and knowledge from the past, even though
some of these practices have been labelled witchcraft, and individuals
have introduced new "non-Navajo" religious configurations, such as peyotism
and syncretistic rituals (Cooper 1978), which have proved beneficial to
many Navajos. Individualism can thus fund Navajo culture with a range of
religious responses to changing circumstances. There will be continuing
debate among Navajos over the place of some of these elements in Navajo
religion, ensuring that the central issues relating to Navajo identity are
kept in the forefront. There are signs, as noted above, that peyotism is
becoming more integrated as traditional singers attend peyote meetings
and even become peyote leaders or Roadmen (Wyman 1983, 536). The
place of the individual ritual specialist will continue to be of central importance in the evolution of Navajo religion.

Thus, although there is a tension between individualism on the one
hand, which at its extreme is manifested in anti-social or "non-Navajo"
practices, such as witchcraft or peyotism, and a traditional system of order
embodied in a well-defined body of knowledge and practice on the other,
it is the creative tension between the two which allows individual input
and expression in the culture while simultaneously maintaining a sense
of order and coherence. The evolving process of a distinctly Navajo religion and culture is maintained through a continuing assessment and ques-
tioning of what elements should form part of a Navajo identity and a
Navajo response to the challenges facing their culture. That these issues
should center particularly around religious concerns[4] should be no sur-
prise; it is their concern with sacred matters that is the hallmark not only
of the Navajo but of all native American peoples.

NOTES

1. It must be remembered that the term "traditional refers to a particular stage
in a culture's history and that all cultures have developed and undergone change
and been affected by outside influences. The term "traditional" here means those
aspects of the culture which are indigenous (i.e., not introduced by white culture)
and thus follows the customary understanding of the term.

2. I met a Navajo who stated that his Grandmother forbade any member of her
family from learning or speaking English and none did so until 1965.

3. Kluckhohn notes that in the particular group he studied those knowing at
least two ceremonials of three or more nights were called singers. Wyman restricts
the term to those who know thoroughly a five-night ceremonial (Kluckhohn
1938, 361).

4. Aberle (1983, 569) notes that peyotism has been successful when other, non-religious, struggles have been less so and points to its "moral code, its effort to maintain community against corrosive atomization of Indian groups, its significance as a vehicle for Indian identity" as reasons for it success.

BIBLIOGRAPHY

Aberle, David. 1983. Peyote religion among the Navajo. In *Handbook of North American Indians*. ed. A. Ortiz, 10. Washington: Smithsonian Institution, 558–569.

Benedict, Ruth. 1923. The concept of the guardian spirit in North America. *American Anthropological Association Memoirs* 29. Menasha.

Bergman, Robert. 1973. A school for medicine men. *American Journal of Psychiatry* 130:663–66.

Cooper, Guy H. 1978. Fieldwork notes.

1984. *Development and stress in Navajo religion*. Stockholm: Almqvist and Wiksell.

Frisbie, Charlotte Johnson. 1967. Kinaalda: A study of the Navaho girl's puberty ceremony. Middletown, Conn.: Wesleyan University Press.

Gill, Sam D. 1979. *Songs of life: An introduction to Navajo religious culture*. Leiden: E. J. Brill.

Harman, R. 1964. Change in a Navaho ceremonial. *El Palacio* 71:20–26.

Hill, W. W. 1938. The agricultural and hunting methods of the Navaho Indians. *Yale University Publications in Anthropology* 18.

1940. Some aspects of Navajo political structure. *Plateau* 13:23–28.

Hultkrantz, Åke. 1987. *Native religions of North America*. San Francisco: Harper and Row.

Kluckhohn, Clyde. 1938. Partcipation in ceremonials in a Navaho community. *American Anthropologist* 40:359–69.

1939. Some personal and social aspects of Navaho ceremonial practice. *Harvard Theological Review* 32:57–82.

Luckert, Karl. 1975. *The Navajo hunter tradition*. Tucson: University of Arizona Press.

1979. *Coyoteway*. Tucson: University of Arizona Press.

Matthews, Washington. 1901. A Navajo initiation. *Land of sunshine* 15:353–56.

Morgan, William. 1931. Navaho treatment of sickness: Diagnosticians. *American Anthropologist* 33:390–402.

Opler, Morris E. 1968. Remuneration to supernaturals in Apachean ceremonialism. *Ethnology* 7:356–93.

Sandner, Donald. 1979. *Navaho symbols of healing*. New York: Harcourt, Brace and Jovanovich.

Sekaquaptewa, Emory. 1976. Hopi Indian ceremonies. In *Seeing with a native eye*, ed. W. Capps. New York: Harper and Row, 35–43.

Shepardson, Mary. 1983. Development of Navajo tribal government. In *Handbook of North American Indians*, ed. A. Ortiz, 10. Washington: Smithsonian Institution, 624–35.

Spencer, K. 1957. Mythology and values. An analysis of Navaho chantway myths. *Memoirs of the American Folklore Society* 48.

Voth, H. R. 1901. *The Oraibi Powamu ceremony*. Field Museum of Natural History, Anthropological series no. 61. Chicago.

Witherspoon, Gary. 1975. *Navajo kinship and marriage*. Chicago: University of Chicago Press.

1977. *Language and art in the Navajo universe*. Ann Arbor: University of Michigan Press.

Wyman, Leland C. 1970. *Blessingway*. Tucson: University of Arizona Press.

1983. Navajo ceremonial system. In *Handbook of North American Indians*, ed. A. Ortiz 10. Washington: Smithsonian Institution, 536–57.

"The Rainbow Will Carry Me": The Language of Seneca Iroquois Christianity as Reflected in Hymns

Thomas McElwain

Researchers have been blind to a rich source of information on native spirituality in the native Christian traditions. Just as the Iroquois have the curious habit of dividing everything into halves, researchers have felt justified in neglecting the Christian half of Iroquois religious belief. By calling part of the community Christian, the Iroquois people unwittingly give the impression that Iroquois Christians have conformed to white religion in ways that Longhouse people have not. Despite the many similarities between Iroquois and white Christians, Iroquois Christianity remains an excellent source of specifically native religious values.

I shall examine the Christianity of one particular Iroquois community, the Seneca community. I shall do so from the limited perspective of the language used in Seneca hymns in the first half of the nineteenth century. Hymns are extremely useful in monitoring the kinds of values in question. Seneca hymns are not translations, because the necessity of adapting the Seneca words, which are generally much longer than their English counterparts, to the strict meter of the already existing tunes, prohibits anything approaching translation. Seneca hymns are therefore very loose paraphrases. A paraphrase paradoxically stimulates the selection of expressions equivalent to the English ones on one hand, while giving leeway for native elements foreign to the original text. An examination of the differences between the English and Seneca hymn texts will suggest which values and expressions are shared by the two traditions, and which are not. More importantly perhaps, the examination will show differences in the extent to which shared values are emphasized.[1]

83

I have used as a source a small volume of hymns entitled *Seneca Hymns*, which was first published by the American Tract Society in 1834 and reprinted four times since, the latest in 1978.

Words for God and Jesus

An examination of twentieth-century texts supports the contention that the so-called Christian word for God is *hawęni:yo'*, while the corresponding Longhouse word is some form of *shǫkwatyę:no'kta'ǫh*. But even at the turn of the century that distinction was not so clear. Although *shǫkwatyę:no'kta'ǫh* has always been limited to Longhouse use and appears to be a late lexicalization, nineteenth century Longhouse texts accept *hawęni:yo'* as well. The Seneca version of the Iroquoian cosmology (Hewitt 1903) does not refer to *shǫkwatyę:no'ta'ǫh* but uses both *hawęni:yo'* and its feminine counterpart *yewęni:yo'*. Hewitt translates the latter without comment as "a god," while somewhat inconsistently noting that the former is the name of the Christian God (Hewitt 1903, 228, 244). Christian usage retains an archaic word very probably from pre-Christian times, while the Longhouse in the twentieth century have opted exclusively for forms that were new in the nineteenth century. Deardorff already noted this tendency (Deardorff 1951).

An examination of the 263 hymns in the collection shows the following occurrence of names. Some form of *haya'takwęni:yo'*, literally, "he is the most important one," occurs in 36 percent of the cases. The modern favorite, *hawęni:yo'* or some form of the word occurs only slightly more readily in 41 percent of the cases. Generally, God is referred to by one of these two expressions. However, an expression with a political connotation in reference to chiefs, *hakowaneh* or Great One, is used in six percent of the cases.

Hymn references to God as Father are probably more numerous in English than in Seneca where they occur at a rate of 3 percent. This may reflect selectivity on the basis of the relatively less important role of father in Seneca society. Interestingly enough, there is no reference to God, insofar as I know, as maternal uncle. But the female creator mentioned above is significant. Other epithets account for the remaining 14 percent.

Hymn references to Jesus using the English form occur in 44 percent of the cases. The Seneca form *tsakaǫhe:tas*, literally, "he brings them back to

life," occurs in as many cases. The English form Christ occurs in 10 percent of the cases, and other epithets, English or Seneca in form, account
for the remaining 2 percent.

General archaic terms of deity are adapted to Christian faith. The word
hawęni:yo' could be translated in at least three ways due to the ambiguity
of the second root: his word is good, beautiful, or great. The meaning is
probably that his word is powerful or effective in relation to creating and
controlling the world. The word haya'takwęni:yo' should not be construed
to suggest the greatest or most important in a pantheon of gods and goddesses. Iroquois world views and recorded cosmogony do not support
such Greco-Roman superimpositions. Iroquois cosmology tends to present
dynamic process in orenda pairs, in contrast to polytheistic or monotheistic systems. The monotheism of Seneca Christianity may be colored by
such dualism, but this is probably true of popular Christianity in general
with its conception of the devil. Heaven, hell, and the devil have corresponding expressions in this collection of hymns.

The emphasis on Jesus's role in resurrection is specifically native to the
Seneca. Their mythology abounds in resurrection scenes in which an
orenda-wonderful relative brings his kin back to life after they have been
destroyed by some powerful wizard. The spell used is to place the hands
on a hickory tree and shout that it will fall on the dead ones unless they
get up. Jesus as known through Seneca words is thoroughly Iroquoian.

Native terms for the deity used in this collection of early nineteenth
century Seneca hymns can be summarized. As for God, only native terms
are used. They are chosen from among pre-Christian terms appropriate to
express the concept of a monotheistic deity. The expressions emphasize
creatorship and sovereignty. For this period in Seneca history there is evidence that the marked distinction between Christian and Longhouse terms
did not exist, Christian usage differing only in its own selection of possible native terms for its own purposes. The term hakehjih, Ancient One, for
example, seems to have been rejected, and the term shǫkwatyę:no'kta'ǫh
may not yet have been lexicalized. No English words for God appear in
Seneca vocabulary.

In summarizing words for Jesus, I find a contrasting situation. The
English form Jesus occurs with equal prevalence as the native term
tsakaǫhe:tas. In addition, a number of other English terms occur, all used
as names. The native term for Jesus emphasizes Jesus's role in resurrection, bringing back to life.

"Before Jehovah's Awful Throne"

I shall now examine a number of hymns to discover the similarities and contrasts between particular English and Seneca texts. Although the orthography used in the hymnal itself is perfectly adequate, I have used here the phonemic orthography of Wallace Chafe (Chafe 1963) for the benefit of those interested in the linguistic analysis of Seneca morphology, which is not apparent in the phonetic orthography generally used at the time of composition. I chose Hymn 17, "Before Jehovah's Awful Throne," not randomly, but because I was intrigued by the fact that it emphasizes the same divine attributes as the Seneca terminology for the divinity, that is, sovereignty and creatorship. On the other hand, its expressions and metaphors seem so completely non-Iroquois that I was interested to see how they would be handled.

'i:s nǫ'tejǫȩ jo'tȩ'shǫ'
ne yǫeja'keh jǫ' eshah
he:akat n awȩni:yo;', ne'
tasheswȩnǫhtǫnyatye'.
ne' n aǫhwǫ' n awȩni:yo'   5
shǫkwa:wis ne tyǫhehkǫh, khoh
n ǫkyǫishä:t: haǫhwǫ' khoh
hoio'tashä' he tyǫhe'.
ho'swa:yǫh hotehoka:ȩt
tesheswanǫ:nyǫ:ne'; ne', khoh,   10
ne' ȩswatyeä'tahkǫ:ǫk
ne' tȩsheswaehsȩǫnyǫ:ǫk.
shǫkwe:te:s n awȩni:yo':
hotanitȩǫsyowanȩh;
ne' kho ne koiwayeistǫh   15
'ȩye:kȩ' he nithaiwayei'.

You nations
on the earth, be grateful
toward Haweni:yo', who
is making us do things.
He himself Hawȩni:yo'   5
has given us sustenance, and
breath: and he himself

has fashioned our lives.
Come here, his gates,
Let us come to thank him; and   10
let us continue to use
our songs to him.
He shows us pity, Hawęni:yoˀ:
his mercy is great;
when one does as one should   15
one will see him bring it to pass.

Before Jehovah's awful throne, Ye nations, bow with joy; Know that the
Lord is God alone; He can create, and he destroy. His sovereign power,
without our aid, Made us of clay, and formed us men; And when, like
wandering sheep, we strayed, He brought us to his fold again. We are
his people; we his care; Our souls, and all our mortal frame; What
lasting honors shall we rear, Almighty maker, to thy name? We'll crowd
thy gates, with thankful songs, High as the heaven our voices raise;
And earth, with her ten thousand tongues, Shall fill thy courts with
sounding praise. Wide as the world is thy command; Vast as eternity
thy love; Firm as a rock thy truth shall stand, When rolling years shall
cease to move.

How does the Seneca mind react to awe before anyone's throne? The
answer is that non-Iroquoian feelings and expressions are largely omitted.
There is no name of Jehovah, no awful throne, nothing sacred about joy,
no uniting of creation and destruction in one divine figure, no creation of
men from clay, no wandering sheep brought back to the fold, no awareness of pagans to evangelize (ten thousand tongues), no awareness of
vastness of time and space. In fact, most of the religious sentiments
expressed by Isaac Watts have been rejected.

What remains of the original wording? In the first four lines "nations"
and divine sovereignty remain. Sacred joy is replaced with gratefulness.
Of the original lines 5–12 packed into four Seneca lines, there remains
only the divine fashioning of our lives to remind us of "our souls and all
our mortal frame" being in God's care. The original lines 13/14 are expressed
in the Seneca lines 9–12 with some accuracy, but the content of the
original lines 15/16 is lacking. The original lines 17–20 are replaced with
entirely different content in the final Seneca lines.

Totally different sentiments have replaced eighteenth-century Anglican expression. In fact, the entire content of the hymn, with the exception of the reference to gates in line nine, is wholly Iroquoian in both sentiment and expression. "Come here, his gates" is in fact a reversion to the Biblical Psalm expression which inspired Watts's use of the word, and it does not make sense in the Seneca text. The Hebraism is completely unintelligible.

Anyone with a passing knowledge of the Seneca language who has listened to Longhouse speeches will recognize the words *ne yoejo'keh, jo;eshah, shokwa:wis ne tyǫhehkǫh, khoh n ǫkyǫishä:t, tęsheswanǫ:nyǫ:ne', 'ęswatyeä'tahkǫ:ǫk, shǫkwe:te:s, koiwayeistǫh,* and *nithaiwayei'.* In other words, the same expressions have been retained in present Longhouse ritual, and have their origin without doubt in pre-Christian and pre-Longhouse ritual.

Interestingly enough, there is an expression from the same semantic pool from which the Longhouse word *shǫkwatyę:no'kta'ǫh* was later lexicalized: *hoio'tashä' he tyǫhe',* which does not materially differ in meaning, and only slightly in form.

The only word that is clearly Christian is *hotanitęǫsyowanęh,* a very common word in the hymns, meaning "his mercy is great." The root of the word, which I have translated as "mercy" is the same as the root used in *shǫkwe:te:s,* which I have translated "to show pity for." This root is part of the semantic pool associated with the relationship between people and guardian spirits, but is taken over in Christian vocabulary to refer to mercy and forgiveness. The Wattsian awe before the vastness of time and space is replaced with this Iroquoian awe in awareness of a relationship of pity between natural reality, however conceived, and human beings. This reminds one of vision quest prayers recorded among non-Iroquoian peoples. This is not to say that the very real Christian thought of forgiveness and mercy is not paramount in the text of this hymn. The rest of the words used in the text have a very neutral connotation.

The vocabulary of the hymn paraphrases is overwhelmingly drawn from what was already traditional religious language, whether Christian or otherwise. Certain native religious values are given functional equivalency to white religious values which were perceived to be less appropriate by the Seneca mind. Among these are gratitude and awareness of divine provision in sustenance and breath, which have replaced awe before omnipotence and the sheep metaphor. This may well constitute an extremely astute theological translation of religious ideas that have been far better understood, subjected to systematic philosophical reflection, selected, translated, and assimilated than theologians, anthropologists, or the white laity have heretofore imagined.

Finally, functional equivalency can be seen between Wattsian awe before the vastness of time and space and the relationship of pity on the part of the guardian spirit and resulting in continuing sustenance and breath. This mercy-forgiveness configuration has no other basis for inclusion in a hymn which ignores that issue in the English original. The complexity of the paraphrasing process in evident.

"Guide Me, O Thou Great Jehova"

I chose the next hymn, Hymn 86, "Guide Me, O Thou Great Jehovah," more or less randomly, with an eye only to the fact that there were no particular problems in understanding the words of the text. Of course, the second verse, lines 7–12, was too good to pass by.

takǫ:wǫ:thas, O swęni:yo'
'akya'tahtǫ'ǫ:tye's:
te'ke'ha:ste' 'i:s se'ha:ste'
'i:'takye:nǫ:h ses'ohta'
kā:hkwano:ǫ' kā:hkwano:ǫ'   5
takhnǫ:t 'ęwǫkahta'jih.

O sehotǫ:koh 'otǫ:sho:t,
ne'ho tkanǫhkwa'syǫ:nyǫ':
'o'ha:ot 'ęwǫkhawi'se:k
tyawe'ǫh, hekatha:ine's,   10
O se'ha:ste', O se'ha:ste',
'i:s shǫ:h takhnikǫ:ni:ak.

n o:nę kęhǫk'ah ne Jordan
tękta't, O sahkwih n ohtyǫ:t;
skę:nǫ'jih takya'tawę:ęt,   15
skęǫ:tih khenyękwa:h
kaęnǫ'shǫ tękǫehsa:ǫk
tyotkǫ:t 'ękatęno:tha:k.

Set me a time and place, God.
I am lost:
I'm not strong, you're strong
take hold of me with your hand.
Expensive bread, expensive bread   5
feed me until I'm full.

Open the door of the spring,
there medicines come from the water.
The rainbow will carry me
always where my path leads.   10
O strong One, O strong One,
only you set my mind at peace.

When at the edge of Jordan River
I stand, oh take away my fear;
carry me over safely   15
across the river to Canaan.
Songs I'll sing to you,
always I'll sing to you.

Guide me, O thou great Jehovah, Pilgrim through this barren land; I am weak, but thou art mighty; Hold me with thy powerful hand: Bread of heaven, Feed me till I want no more. Open now the crystal fountain, Whence the healing streams do flow; Let the fiery, cloudy pillar lead me all my journey through: Strong Deliverer, Be thou still my strength and shield. When I tread the verge of Jordan, Bid my anxious fears subside; Bear me through the swelling current; Land me safe on Canaan's side: Songs of praises I will ever give to thee.

The following expressions in the original English were rejected in the paraphrase: "pilgrim through this barren land," the word "crystal", the leading of the "fiery, cloudy pillar," "my strength and shield," and going through the "swelling current."

The replacements and additions of the Seneca paraphraser are most interesting and enlightening. The Seneca word for guidance, *tako:wo:thas,* has a different connotation than does the original. Chafe (1967,78) defines the root to mean "indicate, point out, show, set a time or place." Some of the subservient stance of the English is missing here. This word is also typical of the Dream Guess ceremony. The pilgrim in a barren land is a religious motif in Christianity, but is foreign to the Iroquois, who are less likely to feel out of place in a wilderness. The danger of losing one's bearings in the wilderness is within Iroquois awareness: hence the use of being lost rather than being a pilgrim in line 2.

The words for being strong in line 3 are found in mythological contexts where sorcery and such abound, but they are used in neutral contexts as well. No special significance in terms of orenda or witchcraft should be read into this vocabulary. In line 4 the word for grasping is an accurate translation, but there tends to be a connotation in Seneca of reciprocity and mutual aid rather than subservience.

Bread of heaven in English evokes images of the manna in the wilderness, and is intelligible in the original, following the pilgrim in a barren land, but is out of place in the Seneca. The term also evokes Jesus's words referring to himself as bread come down from heave. All of this is missing in the Seneca text. Here the bread is merely expensive. The faith of this paraphraser seems to emphasize economic survival, something perhaps much more appropriate to the situation and time of composition than the mystical manna of the original.

To open the door of the spring is a lame attempt at being faithful to the English original. The healing waters of the original evoke images of the water from the rock in the wilderness, the spring of living water in Jesus's words, and the references to the river of life in the book of Revelation. All of this is lacking in the Seneca text. The healing waters of Oliver become in Seneca something vaguely reminiscent of the collection of water for medicine in the Seneca Little Water Society.

The reference to the pillar of cloud and fire of the Exodus is completely lost in the Seneca. Instead, we have a fine example of Iroquois sensitivity to natural beauty and the religious significance of the natural world, which some researchers tend to ignore. Anthropologists with their quaint romanticisms tend to overlook the strength of the bonds attaching the Iroquois to the natural world because it is generally not given the kind of expression expected. Here the expected expression occurs, but it is far shallower than the reality of the sensitivity of ordinary Seneca people today who step out morning after morning and always draw new strength from the hills overlooking Jimmersonstown.

Although the paraphraser of this hymn does not seem to have the same philosophical sophistication seen in the preceding hymn, something of the sort may perhaps be seen in the replacement of "Be thou still my strength and shield" with a reference to peace of mind. Setting the mind at peace, different forms of this word, are prevalent in this collection of hymns. It seems to have a function similar to salvation in English. State of mind is an important emphasis in Iroquoian spirituality, and is even found expressed at the end of each section in the Thanksgiving Address recorded from Chief Corbett Sundown by Wallace Chafe (1961).

The unity of the hymn in English was not perceived by the paraphraser. The references in the last verse, however, may well have influenced him to make an accurate translation of that portion. The whole wilderness experience leading up to Jordan and Canaan have nevertheless escaped him. There is no doubt that these wilderness-wandering metaphors do not speak to Iroquois people in the way the author of the English hymn intended. These metaphors were mere blanks to the paraphraser, and he filled the space with expressions of his own faith, which was, of course, highly colored by the spiritual expectations of his own culture.

The references to God use the terms *Sweni:yo'* (vocative form of *hawęni:yo'*) and *se'ha:ste'*, Strong One. The context suggests a providential concept of the natural world. These terms are consistent with the idea of God as sustainer of that world. Although in theory there should be no contrast between the cultures here, the one, in fact, needs a divine shield from the world, while the other is intimately bound to it by the rainbow.

Seneca Hymns Based on Bible Paraphrases

A great many Psalm texts are found among the Seneca hymns. After all, the hymn was only at that time beginning to replace the metrical Psalm in the more liturgical English traditions, and had become prevalent only a century before among Baptists and Methodists. The Presbyterian mission to the Senecas stimulated the composition of these hymns, and Psalm-singing Presbyterian groups exist to this day.

What is perhaps more remarkable in the Seneca hymnal is the predilection for Bible paraphrase in congregational singing. Similar interests appear among white Christians only fifty years later, and then only on a more limited scale. A favorite gospel story set for congregational singing among white Christians is the stilling of the storm. Peter walking on the water is another of the gospel stories found in the Seneca hymnal (Hymn 215).

Miracle and healing stories, such as the healing of blind Bartimaeus and others, are drawn from the Gospels. The interest in miracle stories is reminiscent of the sung origin myths of the secret Seneca medicine societies. Christian participation in the medicine societies has been documented. An aversion to the Handsome Lake Longhouse religion is not necessarily associated with a rejection of the medicine society. In fact, the Handsome Lake religion rejected the medicine society, which went underground, and the Longhouse institution only began to accept it about the time these hymns were composed.

Warnings of judgment are found, along with stories such as the house built on the rock. About half of the sermon on the mount is set to music, including the Lord's Prayer, the Beatitudes, and the section on divine providence (Matthew 6:28–33).

Although a number of humn paraphrases exist in which the agonies of the cross are mentioned, the Seneca gospel paraphrases skip over the torturous aspects of the cross. There is a fascination with the reactions to the crucifixion in nature: the darkness and earthquake, the rending of the veil in the temple, as well as a marked interest in the thief on the cross and other human reactions to the crucifixion. The lack of interest in the torture itself is interesting in contrast to white hymns. Torture is a means of displaying and increasing orenda, the so-called mystic power of the Iroquois though that idea is not transferred to the crucifixion of Jesus.

Instead, the paraphrases focus not only on natural phenomena, but on the Gethsemane experience. The Seneca Christian mind seems to find something of greater value in Jesus's prayer experience before the cross, the agony expressed in this story making a strong impression. The fasting vision quest, which this story suggests, is not an institutionalized part of traditional Seneca ritual but does play an important role in personal ceremonial, especially in connection with hunting. Christians have the most precisely preserved personal ceremonial, so it is hardly surprising that the Gethsemane scene is so moving from the Seneca point of view.

Not unexpectedly, favorite paraphrases from the Book of Revelation are those drawn from the two final chapters describing the paradise awaiting the saints. In this, Seneca expectations hardly differ from those of other Christians.

There are also five extensive passages from the Old Testament preserved in the Seneca hymns: Exodus 19:16–20; Leviticus 4; Ruth 1:16–19; Isaiah 55; and Ezekiel 37:1–14. Each of these passages, with the possible exception of Leviticus 4, is particularly relevant to Seneca Christianity.

Considering that the paraphrases of the Old Testament are fairly limited, it is surprising that such an obscure text as Leviticus 4 is included as Hymn 107, a cumbersome text with long lines detailing the Hebrew sin offering. Animal sacrifice was in fact known to the Senecas at the time of composition, since the white dog sacrifice was discontinued only in the twentieth century. There is no way of knowing whether this might have made the Hebrew sacrificial regulations of more interest to Seneca Christians or not. Needless to say, among the small number of Seneca hymns still being sung, this one does not appear.

The text from Ruth is most familiar. "Entreat me not to leave thee . . . " needs no justification for inclusion in this select group of paraphrases. Nevertheless, the story as a whole, and this text in particular, express the thought that a person of foreign and pagan origin might be chosen by God even before one of the holy people. This preference for a convert from paganism cannot have been lost on these early Seneca Christians.

Similarly, Isaiah 55 is a text whose inclusion needs no justification from a Christian point of view. It is the well-known "Come everyone that thirsteth. . . . " Interestingly enough, however, it also expresses in clear language a preference for the converted pagan. Passages which combine Christian familiarity with and a preference for pagan converts are among the favorite texts chosen for Seneca hymn material.

The final passage, Ezekiel 37:1–14, is also a familiar one to Christians, but its inclusion here is surprising nonetheless. The famous story of the dry bones coming to life is unique in the Bible, but contains a typical motif of Seneca mythological tales. The humorous aspect of the dry-bone resurrection is often expressed in the mismatching of bones as well as in the dramatic rustle of their coming together. This vivid picture from Seneca storytelling was no doubt too tempting for the hymn-writer, and one may well imagine the enthusiasm with which Hymn 76 was sung, perhaps to the slight discomfort of the missionaries.

The Old Testament passages used appear not only to reveal mere Christian familiarity but a real perusal of the Bible and an interest colored by typically Seneca expectations in subject matter and a preoccupation with ethnic and cultural questions. The same can be said for the gospel texts in general. The gospel texts specifically touch familiar Christian themes: healing and miracle, the agony of prayer, and the awesomeness of natural phenomena. The Biblical possibilities for personal vision and torture remain untouched, perhaps revealing a trend in Seneca thought also evident in the so-called pagan Longhouse religion.

A perusal of the Bible text of Exodus 19:16–19 will show that the paraphrase of Hymn 53 selects the expressions dealing with attention-catching physical phenomena, that is, fire, thunder, clouds, noise, the trumpet sound, and the voice of God. The rest of the Bible text is seen as incidental and is omitted. The time of day, the movement of the people to the foot of the mountain, and the speech of Moses are all removed. What is left of the text is enclosed in a call to praise and a reiteration of the power of God.

ha'hastesyowanęh
a aya'takwęni:yo',
ha'teyoto'k tekaęhsa:ǫ'
he niohsęno'tę:h.

Sinai tyonǫtate'
ne'ho thotya'tęhtǫh,
kakwe:kǫh he niyonǫta'
we:so' wa'a:ǫta't.

we:so' kayę'kyǫ:nyǫ';
kawęnǫta:tye's khoh; —
thotya'tęhtǫh n ojistakǫ:h,
ne shǫkwawęni:yo'.

'otkae'ni:h, niyo:to'k,
n otha:h ne yęǫ'tashtha': —
'o:nę ta:snye't ne ahwǫ',
he:ǫwe n ohji'kä:tęs.

ne' ho:ǫwe shǫkwa:wi:h
n oyaneshäkwekǫh:
ne' niyo:to'k tekaęhsa:ǫ'!
O! ne' twaiwano:ǫk!

His power is great
He is the Great One.
Complete a song of praise
to His name.

On Mount Sinai
He came down,
the whole mountain
greatly trembled.

It greatly smoked:
and it thundered; –
when He descended in fire,
our God.

When the noise ended,
He took the trumpet
then He Himself spoke,
from the thick clouds.

From there he gave us
all His law:
Complete a song of praise!
O we who love His word!

The event is the giving of the law, but the text chosen expresses the natural physical manifestations of the event rather than the familiar content to be found in the next chapter. It is tempting to emphasize the overwhelming sensual vision described here to the possible detriment of the content of the law. A Seneca meditation on the law might include visual images of the fire and mountain, possibly even the audition of thunder, trumpet, and noise. This might be in contrast to a rabbinical style of legal application or a Christian catechistic style. The law may very well be situated within the context of natural reality rather than the imposition of a divine will clearly distinct from the natural world. In that case the Seneca viewpoint might be closer to the original psychology of the text than either rabbinical or Christian tradition.

The vocabulary of the paraphrase follows closely that of the original text in contrast to the hymns already examined, which depart from the vocabulary of the English hymn-writers. To the extent that the Seneca paraphraser finds that the vocabulary converges with Seneca thought, the paraphraser will follow the vocabulary of the hymn-writer, but in other cases depart from it. In the case of a Bible paraphrase, the Seneca para-phraser remains close to the vocabulary of the text, using only selection to accommodate to Seneca thought.

All three of the hymns examined in detail have shown strongly con-trasting traits vis-à-vis corresponding English hymns. The three examples generally illustrate the kinds of contrast to be found and the means of attaining them. Two kinds of hymns remain: those showing little relevant difference between the Seneca and English texts, and those which are entirely original in the Seneca. A significant number of both types exist, in fact, in the Seneca hymnal. An example of the former kind is Hymn 35, which is a reasonably close translation of the English hymn "Awakened by Sinai's Awful Sound." An example of what seems to be an original hymn in Seneca in the following Hymn 88.

ne'ho niwakyǫ:yakę:h
'i:' ha'tewakahsé thwéh
n aya'takwęniyo'keh,
ne' tih n akathǫta:tǫh.

ne' n aya'takwęni:yo'
hakasteistǫ:tye's;
ne' hakyenówó'se:nó':
ne' n i' tęęhsęǫnyǫ:k

ne' nęwǫkatęnota'k
ne satanitęǫshä'
'i:s taesahkwa'tǫ:ǫk
kęǫya'keh n :etkę:kwah.

ne satanitęǫshä'
ne' si:kwah kęǫya'keshǫ'
ne' n i:s tisaiwayeistóh
hetkę nǫ'ohji'kä:tih.

ne' ne tęehsęhsęǫnyo:'
O 'i:' n akathwaishä',
sę:nǫh jisa'nikǫ:hęh
hotanitęǫsyowanęh.

I see the sky
It is I who weep
in the Great One,
now then he obeys me.

The Great One
takes care of me,
He helps me:
I sing praise to him.

I'll continue to sing
your mercy
you continue to provide
from the sky up there.

Your mercy
away in the sky
you do as you should
up there on the other side of the cloud.

I'll praise his name
O my soul.
Do not forget
his great mercy.

I have chosen a middle road in translating these words. Sanctimonious language may be used because in Seneca there is no distinction between "heaven" and "sky"; between "praising," "thanking," and even "greeting"; and between "he feels very sorry for," and "his mercy is great." This hymn may sound either very sanctimoniously Christian or rather pagan just by the words chosen in translation.

The direction is completely skyward and emphatically so, with the inclusion of particles redundantly indicating an upward direction. The archaic belief in sky guardians has undoubtedly influenced this hymn. Consistent with petition to a sky guardian is the reference to weeping on the part of the petitioner, to feelings of pity on the part of the sky guardian, and the rather strong expression, "he has obeyed me," which might be more literally translated with the archaic "he hearkened unto me." Also consistent with the sky guardian motif is the type of relationship described.

God cares for the petitioner, He helps him, He takes pity on him, He provides for him, and He continues to fulfill His obligations in the sky.

The relationship on the part of the petitioner is also typical of pre-Christian thought. The petitioner draws attention to his need and pitiable state with reference to weeping; he thanks the sky guardian; he refers to continuity of gratefulness and to the ritual formula that his mind should continue in that frame.

We are faced here with a raw, pre-Christian petition to God as a sky guardian rather successfully molded into a 7.7.7.7 meter sung to an Anglican hymn-tune. One would hardly be surprised to encounter a reference to the rising smoke of tobacco. The stunning beauty of the traditional, pre-Christian Seneca prayer is entirely intact. The old cosmology is maintained. Everything continues to perform its obligation, even the one on the other side of the cloud.

Faced with the broad spectrum of religious accommodation already noted and the conservative resistance of this hymn, one is tempted to speculate on the dynamics of how these different positions were actually integrated in particular individuals and in the community. Unfortunately, the bare text of the hymns does not give the information necessary for drawing conclusions on those fascinating areas. Perhaps it is enough that they existed.

Summary

Although the examination of the Seneca hymn material here is sketchy and brief, it has been fruitful. Many other fruitful materials exist on Seneca Christianity which have been virtually untouched by researchers. Christian vocabulary is only noted in passing in the linguistic studies of Wallace Chafe, while extensive material is given for the Longhouse. This study does not enter this area either, although the hymns are a fine source of such material as the following brief appendix indicates.

Much work should be done on the present Christian usage of Seneca hymns. Hymns are in use on all three reservations in western New York, and many of them are newer productions not found in any published source. The role such hymns play in liturgy, theology, and social interaction within the congregation ought to be documented.

A number of discoveries are noted, however, in this study. The source of the language in Seneca Christianity is first of all pre-Christian ritual expression, augmented by special lexicalizations to express new, Christian ideas. In some cases direct, literal translation into Seneca of Christian expressions results in language normally inconsistent with Seneca expression and incomprehensible to an outsider of the tradition. Finally, a few words, such as Jesus, Christ, and place names, are directly taken over from the Bible.

The variety of theological motifs follows a similar pattern. A large portion of the hymn material reflects pre-Christian cosmology and ceremonials. Sometimes accommodation takes the direction of rather sophisticated philosophical equivalence between purely native ideas and Christian ones. A further accommodation seems to express new, Christian ideas in old Seneca language. Finally, there is evidence that Christian ideas have been accepted wholesale and show no particular influence of Seneca religious values.

These differences may not correspond to any factionalism ever existing in the community. They certainly do not reflect a narrow pagan versus Christian dichotomy. Rather, I suggest that individuals exhibited a combination of traits varying from person to person, and from time to time. The body of hymns at least suggests such diversity, no matter how it was distributed.

The orthography of the collection is uneven, suggesting that it is the work of many individuals. There is even an indication of idiolectal differences in speech. The differing levels of accommodation and retention of native values that have come out in this study may well represent diversity on the individual level. The collection is useful in giving a cross-section of the native congregation, with hymns produced by individuals so widely differing in acculturative levels.

Another area of interest is that such individual differences indicate conscious adaptation with rigorous philosophical methods on the part of some, and exteriorized, determined accommodation by others. All the hymn writers evidence a strong and vital spirituality as might be expected, and in that sense may very likely be set off from the community at large.

The hymns reflect particularly what is appropriate to corporate ritual among the Senecas. This no doubt explains the lack of reference to personal vision despite the convergence of Biblical precedent and a native American tendency to expect such behavior. The equation of the Christian God with a native sky-being is hardly surprising. Nor is it surprising that earth-bound helping spirits are absent from the hymns. This cannot be explained, however, merely as a Christian rejection of pagan values, belonging as it does to the medicine society and personal ceremonial. For this reason, both Christianity and the Longhouse are parallel in petitioning the sky-world in public and the possibility of relating to earth-bound spirits in private. There is evidence that a segment of the Christian population continues to do so even today, although in all fairness it ought to be pointed out that many Seneca Christians reject society ritual and mythology emphatically. The very emphasis of their rejection, however, indicates how widespread might be the temptation to do otherwise.

As might be expected, Seneca hymns express both Christian and pre-Christian values in language perfectly adequate for the task. Other hymns exhibit fusion of values, again as might be expected. Considering the attention that has been given them, they are a rich source of cultural and religious data and deserve the attention of scholars in the future.

NOTES

1. My findings would be extremely tentative without the help of Mr. Arnold Doxtater of the Cattaraugus Reservation and Mrs. Dema Stoffer of the Allegany Reservation in western New York State, who inspired my interest in the subject. Mrs. Stoffer pointed out the neglect of Christian tradition as a source of native values. She believed that much archaic tradition that has been discarded by the non-Christian Longhouse people survives among some Christians. She also felt that such values are currently threatened by what she termed "fundamentalism." My experience is that her perceptions are intelligent and clear- sighted. Mr. Doxtater was another active Christian who was not afraid to find a native American contribution in his faith.

APPENDIX: A SHORT GLOSSARY OF CHRISTIAN VOCABULARY

This short word list includes words in the form they occur in the hymns numbered with the hymn and line from which the word is taken. Although their roots may be found in Chafe's dictionary, these words are used in a sense which the dictionary does not indicate. Most of the Christian usages noted in the dictionary do not appear here. I have tried to take only lexicalized expressions that are recognized equivalents of English words, but the examples I have taken may not necessarily be the most commonly used equivalents in every case. They are significant because they occur in the hymn texts. Some of these words are also typical of the Longhouse, but may be used differently there. The word for "angel," for example, refers in the Longhouse to one of the four beings who appeared to Handsome Lake. The word for "gospel" is the same as used by the Longhouse for the "Good Message," although a slightly different form is attested here. The word for "sin" is the same as used in the Longhouse.

ALMIGHTY. sekowanęh "you are great" 9:1.

ANGEL. hatiǫya'ke:onǫ' "sky-dwellers" 208:2.

BLEED. hotkwęhsaiǫh "he has bled" 181:1.

BLESS. takwatę'swiyostęh "bless us!" 42:2.

BLEST. 'o'nikǫiyoste:' "it makes the mind good" 35:14.

BORN AGAIN. hęjonǫkä:t "he'll be born again" 29:5.

BE CONVERTED. nǫ'twakatenyę'to'k "I changed completely" 29:10.

CROSS. tekayahsǫ:t 168:2.

CRUCIFY. tsiǫwǫya'tha:' "when they crucified him" 133.1.

ETERNAL. tkakǫ:t "irrevocably" 157:23.

GOSPEL. kaiwiyosta'k "good word" 162:23.

GRACE. watanitęǫsyowanęh "his great pity" 181:7/

HEAVEN. kęǫya'keh "in the sky" 137:2.

HOLY SPIRIT. sathwaishi:yo:h "your spirit is good" 97.1.

KINGDOM. honǫhsatokęhti' "his house is straight" 218:3.

LAW. hoyaneshä' "his law" 29:2.

MERCY. takwatkathoh "look at me!" 76:1.

PITY. taki:teh "pity me, have mercy on me" 14:1.

PRAISE. te:hsęhsęǫnyǫ:ǫk "let me praise him continually" 25:2.

PRAY. shetwatǫisyǫh "we pray to him" 157:5.

REDEEMER. shakǫhetǫh "he makes them alive" 106:2.

RIGHTEOUS. saiwayeistǫh "you do as you should" 120:1.

RISE (from the grave). tethotkęǫh "he has risen" 27:1.

SAINT. swęǫya'ke:onǫ' "you sky-dwellers" 64:2.

SAINT. swaiwiyostǫh "it makes your word good" 186.1.

SALVATION. tsakoya'takwatha' "it makes him take up their bodies, accept them" 87.1.

SERVANT. hoha'shä'shǫ' "his hired help" 20:1.

SIN. swaiwane'akǫh "you have sinned" 49:2.

SOUL. 'akathwaishä' "my soul" 55:1.

THRONE. katyętahkwa' "it is used for sitting" 73:48.

WRATH. honǫ'khwęshä' "his anger" 29:14.

BIBLIOGRAPHY

Chafe, William L. 1961. *Seneca thanksgiving rituals.* Bureau of American Ethnology Bulletin, no. 183. Washington, D.C.

1963. *Handbook of the Seneca language.* New York State Museum Bulletin, no. 388. Albany, N.Y.

1967. *Seneca morphology and dictionary.* Smithsonian contributions in anthropology. Washington, D.C.

Deardorff, Merle H. 1951. *The religion of Handsome Lake.* ed. William N. Fenton. Symposium on Local Diversity in Iroquois Culture. Bureau of American Ethnology Bulletin, no. 149. Washington, D.C.

Hewitt, John N. B. 1903. *Iroquoian cosmology.* Bureau of American Ethnology Annual Report, no. 32. Washington, D.C.

No author. 1936. *Seneca hymns.* New York, N.Y.: American Tract Society.

No author. 1847. *Christian psalmody.* New York, N.Y.: American Tract Society.

Shamanic Images in Peyote Visions

Paul B. Steinmetz

The purpose of this paper is to show how Peyote visions in the Native American Church are the source of shamanic images which heal through the imagination.[1] Jeanne Achterberg describes the relationship between shamanism and the imagination: "Shamanism is the medicine of the imagination. . . . The shamans claim to have special skills for journeying to the planes of the imagination where healing of the body and healing of the planet are possible" (Achterberg 1985, 6). "The shaman's work is conducted in the realm of the imagination" (11). During states of ecstasy the shamans "ascend to the sky or descend to the underworld of the imagination . . . . shamans have been recognized throughout the recorded history of the human species as having the ability to heal with the imagination, par excellence" (13). "Shamanism is the oldest and most widespread method of healing with the imagination" (15).

Not surprisingly, shamanism played an important part in the use of peyote among the Mescalero Apache. Opler states,

> The man who had meaningful experience with Peyote, or who learned a ceremony from one who had been vouchsafed such an experience, became a Peyote shaman with the same validity and justification with which one who had supernatural traffic with bear or learned a bear ceremony or became a bear shaman. These shamans became the leaders of the peyote camp or the "peyote chiefs" and were in charge whenever a peyote ceremony took place. (Opler 1936, 149)

My intention is to show how the peyote visions experienced on the Pine Ridge Reservation are shamanic in nature since they heal with the imagination in a visionary experience akin to ecstasy. The visions were shared with me during the late 1970s. Although most of them have been taken from a previous work, some in a condensed form (Steinmetz 1989), I comment on them here to bring out their significance.

Lawrence Hunter relates that a Navajo couple came to a meeting with a little girl who was so sick with pneumonia that they had had to put her in the hospital. When the staff came to Hunter, he told them that he would try to help the little girl through his songs.

> I started singing but somehow the song was different. It make me wander around in some hills as I closed my eyes. I had this long stick and I was poking around for something I was trying to find but could not. So I cut the song off and started the second one. I kept going like that and I couldn't find what I was looking for. I opened my eyes and I saw that I was making the people restless the way I was singing the song. I started the last song. That song came to me. I found the thing I was looking for. It was a root. I picked it up and I put a piece in my mouth and started chewing it and I stuck a piece in my pocket. About that time the roadman started blowing his whistle and started yelling, "Heya, heya." Everybody started flapping their feather fans and I kept singing that song and I got through. The girl's mother came over and grasped me and said, "Thank you. As you sang the last song my little girl came to the door [in vision] and she was well." After the meeting the parents brought the girl back from the hospital and she was well.

The image of wandering around the hills without discovering the sought-for object made it impossible for Hunter to sing the songs properly and made everyone at the meeting restless. However, the image of finding the herb resulted in the mother having a vision of her daughter recovered at the door and the daughter actually being cured. According to Lakota belief, the Peyote Spirit used the images as sacramental signs of healing. What gives one an understanding of religious phenomena in primal religions, including native American religions, is the sense of sacramentalism, which must exist within a belief system. I have shown elsewhere in an extensive survey of the Sacred Pipe that sacramentalism is the most essential characteristic of that religious symbol (Steinmetz 1984). Consequently, in the peyote visions it is the inner images that God or the Peyote Spirit uses as sacramental signs of healing power that best explain what has happened. Without belief in the sacramental power of images, there is at most an incomplete explanation. One must understand religious experience within a belief system, although one doesn't have to accept personally the faith of the person studied. Until anthropologists discover the sacramentalism of native American religions, they will never be able to understand them, as, for example, W. E. H. Stanner's important contribution to the study of Australian aboriginal religion, in which he develops the sacramental nature of totemism (1960).

Beatrice Weasel Bear tells the story of Joe Sierra's vision of inner healing.

> Joe Sierra had tuberculosis real bad. The hospital said he was going to die. He went to Oklahoma and they doctored him and gave him a lot of medicine. Pretty soon he had a vision. He was wandering off in some desert. Somebody told him to pray to his grandfather. At first he thought of his natural grandfather. But the voice kept on repeating, "Remember your grandfather." Then he thought of his great-grandfathers and other grandfathers in an Indian way. But he kept on hearing the voice. Then, all of a sudden it dawned on him what the voice was saying and he prayed to Grandfather, the Great Spirit, and he came out of it and got well.

Until he recognized the voice for what it really was, the voice of the Great Spirit, it kept on repeating itself. But when it is recognized as such, the image becomes a sacramental sign of God's healing power.

Beatrice Weasel Bear tells of a vision of inner healing. She looked at the half-moon fireplace with the ashes shaped like a water bird.

> When I looked at that, I saw the Half Moon and the Peyote sitting up top, way up there. It looked real smooth and nice up there. The Peyote was way on top like a crown. In between I saw a dark abyss. The body of the water bird was shining and sparkling. That was a real shiny city sitting there. When I looked at that city, I saw a lot of evil things going on there. Further on down there where the tail part was, I saw human skulls and bones covered with snakes. I thought that if a person stays up on top, he will be all right. But if he falls down into the abyss and the city, he will end up with the bones and the snakes. If a person doesn't follow the Peyote road and goes down into the wicked city, he

will end up with the skeletons. That's real death. That was years ago, and it is still vivid. Another time I saw a man standing with arms reaching out. He was Jesus. I looked again and I saw a whole bunch of snakes. I shut my eyes and prayed and when I looked again Jesus was there. When I first started taking Peyote and going to meetings I used to see snakes in the fireplace. Pretty soon I saw them once in a while and pretty soon they were all gone.

These are images of inner healing. Beatrice is empowered to face the dark side of herself symbolized by the skeletons and the snakes because of the redeeming image of the peyote road with the Chief Peyote "on top like a crown." The image of the peyote road is a source of great strength among members of the Native American Church. This vision enabled Beatrice to accept a genuine moral conversion and to practice the peyote ethic. The frequent image of snakes crawling over skeletons, which disappears and gives way to the image of Christ, indicated a psychotherapeutic development, since the images coming from her unconscious changed from one of death to one of life.

Bernard Ice shares a vision of a Lakota woman who became sick during a meeting and was given peyote. She lost consciousness and doctoring her did no good. He describes the second meeting they conducted.

The staff made one complete round and then her brother came in and sang. She moved when he was singing. Emerson Spider put cedar on the fire and fanned her with an eagle feather. Her hand went up over her head. She got up and tried to grab something like she was sleeping and just got up. Later she told me her vision. She saw an eagle. She wanted help but the eagle didn't look at her. He looked the other way. When her brother was singing, a boy about ten to twelve years old, the eagle looked at him and then at her and she started moving at that time. When Emerson fanned her with the eagle feather, the eagle started flying towards her and she tried to grab the eagle's legs. That is what she was grabbing for. If she could grab the eagle's legs, she could get up. The reason she got that way was that she was trying to pray for everybody in the meeting. They were all sinful. She prayed that she would take all the sins on her even if she would have to die. When she prayed like that, it did happen. It was like a big sack, real heavy. So that weight was on her and she couldn't move. She tried to find a way out. She was in darkness too. She saw a small hole that she could go through but she could not find her way towards it. When her brother was singing, there was a little feather that showed her the way out. Her brother was singing and he was a little boy and he was sinless. His voice represented that little feather that showed her the way out. So she was able to grab the eagle's legs and he took her out through the hole. When Emerson put cedar on the fire, the big sack of sins was thrown into the fire and burned up.

In the peyote belief the woman becoming unconscious was the result of a spiritual cause, being overwhelmed by the weight of sin. It was appropriate that the voice of her sinless brother showed her the way so that she could grab the eagle's legs. The images of the feather floating towards the hole and of grabbing the eagle's legs were the healing images which were the source of her revival from unconsciousness. The image of the eagle represents a mediator and becomes a symbol of salvation.

Emerson Spider tells of a vision Tom Bullman had at a meeting when he was sick:

He saw a log house just about to fall over. So they braced it with other logs so that it wouldn't go over. So he went into this house and it was all messed up inside. All kinds of trash was laying all over. So he started to clean up and he noticed that there was someone there helping him clean it up. Pretty soon they pushed all the trash out of there. And here he came to and the house he saw was himself. The sickness was about ready to get him down and make him fall over. The logs bracing the house were the prayers that were said for him. The man that helped him sweep it out was the Peyote. It cleaned him out and that morning he was well.

Through the image of the logs bracing the building Tom felt the support of the community praying for him and the power of peyote itself. The healing power of peyote is expressed through an image of the man cleaning up. This shows how closely peyote is associated with the images arising from the unconsciousness. Through peyote the depths of the psyche become sacramental.

Joe American Horse tells of a vision that his father, Charles, had.

Charles had buried two previous wives. Then he took sick and was given six months to live. Since Peyote was outlawed on the Pine Ridge

Reservation, he went to Nebraska and attended meetings among the Winnebago. He saw a man coming towards him wearing what looked like a dark suit. But, as he came close, he saw that it was his skin which was all black and shriveled up. He thought the man had been smiling. But close up his mouth was all peeled. He looked at the man and saw that it was himself. He looked at himself and saw that he had good clothes and a home but it was his soul. His soul was going to determine whether he was going to live or die. His sickness was from his soul.

When the source of Charles's sickness was determined, he was healed. Today the sickness would be attributed to a psychological source and be considered psychosomatic. A vision can perform some of the same functions as psychotherapy, which is also a form of healing through the imagination.

Emerson Spider relates an out-of-body experience he had in a vision. He was crying over the great pain which he felt in his leg, and he had taken to peyote to be healed. The vision begins with his sister, who is without sin, crying. Emerson cries this time for his sins. While he was crying, he could hear himself as a young child. His voice had changed, and he cried just like a little baby, indicating the depth of the experience. Then a shining man appears and invites Emerson to come after him to teach him things he had never learned. But first, he would review the events of his life like a telecast, exactly as they happened.

> So it came time for the man to come after me. "Have this place cleaned up," he said. "Sweep it up. I will come after you in the spirit." I told my mother about this so she cleaned it all up. As the man approached, I told my mother not to come near. The man said that I had to die to be with him so that he could teach me things I didn't know. So my mother saw me and started hollering for help. She said I was dying now. I had some uncles and they came running into that place. I was already out of my body. I saw my body laying there with eyes wide open and ready to pop out like. And that man was coming after me. He stood at the doorway. He didn't come in because these people were hollering. They told an uncle to tell the relatives I was dead. So I was in the center of the room and I didn't know what to do. I had a chance of going with the man that came after me. But again in my mind I was thinking what would happen to my father when he comes back and

sees me dead. I always pitied my father because he favored me being I
was the oldest child. So I made up my mind to go back into my body
and stay there. This is what I did. I went back into my body and got
up. I started singing songs which we never used before in the meeting.
I think it is the power that sings through me. I didn't really sing them
since it seems that somebody was singing them through me. So they
tied the drum and had a meeting that night and the next morning I got
up and walked around and all the pain was gone.

His mother cleaning the room was symbolic of the purification Emerson
required for his spiritual experience. Telling his mother not to come too
close indicated the dangerous power of the sacred which can be considered a taboo that has to be observed. The songs came from an out-of-
body experience, an experience of the transcendent world. Through these
songs these images became one of healing power. What knowledge Emerson
would have obtained if he had followed the man and risked leaving his
body, he will never know. But images do have an effect on the body and
continuing the journey could have resulted in death, a risk he did not
want to take because of his father.

Lawrence Hunter recalls doctoring a traditional medicine man during a
meeting. He gave him four peyote buttons with a star shape on them.

Towards morning I sang the morning water call song, "They say get on
your fast horses because Grandfather is coming; I want to get everything completed before He comes up and starts a new day." As I sang
that song the medicine man sat up and asked for the staff and he sang
four songs in a voice that came out clear. He could only talk in a whisper. We went outside and the medicine man told me, "See those people over there? They are coming after me. They are my parents, my
mother I have never seen and my father that I had known only vaguely,
and some of my other relatives. They are standing there looking at
me." I kind of got scared. He got through going to the toilet and so we
came back to the fireplace. As we were about to enter, the morning star
came up and went down again. It came up four times. Four times the
medicine man raised his arms and yelled. I helped him by saying, "Ha
ho, Grandfather, thank you. You heard us for what we said. You heard
us. Thank You." We went back in and everybody looked at us. The
paleness in the medicine man's eyes was all gone.

In order to appreciate these healing images we must be aware of the associations they had for the medicine man. The morning star is a traditional symbol of a new beginning. Four is a sacred number and the image of the morning star rising four times is very sacred. This is a symbol of the spirits gathering from the four directions with the power to bring back the medicine man from near death. The vision of the medicine man's relatives coming after him indicates his close proximity to death. In the morning water call song, God is associated with the morning star, thus becoming a sacramental sign of His healing power.

White Bull wanted to be baptized but his father didn't believe in it. So White Bull had the following vision.

He was at a meeting and all of a sudden, his vision went blurry and he was unable to see the people there. He thought to himself, "That's alright; I can still hear them." All at once, he could not hear. The Peyote had stopped his hearing. So he thought, "I can't see nor hear but I will just sit here and think about tomorrow, about seeing my girl friend and going to a pow- pow." But the Peyote continued to work on him and pretty soon all he could think about was himself. So he thought, "I will just sit here on the floor and lean against the wall and go to sleep. So he was trying to touch the back of the wall he was leaning on but he could not do it. He almost fell backwards. "So I don't have to go to sleep. I will just sit on the floor." All of a sudden the floor was moving. He looked down and saw that the floor was just a layer of bricks, no cement in between. He could see nothing since it was dark. He felt the bricks were going to fall over and he wanted to die. He thought he might not be high enough and falling would only result in broken bones and a hard life. He took a deep breath and held it. Then, he heard voices behind him, shouting and crying and laughing. He found himself on a prairie, on level ground. In back of the people there was a big fire coming. The people were running away from the fire past him. He ran with them to a town. All the buildings were churches. He wanted to go with some people but he didn't belong there. So he went to a church and knocked on the door. The minister looked at him and closed the door because he didn't belong there. So, he thought to himself, "As soon as I can, I am going to get baptized and belong to a church so that I won't get caught by this fire." That morning he got baptized.

The peyote made him withdraw from all that he saw, heard, and felt so that he was no longer on solid ground. He experienced a dismantling of his personality so that it could be rebuilt through the experience of seeking entrance into a church to escape the fire. A similar process is used in various forms of therapy.

Jim Blue Bird, one of the charter members of the Native American Church on the Pine Ridge Reservation, received a song through a peyote vision. After taking peyote he ran away from the meeting until he came to a haystack, which he climbed. He looked toward the east and in the coming daybreak saw a vision of Christ surrounded by angels singing a spiritual song. The words were, "Jesus is the Light of the World; Jesus is the door of the Kingdom of Heaven." Thus, the song is used in the Church because of Jim Blue Bird's visions. Songs having power are given in peyote visions just as they are in the vision quest with the Sacred Pipe.

Lawrence Hunter had a vision of being inside the drum used at a meeting.

> Every time I beat it, it looked like the water was coming up. I wanted to get out but I couldn't. As I beat it slow, the water kept going down but I couldn't get away from it. The last song I remembered was a chief song. As I sang it, God knew I was in this state. I kept muttering to myself, "Great Spirit, have pity on me." As I kept drumming, I kept saying that all the time. And as I looked at the Chief Peyote, he was just a little old man, wrinkled up, stringy grey hair, barefoot. He was sitting on the mound. I couldn't get past him. I couldn't go around him. He just sat there and looked at me. And I couldn't hide anything that came to my mind because he knew it all. And I got to singing and I came out of it. The only thing he told me was, "Try and do it right." He said that if I didn't, I was going to hurt myself and somebody else too.

Images in peyote visions can be drawn from many different traditions. Blue Bird had an image of Christ while Hunter had the image of the Great Spirit having pity on him, prominent in the Lakota Sun Dance. Hunter had to face the little old man because he was the Peyote Spirit, an expression of the archetype of the wise old man, and there was no way of getting around him. But it is an archetypal expression which is characteristic of the peyote way.

Emerson Spider had a vision which enabled him to seek the center of his self.

As a young man at a meeting I thought I heard the noise of a car. But the fireman told me there was no car outside. Then I thought it was from the drum. So the drum stopped but the sound was still with me. So I looked all over the room. It was getting closer as I looked at the altar. All of a sudden I saw the Chief Peyote that was sitting in the midst of the people and that is where the sound was coming from. The Peyote was spinning real fast, and it was making the sound. It was sort of a plate that was spinning fast. And in there were classes of people sitting on the plate. The ones that were trying to live according to God's Word were sitting towards the middle. And all those who were not obeying the laws of God were sitting way on the edge of that plate like. And I heard people hollering and crying and I saw jails and other places that did not belong to Christ on the outside of the plate. And I was on the rim of it and I was hanging on and praying that I would live a Christian life. And I was praying real hard and hanging on. And all of a sudden I came out of the vision and I was sitting on the floor and hanging on to my cushion.

This is a centering vision with a great deal of affect similar to a mandala. The image of hanging on the rim of the plate in peril of falling into evil places caused him to be afraid, while being at the center was a source of peace and strength. This is the image that enabled Emerson to live a good Christian life. Moral conversion is very difficult, and there is an inner healing that takes place here.

Bernard Ice had several visions. The first one involved the symbolism of the gourd.

One time I had a gourd but I didn't have any rocks in it. I was sitting at a meeting and thinking about it. Then in a vision I saw a gourd laying on its side with little rocks coming out of it, two or three inches thick, just the size I wanted. When I looked up there was a road going up. As I walked the rocks were getting better, like agates, then like marble, pearls, and finally silver and gold. They turned out to be diamonds way up in the sky. The instruments can help you have a vision of the good road to heaven. Even those little rocks can do this. Maybe some day I will have diamonds in my gourd when I get to heaven.

The images of the rocks becoming precious stones raised the mind and heart of Bernard to God, that is, bestowed on him the gift of prayer. It gave him an image of heaven, a gourd with diamonds, which was relevant to him.

Bernard also shares a vision of the morning water woman.

> I had a vision of the morning water. I saw the big dipper. When the handle is up and the dipper part down, it is the morning water time when the woman brings the water. At that time the dipper is tilted over the clouds and the water drips out and hits the clouds. It lightnings and the water comes through in a shower and hits the mountains and the hills. Streams start flowing down to the creek. The water woman comes up to the creek and gets the water in a bucket. She was facing east in my vision with her hands up in prayer. She got the water that came from the dipper and took it into the tipi and blessed it. I saw it come from the big dipper.

The image of the water coming from the big dipper brings a feeling of transcendence which is a source of blessing far greater than the power of the water woman. She is simply the sacramental sign of God blessing through the water.

Emerson Spider shares a vision of his father's casket.

> While I was in the power of the Lord through the holy herb [peyote], I saw a vision of a casket. It was set before me like a door. It was a door and all men have to go through that door. I could see my father standing right in the doorway. He was facing the other way. I looked beyond the door and I could see that light. I noticed that it was a real shining place and that it was a real good place to be, where my father was going.

One can tell a person that his father is going to heaven. But the power of the image is greater than rational thought. This is especially true of an image coming from a vision, which is perceived as coming from God.

Bernard Ice had a vision which confronted him at the loss of his son.

> I had a vision of my boy's grave. Dirt was piled up and flowers were on it. I started crying again. All of a sudden it changed into the Peyote altar. It was earth like a grave. Here the altar was a grave and the ashes were in the fire. The altar was like the beginning and the end. God made the earth at the beginning and the ashes were the end of the

world. In between there are the Old and New Testaments. All of our beloved ones are beneath this altar, the earth. There is a road on the moon [the dirt mount]; this is the road of life. That is where God is taking care of the souls of our beloved ones. He has a place for them. I am going to go underneath the earth and from there the Peyote grows. There is a spirit in the Peyote; God put it there.

The images are understood through association. When the grave becomes the altar, it becomes a sacred place, including all life from the beginning to the end and containing the peyote road which leads to God. It is good to be buried in the earth because that is where the peyote grows. Through these associations the image of the grave becomes a healing image that reassures Bernard of his son's happiness.

These images are beautiful and powerful expressions of the native American unconscious. They enrich all those who allow them to touch their own inner depths. There is a common substratum of healing through the imagination which underlies shamanism and these visions. Consequently, through these visions we can appreciate the connection between shamanism and guided imagery or psychotherapy. These visions show how the method of the association of images gives up an insight into the nature of religious experience. They give us a sense of the sacramentalism at the heart of that experience, giving us the feeling of being overwhelmed by the transcendent. They contain shamanic images since they heal through the imagination in an experience akin to ecstasy. They are indeed a source of blessing in our lives.

NOTES

1. As a doctoral student of Dr. Åke Hultkrantz at the University of Stockholm I learned to appreciate native American religions as religious experience, as a transcendent experience expressed through symbolism. With Dr. Hultkrantz as my mentor, I discovered the common religious substratum of diverse religious experience through the use of a phenomenological approach. With deep gratitude I dedicate this article to him.

BIBLIOGRAPHY

Achterberg, Jeanne. 1985. *Imagery in healing: Shamanism and modern medicine.* Boston: Shambhala.

Opler, Morris E. 1936. The influence of aboriginal pattern and white contact on a recently introduced ceremony, the Mescalaro peyote rite. *Journal of American Folklore* 49:143–66.

Stanner, W. E. H. 1960. On aboriginal religion. *Oceaniaa* 3(4):245–78. Reprint *Oceania Monograph* 11:25–58.

Steimetz, Paul B. 1984. The sacred pipe in American Indian religions. *American Indian Culture and Research Journal* 8:27–80.

1989. *Pipe, bible and peyote among the Oglala Lakota: A study in religious identity.* Knoxville: The University of Tennessee Press.

III. MUSERS AND ABUSERS

Reflections on the Study of Hopi Mythology

Armin W. Geertz

Most of the literature concerning Hopi studies has serious problems, but some of it, such as *Book of the Hopi*, is of such literary caliber and imitates professional results so well that even academics outside of the field of Hopi studies become ensnared. And lay readers find such literature compatible mostly because persuasive style is confused with ethnographic accuracy. But this literature leaves the academic and lay readers floundering at the fine dividing line where only specialists can separate the dependable data from the nonsense.

Literary Genres and Academic Studies

Frank Waters' *Book of the Hopi* is *not* an authoritative source book on Hopi mythology and religion. Waters has committed the cardinal error in the study of non-Western cultures, namely, the construction of an interpretative framework based on faulty data and methods in fulfillment of a soteriological dream of how humans *ought* to be. Because of this, Waters' book is normative and theological in scope and effect. This may seem harmless to some, but it is of crucial importance in the non-sectarian, objective study of religion. From the latter point of view, it makes a great deal of difference whether the description of another culture coincides with empirical reality to a sufficiently high degree.

Walter Watson noted that there are three sorts of conditions essential to the objectivity of scholarship: "mutual criticism, freedom from political control, and a thorough knowledge of one's own cultural roots" (Watson 1985, 303). It is the epistemological self-scrutiny which all truly scientific, academic research uses in its continual efforts at self-renewal, at furthering methodological awareness, and at increasing the accuracy of humanistic knowledge which contrasts scientific inquiry from poetic inquiry. The latter form of inquiry has a different goal, namely, an aesthetic expression of conceived Truth, a statement to be made to a more or less wider audience. Often the problem is that the wider the audience, the more inaccurate the data. But although the goals of these two contrasting genres may be different, the means are sometimes the same, especially when the topic is ethnographic or historical, such as in "historical" novels. This means that the poet uses some of the same ethnographic or historical methods as the academic but is not hampered by the latter's methodological awareness and restraint. The poet prefers to see the problem in another light. What is at stake for him is an intuitive sensitivity to the subject at hand, as opposed to the boorishness of documentary science. Frank Waters presents his book in exactly this light:

Its aim as a free narrative was to achieve the full spirit and pattern of Hopi belief, unrestricted by detailed documentation and argumentative proof. As such it conflicts in innumerable instances with the scientific views of the Hopis held by outside academic observers. The documentary scholar may question whether an ancient primitive people could have evolved such a rich belief and preserved its full tradition for generations by word of mouth. He may assert that the interpretations of the myths, legends, and ceremonies are largely my own speculations. He will certainly deny that invisible spirits manifest themselves as described. To these doubts and denials my only answer is that the book stems from a mythic and symbolic level far below the surface of anthropological and ethnological documentation. That it may not conform to the rational conceptualization ruling our own beliefs does not detract from its own validity as a depth psychology different from our own. It stands for itself as a synthesis of intuitive, symbolic belief given utterance for the first time. (Waters 1963, xxiii)

Waters reiterated this view after reading my 1983 criticism:

It [the article] illustrates the scientific mode of thought which is different from my own in viewing the mythical, symbolic, and intangible essence of Indian thought and feeling. The foreword to *Masked Gods* by Clyde Kluckhohn of the Department of Anthropology at Harvard University, from which you quote part, points out that the difference in such approaches was manifested as early as Plato and Aristotle. He shows an objectiveness and tolerance which is lacking in the curiously indignant and angry criticisms so often written of various Indian books of mine by other lesser professional ethnologists and anthropologists. The analytical approach of science is prevalent in this age dominated by science. It is of undoubted value, though perhaps not the highest. I myself have gained much from the academic studies with their ethnological documentation, and I believe my own writings also benefit members of the scientific community unconsciously or consciously. There is in all of us an innate intuitive perception of old truths too deeply buried beneath our modern intellectual facade to be exhumed and voiced by any one spokesman. (Personal communication November 15, 1983)

We are in agreement on the nature of the problem. The above-mentioned foreword by Clyde Kluckhohn is by no means unequivocal. In fact, Kluckhohn exonerates himself from identification with Waters' methods and writes that it's healthy for the scientist to have his *a priori* premises questioned by a poet now and then, but if it were up to him, he would rather have conclusions tested by independent observers and the "scrupulous workmanship in detail" of the great scholars of southwestern ethnography.

The problem is that the *Book of the Hopi* is poor ethnography. Waters' report lacks methodological clarity, documentation, and citation. In other words, his report lacks techniques which were evolved in order to provide the reader with a more or less transparent view of the boundary between the empirical data, on the one hand, and the subjectivity of the author, on the other. Ethnographic documentation does not necessarily imply that all scientists doubt the spiritual substance of their subject, it only implies that, difficult as it is, the scientist wishes to approach his subject on its own terms.

The Book of the Hopi has become the all-time best-seller in the literature about the Hopis, so we cannot afford to turn a cold shoulder to it. And since Waters insists on calling it the "Hopi Bible" (Waters 1963, xxii), it will sooner or later be taken seriously by academics from other fields and by the intelligent reading public. But this reading public must be assured that the materials at hand have been handled by competent people. Everyone has the right to express opinions, which is part and parcel of a democratic world view. But the data, which is so important in opinion-making, must be as pure or as close to the source, or to a truth, as possible.

I am not advocating an academic form of isolationism. I am only making an appeal to all students, academics, and poets of non-Western cultures to keep the ultimate goals of each genre in mind and to keep them separate.

An apt quotation from Walter Watson is instructive at this point:

> Recalling Aristotle's conception of the educated man, there are three sorts of interests which are essential to us all and which we all potentially share. These are interests in what is true always and everywhere, in the enjoyment of art, and in the appreciation of the values realized in men's lives. All relate to objects which are the same for all men and thus cut across the differences of cultures. The cosmos in which we exist is the same for us all, the enjoyment of art so far as it is grounded in what the work is is the same for us all, and however different our values may be from those of others, these values, to the extent that they are genuine, provide a ground for the appreciation of values different from our own. But the sciences and the arts and the actions and institutions of men are all cultural products. And so in this world of many cultures the essential interests of man depend of the perception of other cultures and their achievements. Any national culture, however great its achievements in science or art or action, represents only a small tributary to that great variety and richness of cultural objects arising from the confluence of all the cultures of the world. This is today the common patrimony of all mankind, and it is our interest in this which orders our interest in other forms of intercultural perception. The scholarly interest in truth provides us with cultural objects requisite to the essential interests of men, and on popular perception, with all its narcissism and distortions and pathological projections, depends the continued existence of the scholar, the populace, and mankind. (Watson 1985, 310)

Hopi Ethnography

Thus, I believe that Waters is confusing the issue when he writes:

Today, more than a half-century later, almost every Hopi ceremony has been reported with painstaking accuracy by a host of professional observers. Yet their studies are limited to minute exoteric descriptions of ritual paraphernalia and how they are used. The esoteric meanings and functions of the ceremonies themselves have remained virtually unknown. This is not wholly due to traditional Hopi secrecy. Professional scientific observers themselves have never granted validity to those aspects of Hopi ceremonialism that border the sixth-sense realm of mysticism. Indeed the rationalism of all the Western world vehemently refutes anything that smacks of the unknown or "occult." Hence Hopi belief and ceremonialism have been dismissed as the crude folklore and erotic practices of a decadent tribe of primitive Indians which have no relationship to the enlightened tenets of modern civilization. (Waters 1963, xvii)

It is most unfortunate that the problem with the scientific study of the Hopis is of another kind than that bemoaned by Waters. His description is correct with reference to the earliest studies of the Hopis. But a more serious problem is that the collection and publication of Hopi myths has only recently left the so-called "Museum Period" of American anthropological history (1860-1900); and time is running out. The more stringent "Academic Period," introduced by the work of Franz Boas and his students, seems to have by-passed the field of Hopi studies, except perhaps for the work of the missionary H. R. Voth. The Boasian high standard of recording and publishing myths, songs, and speeches in the original language never became an important factor in Hopi studies, not even in linguistic studies. And although we have excellent studies by ethnographers and social anthropologists, there were virtually no published primary source materials in the Hopi language until the late 1970s. None of the researchers in Hopi studies, such a J. W. Fewkes, A. M. Stephen, E. C. Parsons, M. Titiev, and F. Eggan, have worked seriously with the language. In fact, the first serious bilingual collection of Hopi myths ever to be published (disregarding Kennard's primary school materials of the 1940s and a similar series of the 1960s) was made by the German linguist Ekkehart Malotki in 1978.[1] This means that the bulk of Hopi studies are still bound to the standards of the Museum Period of almost a century ago. Hopi studies have been weakened by a silent, accumulated consensus which has given birth to an accumulated body of untested opinions and data as a by-product.

Ekkehart Malotki dramatically broke the consensual silence in 1979 and again in 1983 with his two works on Hopi time and space which have disproved once and for all most of Benjamin Lee Whorf's theories about the Hopi language, and yet the much-vaunted new *Handbook of North American Indians,* which will serve as a source book for at least the rest of this century, contains an article on "Hopi Semantics" which is an inexplicably uncritical recounting of Whorf's speculations on the Hopi language (Voegelin et al. 1979). Even though this article came out the same year as Malotki's 1979 work, it is not just a question of one more example of authorities disagreeing with one another, but a question of paradigmatic blindspots on the part of the Voegelin team.

Frank Waters: *Book of the Hopi*

My criticisms of *Book of the Hopi* focus on four major areas: the backgrounds of the authors, their methods of approach, the informants involved, and the end product.

The Authors

Frank Waters' position has been made clear above. It is enough now to indicate that he does not have an academic background, that his subjects are especially Southwestern Indians, and that he is interested in occultism, Jungian psychology, and those elements common to humanity in the areas of values and philosophy. Waters' sincerity and integrity are beyond question, but as I have indicated, my criticisms of Waters are methodological and epistemological.

Oswald White Bear Fredericks was born in Oraibi in 1905. He has a long record of schooling from Phoenix Indian School to Haskell Institute and Bacon College in Muskogee, Oklahoma. Here he became a devoted Christian and worked many years for the Boy Scouts in New York, the YMCA in Newark, and for Fred Waring at Shawnee-on-the-Delaware (Waters 1969, 15). He has served on the Hopi Tribal Council, as Tribal Judge, and as the Governor of Kykotsmovi. He is a member of the Coyote Clan, and even though he is the nephew of the late Chief of Oraibi, Tawakwaptiwa of the Bear Clan, he holds no traditional religious posts. The publication of *Book of the Hopi* has unfortunately placed him in an uncomfortable position among his own people.

Waters has described his association with Fredericks in his book *Pumpkin Seed Point* (1969) and has provided a detailed description of him. In Waters' own estimation, White Bear's ignorance of his own traditions was only equalled by the missionary zeal which grew in him during the collection of the materials for the book. White Bear came to regard himself as a prophet. On the back of his pottery ashtrays for the souvenir shop was imprinted his signature: "White Bear, Expert on Hopi Religion" (Waters 1969, 158).

This new-found identity encouraged an authoritarian bend which influenced the sessions of collation and interpretation. White Bear would counter Waters' objections with:

> I know you now! You go by these ethnologists who have lied about my people! You won't accept my word as the spokesman for my people. You got to print just what I say or I'll quit! (Waters 1969, 87)

White Bear did not, however, enjoy the support from the very people whose information led him to believe in his role.

> I was worried about him. He was now fully possessed by his archetype. Reality of course did not justify his assumption of the role of messiah for all his people or a spokesman for any group. A relative of his, Thomas Banyacya of New Oraibi, was now recognized as the official spokesman for the Hopi Independent Nation, as the Traditionalists now called themselves, indicating that White Bear's assumptions were ignored. Here on the Reservation he was still abnormally shy and retiring, not accepted as a member of any village group of Traditionalists, and still generally known as Oswald Fredericks. Only in the white world outside could he confidently assert himself as the Hopi prophet, White Bear. (Waters 1969, 170)

This is a revealing indictment from a man who would have us believe that the data, collected and single-handedly translated by (with absolutely no controls by a competent linguist) just this White Bear, should seriously be accepted as the Hopi Bible! Others who have had field experience can sympathize with Waters' trials, but there is no doubt in my mind that White Bear was a definitive barrier between Waters and the Hopi tapes.

Methods of Approach

The methods employed were simple enough:

> White Bear collected most of our research material. He would take
> down on a little battery-run tape recorder the discourses of our Hopi
> spokesman. Later he would play them back, translating them into English
> to his wife who would type them for my use. He also served as my
> interpreter when I interviewed Hopis, guided me to all the mentioned
> sites of ancient ruins and hidden shrines, and made drawings of pic-
> tographs and petroglyphs carved on rocks and cliffs. (Waters 1969,
> 14)

White Bear's wife is a businesswoman born in Waukegan, Illinois. She has
no academic training and has no understanding of the Hopi language. Yet
she has had an important hand in the editing. Waters noted, as an example, how she persisted in typing all references to "Spider Woman" as "Spider Lady" "because as she said, a lady was more dignified" (Waters 1969,
86). Even though this example is seemingly harmless, how many other
attempts made by Naomi Fredericks to make sense out of White Bear's
English went unnoticed by Waters? All of us who have struggled with
translating this and other non-Western languages know that an ill-placed
pronoun or misunderstood particle can lead to total misunderstanding.

As far as I have understood Waters, the tape-recorded Hopi source
material was roughly translated into English by White Bear, and then considerably edited by Waters as well (Personal communication January 8,
1974). This method is highly suspect, although unfortunately widespread
in anthropological literature. Again and again one finds in all fields, from
the Americas to Africa, Asia, and the Pacific, text collections, perhaps
tape-recorded in the original language, but translated by a bilingual informant and polished by the monolingual anthropologist. In the Hopi field
there are even worse examples, such as with H. Courlander, H. Lockett,
and L. W. Simmons, where a bilingual informant relates his or her narrative in the foreign language alone. Hopis with a dependable knowledge of
English are difficult to find. None are so well-trained as to be proficient in
expressing Hopi religious thought in the often inadequate English idiom.

Hopi source material in unedited form can be ungrammatical, repeti-
tive, and difficult to understand for an outsider. The crucial suffixes are
often slurred in a narrative, sentences can be frustratingly imprecise and

often idiomatic, and the language utilizes a large number of pronouns, especially indefinite ones. The result is that at times one has only the context as a guideline in distinguishing subject from object or even the type of action being verbalized.

In combination with an interpreter who had his own goals in mind, Waters was in a dangerous situation. To make matters worse, there does not exist – even at this late date – a comprehensive grammar, nor, a comprehensive dictionary with supportive text material. Thus, even if he wanted to, Waters was in no position to check on White Bear's translation without devoting years of effort to it. Can this be anything else than a fatal error?

Not only are we confronted with the specter of an unimaginable number of technical errors, but realizing that translation is *always* interpretation, we are confronted with the unpleasant fact that the "translator" of these tapes was a man obsessed with an idea: a missionary for the Hopi religion, a religion that *a priori* is not interested in missionizing.

These problems are further compounded by the fact that the source material has also passed into the hands of another man with a mission. Waters wrote to me about this very problem:

> The original material on which my book is based is voluminous, repetitive, and redundant. My effort was to condense it in ordered form to bring out the complete pattern of the progressive annual ceremonial cycle. This had never been perceived or conceived by anthropological observers. It is true to fact, as attested by the text. But it is also true that no recording of any fact or event – even a newspaper reporter's reportage – is completely free of an unconscious bias of some kind. The spirituality is there: in the myths and rituals derived from the ancient past; and in the hearts of the contemporary priests and leaders. But one must have the heart, the bias, to perceive it – just as surely as "it takes a thief to catch a thief." And this unconsciously was perhaps one of my purposes in doing the book, although I'm not a proselytizer – to help awaken in others the faculty of perceiving the spiritual basis of these Hopi Mystery Plays before they are swept under the rug of Progress. (Personal communication February 26, 1974)

Waters' point on unconscious bias is well-taken. However, romanticized and uninformed empathy cannot secure reliable insight.

The hermeneutical problems have not been solved by Waters' intuitive empathy. On the contrary, it complicates matters by replacing the open-ended hermeneutics of humanistic science with a normative universalism, i.e., that all of humanity has the same set of transcultural, absolute truths and values which any person in any culture can approach intuitively and perceive directly and truly. There is a sufficiently voluminous amount of evidence to the contrary to make such a position unwarranted and untenable. However, Waters is not alone in maintaining the universalistic stance, this being the major dogma of the Jungian and quite a few other disciplines and sciences. But, surely, even universalists must admit that the soteriological purpose of "awakening" the reader is hardly conducive to the reproduction of reliable information!

The problem of bias is all the more reason to resort to documentation and argumentation. My question, in the face of such inadequately processed source material, is this: whose view has Waters really perceived?

The Informants

Waters mentions his thirty or so "spokesmen" in his introduction (Waters 1963, xxi). The most important of these informants is Wilson Tawakwaptiwa, the late Village Chief of Oraibi, and his brother (White Bear's father) Charles Fredericks. By comparing with previously published material from Tawakwaptiwa (James 1940, 9–12; 1974, 2–8; Titiev 1944, 73–74), we find that he played no role in the first section on the "creation" myths. This section is the theoretical basis for the rest of the book, and yet, it stands out as being the only account of its kind in the literature.

Who, then, if not the Village Chief, has provided the structure for this unique systematization? As far as I can tell, one man, the late Otto Pentiwa (Kachina Clan, Kykotsmovi) has provided Waters and White Bear with the material made for poets (Waters 1969, 55–57 and Blumrich 1979, 19). I do not know any more about the man, but he provided Waters with the whole idea of psychic centers and other occult matters, as well as adding details about the three previous mythical worlds. All of these ideas are unique for the literature by and about the Hopis, which goes back to the 1860s.

There are a number of important interpretations made in the *Book of the Hopi* of the many petroglyphs both in the area and scattered all over the Southwest. Those interpretations not made by White Bear were made by John Lansa (Badger Clan, Oraibi). He has also provided much of the material on the ceremonies, especially the interpretative material (Waters 1969, 74–85). He is a leading figure in the highly controversial activist group called the Traditionalists, or more correctly, the Hopi Independent Nation. This group is unfortunately represented by a significant number of Waters' informants.

This is a small group of very active, determined, and highly visible politicians whose main goal seems to be the overthrow of the Hopi Tribal Council. Their leader was, until shortly before his death, Dan Qötshongva (Katchongva to his white followers) from Hotevilla. The leadership passed to his even more controversial former aid and political rival, David Monongya. There is at present another power struggle going on at Hotevilla for the new leadership, a struggle which has been going on for the six years or so before Monongya's death in 1988.

There are certain things which characterize this group: they are *not* anointed, duly-appointed spokesmen of the Hopis any more than White Bear is. They are active fund raisers in the U. S. and Europe. They have intimate contact with, and support from, the generation of the sixties, which found in Hopi land the occult Mecca of the American continent, and the Traditionalist "spokesmen" as the messiahs of the coming End of the World. Finally, they have developed through many hours of discussions among themselves and with non-Hopis a coherent, systematic series of "prophecies" concerning the end of the world and the coming world renewal.[2] This group has always used their mythology for political purposes, as Goldfrank (1948) has shown.

An educated guess would place anywhere from 8 to 14 of the 27 names in this group (Waters 1963, xxi). This is unfortunate, since the group in question, among all of the Hopi groups, panders to and comes closest to Waters' decidedly occultist-Jungian eclectic world view (Waters 1969).

The End Product

Considering the authors and the informants involved, what else can be expected than an enigmatic "Book of the Hopi"? Waters is certainly correct in writing that "this great cooperative effort could not have been obtained before, nor could it be obtained now . . . " (Waters 1963, xxi). But I am firmly convinced that this is so by reason of the individuals involved and not because Waters has somehow discovered the esoteric mysteries of the Hopis.

Not only is Waters' book filled with factual errors, but his decision to dispense with the boorishness of documentation leaves the reader with no indication of the differences between paraphrases of native accounts, his own eyewitness observations, and information stemming from other published accounts. Hopi interpretations are indistinguishable from his own. All these various forms of information are presented as one undifferentiated mass of "truth", seemingly objective in tone, but hopelessly mixed with the author's own subjectivity. Of course, any author of any book can hardly avoid consciously or unconsciously influencing the content and the tone of this or her book. That is why the reader has a right to know what the sources are and who is narrating and interpreting what.

Leaving aside the technical weaknesses of the book, there are two principle weaknesses which make the text material and the book as a whole unreliable.

The first principle weakness is that Waters has, for the first time in the history of the literature about the Hopis, provided a fully integrated cosmology, cosmogony, anthropogony, and eschatology. This is a remarkable achievement—which is precisely why he should have used every precaution and form of argumentation in order to prove his case. Waters postulates that the highly heterogeneous conglomeration of major ceremonies, which are performed every year, are strictly and consistently patterned upon the symbology of the Creation process, which has been revealed to us for the first time in the first 36 pages of *Book of the Hopi*. However, Hopi religion does not consist of a common national religion—a pan-clan, pan-mesa ideology and ceremonialism.

Each clan owns a set of traditions with appropriate rituals and ritual objects. The traditions relate not only the beginnings of the clan, but its migrations. Each clan has its own place and destiny in Hopi history. These clan traditions are mutually incompatible, and accounts—even within a single clan, especially from other mesa villages—are conflicting and based entirely upon the knowledge and hierarchical status of its members. Acculturative processes have distributed this situation further, in some instances to a considerable degree. The religious brotherhoods, on the other hand, have served to coordinate these disparate clan traditions into a workable ceremonial homogeneity at each village. But as soon as the ceremonies begin disappearing, the disruptive nature of the clan philosophies becomes more evident, as is the case today in Hotevilla. Thus, no clan has a "complete" version of the Four Worlds Mythology, because there is no such complete version. Each clan jealously guards it own version as being autochthonous and complete in its own right. All the versions of the Four Worlds Mythology that have made their way into print are, without exception, the products of amateurs with little sense of textual criticism.[3]

The second principal weakness with the book is that the account contains no Emergence Myth. This type of myth is brushed aside as being a "popular anthropological belief" (Waters 1963, 31). But this assertion is patently absurd. What is by far the most questionable part of Waters' book is that the architecturally-storied series of worlds is absent and we find, instead, the Hopis coming to the continent from the west on reed rafts (Waters 1963, 23ff.). If Hopi story-tellers agree on anything at all, it is that the Hopis, together with most of the other races of the world, gathered together in the *subterranean* Third World in concern over the growing number of calamities, and magically produced a gigantic reed plant which pierced the sky, providing an escape route upon which to *climb up* to the world above, which is the present world. The place where the reed pierced the sky of the Third World is called Sipaapuni, and is believed to be located at a specific spot in one of the side canyons of the Grand Canyon system. In fact, this place has until recently been visited regularly by pilgrims in connection with the initiation of the young men (Geertz 1984a and 1984b).

There can be no doubt that this book will continue to be a source of inspiration for thousands yet to come. We are talking about a book which somehow fulfills deep-seated needs that plague our Western culture. Where scientists fail to satisfy, journalists and novelists will succeed. And instead of something resembling the truth of the matter, the results are often simply reflections of ourselves clothed in exotic forms.

As Needham wrote:

The very people who were most firmly committed to the interpretation of the exotic found their reasons, some of these doubtless excellent, for declining to meet the general desire for narratives conveying the piquancy of the outlandish. But the desire is not to be denied, and if professional ethnographers as a class do not satisfy it then others will. (Needham 1985, 189)

Conclusion

Which brings us to one last problem. It is interesting that anthropologists have so often been accused of unethical behavior because they publish their data, secret or otherwise. And yet, the *Book of the Hopi*, which pretends to be final revelation of the esoteric secrets of the Hopis, has not suffered the stigma of "unethical conduct."

This fact in itself is enough to indicate the caliber of the book. *Book of the Hopi* has created a new Mecca for many of its readers. The Hopis themselves are appalled by the book and by the presence of the thousands of pilgrims who visit their land every year. There have circulated a large number of generally negative stories and jokes among the Hopis about these pilgrims for over twenty years now. This stream of unwanted visitors has also led to an increase in confrontations between political Hopi factions on the Reservation, accompanied by isolated incidents of violence.

One cannot simply disregard the situation because the problem is cumulative and therefore not immediately discernable until it reaches epidemic proportions. *Book of the Hopi* and a whole series of other similar types of writings are expressions of an accumulation of eclectic bits of information, pulled out of their cultural and religious contexts, and used to reinforce a holistic world view, presently called "New Age", which perceives the multifaceted world and its problems in a highly stereotyped manner. This "grass-roots" philosophy is no longer the search for "understanding, in the form of esoteric knowledge; authority, in the relationship of respectful submission to a master; achievement, by way of hazardous or strenuous training" which "orectic ethnography", such as Carlos Castaneda's *The Teachings of Don Juan*, fulfill, as noted by Needham in his perceptive essay "An Ally for Casteneda" (Needham 1985, 190, 217); but a totalitarian[4] and fundamentalist alternative to technocratic greed and sloth. The need to check the excesses of technocracy is necessary of course. But the baby has been thrown out with the bath-water, since the open-ended tolerance begun by the Enlightenment disappears in the haze of a series of politically volatile issues. Thus, if one criticizes the harm done to the Hopis, one is in reality criticizing an integrated world view, a world view characterized by its own exponents as an "amorphous cultural transition" without creed, dogma, or leaders, but which integrates such concerns as "environmentalism, holistic health, women's rights, social responsibility, and personal spirituality."[5]

My quarrel is not necessarily with one or another viewpoint on these important issues. My quarrel is with the *way* native peoples, who have had little or no part in these issues, are used by proponents on both sides of the issues. The overly romanticized and nostalgic view of American

Indians as noble savages, born born with an environmentalist tempera-
ment, is just as harmful as the view propounded by industrialist tyrants
laying pipelines on the lands of those same supposedly backward savages.[6] Each group has a vision of it own which has little to do with the
Hopi reality.

Notes

1. Malotki (1978). See as well his series of publications together with Michael
Lomatuway'ma (1984, 1985, 1987b, and 1987c). Other texts published in Hopi
with parallel translation are in Geertz (1987a).
2. See Geertz (1987). For the exactly opposite opinion, see Clemmer (1978).
3. Cushing (1924) is probably the most reliable source among this category, but
it should be remembered that his field of expertise was the Zuni Indians.
4. See the tyrannical techniques employed by the leader of a New Age com-
mune in Veysey (1973, 279–408).
5. See the opening editorial and the articles in *The 1988 Guide to New Age
Living* published by Rising Star Associates, Ltd., Brighton, Massachusetts. See also
Borowski (1987); Campbell and McIver (1987); and Melton (1986, 107–24).
6. There is a growing literature on this subject and hardly any room in a note
to do it justice, but the classic work of Vine Deloria, Jr. (1969, 1973) should be
mentioned along with more recent literature such as Berkhofer, Jr. (1979); Vecsey
and Venables (1980); Gidley (1987); Feest (1988); and Green (1988).

Bibliography

Berkhofer, R.F., Jr. 1979. *The white man's Indian: Images of the American Indian
from Columbus to the Present*. New York: Alfred A. Knopf.
Bharati, A. 1976. *The light at the center: Context and pretext of modern mysticism*.
Santa Barbara: Ross-Erickson.
Blumrich, J.F. 1979. *Kásskara und die sieben Welten. Weisser Bär erzählt den Erdmythos
der Hopi-Indianer*. Wien/Düsseldorf: Econ-Verlag.
Bornemann, F. 1982. Review of *Das Buch der Hopi*. In *Anthropos* 77: 959–60.
Borowski, K.H. 1987. The renaissance movement in the U.S.A. today: An account
of alternative religion in popular media. In *Social Compass* 34(1):33–40.
Campbell, C. and Shirley McIver. 1987. Cultural sources of support for contempo-
rary occultism. *Social Compass* 34(1):41–60.
Clemmer, R.O. 1978. *Continuities of Hopi culture change*. Ramona: Acoma Books.
Courlander, H. 1970. *People of the short blue corn*. New York: Harcourt Brace
Jovanovitch.
1971. *The fourth world of the Hopis*. New York: Crown Publishers.
1982. *Hopi voices: Recollections, traditions, and narratives of the Hopi Indians*.
Albuquerque: University of New Mexico Press.
Cushing, F.H. 1924. Origin myth from Oraibi. *Journal of American Folklore* 36:163–70.

134

Deloria, V. 1969. *Custer died for your sins: An Indian manifesto.* New York: Avon Books.

1973. *God is red.* New York: Grosset & Dunlap.

Geertz, A. W. 1983. Book of the Hopi: The Hopi's book? *Anthropos* 78:547–56.

1984a. A reed pierced the sky: Hopi Indian cosmography on Third Mesa, Arizona. *Numen* 31:216–41.

1984b. Tilbage til moderskødet. Valfart hos to utaztekiske folk: Hopi-indianerne og huichol-indianerne. [Back to the womb. Pilgrimage among two Utaztecan peoples: The Hopi Indians and the Huichol Indians.] *Chaos* special issue 2:5–25.

1987a. *Children of cottonwood. Piety and ceremonialism in Hopi Indian puppetry.* Lincoln: University of Nebraska Press.

1987b. Hopi-Forschung, literarische Gattungen und Frank Waters' *Das Buch der Hopi.* In H. P. Duerr, ed., Authentizität und Betrug in der Ethnologie. Frankfurt:111–36.

1987c. Prophets and fools: The rhetoric of Hopi Indian eschatology. *European Review of Native American Studies* 1:33–45.

Gehlen, R. 1988. Propheten und Narren. Anmerkungen zu den Arbeiten von Armin W. Geertz. In Kunze 1988:137–43.

Gidley, M. ed. 1987. *Representations of Native American cultures.* Special issue of *European Review of Native American Studies* 1(2).

Goldfrank. E.S. 1948. The impact of situation and personality on four Hopi emergence myths. *Southwestern Journal of Anthropology* 4:241–62.

Green, R. 1988. The tribe called Wannabee: Playing Indian in American and Europe. *Folklore* 99(1):30–55.

James, H.C. 1940. Haliksai! *The Desert Magazine.*

1974. *Pages from Hopi history.* Tucson: University of Arizona Press.

Johnston, T.F. 1982. Review of *Spider woman stories.* In *Anthropos* 77(1/2):300–301.

Kelly, R.S. 1988. Spiritueller Imperialismus oder die Vereinnahmung der Hopi. In Kunze 1988: 132–36.

Kluckhohn, C. 1950. Foreword to Waters 1950:xi–xii.

Kunze, A. ed. 1988. *Hopi und Kachina. Indianische Kultur im Wandel.* München: n.p.

Lewis, B.; E. Leites, and M. Case, eds. 1985. *As others see us. Mutual perceptions, East and West.* New York: International Society for the Comparative Study of Civilizations.

Lockett, H.G. 1933. *The unwritten literature of the Hopi.* University of Arizona Bulletin Vol. IV, No.4, Social Science Bulletin No.2. Tucson.

Malotki, E. 1978. *Hopitutuwutsi. Hopi Tales. A Bilingual Collection of Hopi Indian Stories.* Flagstaff: Museum of Northern Arizona.

1979. *Hopi-Raum. Eine sprachwissenschafliche Analyse der Raumvorstellungen in der Hopi-Sprache.* Tübingen: Gunter Narr.

1983. *Hopi time. A linguistic analysis of the temporal concepts in the Hopi language.* Berlin and New York: Mouton.

Malotki, E. and M. Lomatuqay'ma. 1984. *Coyote tales. Istutuwutsi.* Lincoln: University of Nebraska Press.
1985. *Gullible Coyote.* Tucson: University of Arizona Press.
1987a. *Stories of Maasaw, a Hopi god.* Lincoln: University of Nebraska Press.
1987b. *Massaw: Profile of a Hopi god.* Lincoln: University of Nebraska Press.
1987c. *Earth fire. A Hopi lengend of the Sunset Crater eruption.* Flagstaff: Museum of Northern Arizona.
Melton, J.G. 1986. *Encyclopedic handbook of cults in America.* New York: Garland.
Mullett, G.M. 1979. *Spider Woman stories. Legends of the Hopi Indians.* Tucson: University of Arizona Press.
Needham, R. 1985. *Exemplars.* Berkeley: University of California Press.
Ortiz., A., ed. 1979. *Handbook of North American Indians.* Vol. 9. Southwest. Washington, D.C.
Simmons, L. 1942. *Sun chief. The autobiography of a Hopi Indian.* New Haven: Yale University Press.
Skidmore, N. 1970. *Chief Dan Katchongva's message: Hopi prophecy.* Hopi Independent Nation: Hotevilla.
The 1988 Guide to New Age Living. Brighton, Massachusetts: Rising Star Associates.
Titiev, M. 1944. *Old Oraibi. A study of the Hopi Indians of Third Mesa.* Papers of the Peabody Museum of American Archaeology and Ethnology, Harvard University, 22/1.
Vecsey, C. 1983. The emergence of the Hopi people. *American Indian Quarterly,* 7/3 (Summer):69–92.
Vecsey, C. and R.W. Venables, eds. 1973. *American Indian environments. Ecological issues in Native American history.* Syracuse, N.Y.: Syracuse University Press.
Veysey, L. 1973. *The communal experience. Anarchist and mystical countercultures in America.* New York: Harper & Row.
Voegelin, C.F., F.M. Voegelin, and L.M. Jeanne. 1979. Hopi semantics. In Ortiz 1979:581–586.
Voth, H.R. 1905. *The traditions of the Hopi.* Field Columbian Museum Publication 96, Anthropological Series Vol. VIII. Chicago.
Waters, F. 1950. *Masked gods. Navaho and Pueblo ceremonialism.* New York: Ballantine Books.
1963. *Book of the Hopi.* New York: Ballantine Books.
1969. *Pumpkin Seed Point.* Chicago: Swallow Press.
1975. *Mexico mystique. The coming sixth world of consciousness.* Chicago: Swallow Press.
1980. *Das Buch der Hopi.* Düsseldorf und Köln: n.p.
Watson, W. 1985. Universals in intercultural perception. In Lewis et al. 1985:301–10.

When Black Elk Speaks, Everybody Listens

William K. Powers

This paper[1] briefly discusses the Christian life of the Lakota, Black Elk, who was made famous by the poet, John G. Neihardt, and others, after the publication of *Black Elk Speaks,* which in the opinion of some is the most influential book ever published on American Indian religion. I realize that a critical evaluation of an Indian and a book that have reached the zenith of popularity in the United States and Canada, and a good part of Europe, risks touching the nerves of those who today hail Black Elk as a true prophet of a universal way of thinking about the world – far beyond the boundaries of the Pine Ridge reservation where he lived most of his life. But, though nerves may be touched, even exposed, my critique is not so much of a man who lived through the classic period of Lakota history and culture, but of the disciples who were to follow him, praise, him, adulate him, idolize him, deify him, and frequently misunderstand him and the culture in which he lived at the time of his interviews with Neihardt.

My overall contention is that the book *Black Elk Speaks,* and the plethora of other books, articles, reviews, essays, songs, plays, and poetry, in fact, obscure Lakota religion rather than explain it. Further, I will argue that much of what passes as Lakota religion today is the product of the white man's imagination, and that soon the Lakota religion, if it follows the path of *Black Elk Speaks* shall simply be absorbed by other religions or philosophies, and it will be no fault of Black Elk the man, but rather Black

Elk the myth, Neihardt, and his disciples. If the term "disciples" seems to convey at once a Christian image, it is precisely because I believe that *Black Elk Speaks* and the Black Elk myth, as opposed to the Black Elk truth, are so successful because Neihardt and others have consciously molded a character that conforms to the Judaeo-Christian model of worldliness, suffering, and salvation. There are those who would argue that the writing of Black Elk's "teachings," as they have come to be called, was not a conscious attempt to satisfy a largely white and Christian audience, but simply a coincidental merger of world views that exist in some mystical way to explain the irrationality of the white man's world.

I would argue that the best judge of such irrationality might be the *Indian himself* rather than white disciples of Black Elk. However, most elderly Indians on the Pine Ridge reservation who knew Black Elk, and this would include other medicine men and singers, some of them still living and practicing native Lakota religion, would wonder why all the fuss about Black Elk. They would insist that Nick (or Nic), as Black Elk was commonly called even during the time of the famous Neihardt interviews, was a charismatic and versatile man. He was a medicine man, although most would not have remembered him as a ritual curer or dreamer, as has been stated by his disciples. Rather they would know him first as an Episcopal layman and perhaps catechist. They would remember him as someone who took up the Ghost dance religion but explained it to his followers in decidedly Christian terms of damnation. They would indeed remember him as a Roman Catholic catechist, who along with his second wife, spent most of their lives from 1905 until his death in 1950 as leaders in the Catholic church, participating fully in the various Catholic programs that brought thousands of Indians together every several years. More importantly, he was known as someone who could teach in Lakota what he believed to be the tenets of the Catholic church. And he would be remembered for his important role of godfather to the newly baptized, as well as ersatz priest when inclement weather or other responsibilities of the church made it impossible for the Jesuits at Holy Rosary Mission to travel to the outlying districts to perform their priestly duties, particularly in the reservation town of Manderson.

Although time and space prevent me from presenting in detail a biographical sketch of Black Elk that would do him justice, I will attempt here to touch upon the most salient features of his participation in Lakota and Christian religion. DeMallie's recent book[2] provides the best, although brief, history of Black Elk, drawing heavily upon missionary literature.

Also of some note, although likewise rather brief, is Steinmetz's treatment of Lakota religion as a kind of pre-Christian belief system in which the sacred pipe is regarded as a harbinger of Christ.[3]

There is, of course, the potential danger of converting Black Elk too severely – balancing his overdramatized traditional role as medicine man with an equally overweighted dedication to Christianity. However, I shall try here to look at his other life, drawing occasionally on interesting shreds and patches of information from my own field work, which include assessments of Black Elk by Lakota people who knew him. Unfortunately, this is a population that is usually not included among the experts and interpreters that have introduced Black Elk to the white man's world, and of course to the younger generation of Lakota and other Indians.

Black Elk Speaks, contrary to most claims, is not Black Elk's story, or even an outline of the most salient features of his life.[4] The importance of *Black Elk Speaks* lies in its description of a *holy vision* of Black Elk's which he revealed to Neihardt. This vision came to him in an attenuated form when Black Elk was nine years old. He then went by the boyhood name of *Kaȟnigapi* (Chosen), a point which Neihardt is not aware of but which is important to the Lakota. Interestingly, despite the claims of Black Elk disciples that the book has invoked a spiritual renascence among its followers, only a few chapters of *Black Elk Speaks* are focused on Lakota religion. The majority discuss in a rather abbreviated way the growing up of an average Lakota.

If we pare his life story down to its significant elements, we find that Black Elk was born on the following dates: 1856, according to the archives of Holy Rosary Mission where finally he was given religious instructions; 1858, according to the information found on his tombstone; 1862, according to the information give by Black Elk to Brown; and 1863, according to the information given to Neihardt. DeMallie convincingly demonstrates that Neihardt was right, and that 1863 is the correct date. These inconsistencies in his birth date represent only minor controversies that generally surround his life.

I shall not dwell on his early years, which we must surmise were like that of any other Lakota boy growing up on the Great Plains in the last half of the nineteenth century. What we know of specific importance is that when he was nine he received part of a vision, and in 1881 when he was eighteen years of age, he received a great, full-blown vision, which was interpreted by another medicine man, who told Black Elk that he must publicly perform his vision, a common practice in Lakota religion.

That year Black Elk performed the Horse dance. The description of the great vision and the Horse dance figure prominently in Neihardt's book and are frequently interpreted in other works.[5]

Sometime during the next five years, Black Elk converted to Episcopalianism. We have little information about this period of time, but we assume that he participated in all the Lakota rituals. However, two facts help us to reconstruct this period in his life. First is the fact that the Episcopalians were the first and only active Christian missionaries on the Great Sioux Reservation between 1879 and 1888 when the first Catholic mission, Holy Rosary Mission, was built four miles north of Pine Ridge Agency.

Secondly, the Buffalo Bill Wild West Show, which Black Elk was to join around 1886, also required that all Indians must be Christian. In 1886 Black Elk sailed with Buffalo Bill for Europe and stayed for three years. In letters he sent home during this time, he is already quoting, albeit crudely, passages from the Bible.

The disciples of Black Elk usually interpret this period as one in which Black Elk sought to learn more about the white man, more about his origins, more about his power. But in fact, there is no reason to believe that Black Elk behaved any differently from the other Indians who accompanied the Wild West shows to Europe. The reservation system had created a vacuous period. There were no buffalo to hunt and no enemies to kill. The Lakota and others were at last at peace with each other, and they were frankly bored. Old song texts which I have collected from this period of time indicate clearly that the Indians leaving for Europe saw it as a challenge, a potential adventure that had all the daring and adventure of the hunt and the warpath. Some of the men even sang death songs at the train station, believing that indeed they might never return from this far off place located rather abstractly across an ocean they had never seen yet had named in Lakota, the Great Water.

The three years in Europe must have been exciting. Black Elk travelled in England, Italy, Germany, and France, and unluckily was stranded. We know nothing about this period except that later he rejoined Buffalo Bill and finally returned home to Pine Ridge. There he arrived just in time to hear about the new messiah in the guise of the prophet Wovoka in Nevada. Black Elk joined in the Ghost dance, but according to informants on the Pine Ridge reservation his manner of preaching the Ghost dance doctrine was decidedly Christian.

For example, in order to make his Christian followers understand the nature of the cataclysmic event that was to manifest itself in the form of a great upheaval of the earth, with the white man churned under, while the Indian remained safely on the surface to rejoin the old people who had died and the buffalo that had nearly disappeared, Black Elk would fill a paunch with water and bury it in the ground. As he preached he would suddenly stamp on the ground around the paunch of water, forcing its contents to spill over. He would then instruct his followers that the portending cataclysm might very well take the form of the Great Flood of Biblical times, and that all disbelievers would perish in the tide. He also carried gunpowder with him and after building a fire would quickly throw it into the blaze, comparing the explosion and scattering of hot ashes to the punishment of fire in hell. All these methods greatly impressed the Lakota people and even today they remember the proselytizing techniques of these stories.

But after the Ghost dance failed, ending with the massacre of the Lakota by the United States cavalry at Wounded Knee Creek, Black Elk, at least temporarily, again began to exhibit an interest in the old times, conducting Yuwipi meetings, curing rituals held in a darkened room for the purpose of calling spirits who in Lakota belief would instruct the medicine man as to the precise method for curing his ailing patients. At this point Black Elk, like so many other medicine men, was participating simultaneously in both religious systems, drawing upon the protocol and ritual of traditional Lakota religion, as well as on Christianity to help meet daily problems as they arose.[6] The necessity of Neihardt and others to make him uniquely Lakota has obscured the fact that most Lakotas have been and continue to be quite capable of moving between two or more religious systems on a situational basis, drawing from each or all those prayers, songs, rituals, histories, myths, and beliefs that satisfied the needs of the particular time and its attendant crises. The western position that people are supposed to belong to one religion, or at least to one religion at a time in serial allegiance to a singular belief system, has contributed significantly to the myth of Black Elk.

At any rate, Black Elk did not spend all his time cogitating over the mysteries of the universe and particularly that part of the world called the white man. Three years after returning from Europe, in 1893, at the age of 28 or 29, although the exact day is not known, Black Elk married a woman named Kate Warbonnet.[7] A son named Never Showed Off was born in 1893, and another son, Good Voiced Star, was born in 1895. His more famous son, Benjamin, who served as the interpreter for both Neihardt and Brown, was born in 1899. His wife, Kate, was apparently one of the first converts to Catholicism, that is to say, was formally recognized and baptized by the newly arrived German Jesuits. Thus in 1895, the first two sons were baptized in the Catholic church, receiving the names William and John respectively. William died in 1897, and Benjamin was baptized on March 11, 1901. Kate later died in 1903, leaving John and Benjamin.

After Kate's death, Black Elk must have felt very much alone in the world with only his sons. He continued to practice various traditional Lakota rituals, a fact pointed out by John Lone Goose, a neighbor who was also a Catholic and a lay catechist. Apparently, Lone Goose had talked with Black Elk about Catholicism and criticized him for participating in what the Jesuits were almost casually to regard as acts of the devil. It was in 1904, after curing a young Indian through traditional methods, that he chanced upon a Jesuit, named Father Lindebner, whom the Indians called Short Father. Lindebner convinced Black Elk to become a Catholic, and after two weeks of instruction at Holy Rosary Mission he was baptized by Father Lindebner on December 6, 1904, the feast of St. Nicholas. Black Elk was given the saint's name and from then on was known to the residents of the Pine Ridge reservation as Nicholas Black Elk, or less formally, Nick. His godfather was the son of a French trader named Peter Pourier, a Catholic catechist.

On July 2, 1905, Nick Black Elk was confirmed in the Catholic Church at St. Francis Mission on the Rosebud reservation, receiving the confirmation name of William. A year later he married Anna Brings, also known as Anna Brings Back Horses, or Brings Back White Horses. She had been married previously under the name of Anna Water Man, or Waterman, and brought to the marriage one daughter, Emma. Apparently, she was baptized a Catholic, but not confirmed, and in the year of their marriage, 1906, she was confirmed at an Indian Congress on July 7, receiving the name Rosa, afterward frequently going by the name, Rosa Anna.

Together, Nick and Rosa Anna had four children, Lucy, Henry, Mary, and Nic Tom, all of whom were baptized on the day of their births. Much later, Benjamin, or Ben as he was commonly know, was confirmed Benjamin Aloysius on June 15, 1911.

The preceding detailed examination of Black Elk's family lineage conveys the idea that Catholicism played an important part in his life, as did his early participation in other religious pursuits such as Episcopalianism, the Ghost dance, Yuwipi, the Vision Quest, and the public enactment of his most powerful visions. Black Elk was consistent in all his beliefs, but toward the end of his career, Catholicism prevailed. And involvement in his newfound religion was systematic, that is, he participated fully in it according to the rules. All his children were baptized and confirmed. Even his interpretations of old Lakota religion were couched in decidedly Christian terms, such as his fire and brimstone interpretations of the Ghost dance.

Between 1907 and 1930, Black Elk was almost totally consumed by his duties in the Catholic church. He was a member of the St. Joseph's Society, a confraternity of Lakota catechists who served as custodians of the local chapels, and who even held prayer services on Sundays and other important holidays when the priests could not make the journey. His wife became a member of the St. Mary's Society, the women's counterpart. These societies had originated with the Benedictine fathers, who found them a convenient way of organizing cadres of the faithful to serve the needs of the Mother Church. During this time, Black Elk was so popular among the Jesuits that he and one or two colleagues were constantly in demand to travel to other reservations to help missionize the other Indians. Black Elk traveled among the Arapahoes and Shoshonis of Wyoming, the Winnebagos of Nebraska, and even the Dakotas of eastern South Dakota. It is reputed that he was Father Eugene Buechel's favorite.

Black Elk's role as a godfather for baptism was particularly important, his record outstanding. For example, in less than one month after Black Elk had been confirmed, he served as godfather for one Jacob Stead (Steed) at Manderson, the community with which he is most readily identified. Over the next year, he served as godfather for seventeen other persons. Between 1906 and 1910, according to the baptismal records of Holy Rosary Mission, he served as godfather for a total of fifty-nine people. Among these were Mark Big Road, a leading medicine man on the Pine Ridge reservation; a German woman known as Agnes Mary Tašica win; still another by proxy; for Silas Fills the Pipe, who later would become a fellow catechist and colleague in travels to other reservations; his own mother, Mary Leggings Down, known as Mary Nañco win or Tipi Gloucia; and for his own son, Henry. In 1911, at St. Peter's Church in Manderson, he served as godfather for twenty people at one mass baptism.

Between 1913 and 1920 he served as godfather for fifteen people, one of whom was his own son's wife. On May 31, 1917, he was godfather for ten persons. During the years 1920 to 1928, he stood up for twelve people, including Jonas Ground Spider, also known as Jonas Walks Under Ground, a leading peyotist in his later years, and Crispina Pourier, the daughter of his own godfather.

On September 1, 1930, he was godfather for the last time for Mary Iron Crow who was sixty-five years old. This date is important because it was the month *after* Black Elk was first visited by John G. Neihardt. In all, Black Elk, for over twenty-five years, not eight, as has been claimed,[8] stood up for a total of 134 people for which we have documentation.

Black Elk Speaks was published in 1932. There is no trace of Black Elk's Christian life in it. But Neihardt was clearly aware of the old man's participation in the Catholic church. Although DeMallie states (1984, 27) that Neihardt probably did not know about Black Elk's participation in the Catholic church, later in the book he states:

> Black Elk told Neihardt little about his later life, his experiences in the Catholic Church, his travels to other Indian reservations as missionary, and his work as a catechist at Pine Ridge. Neihardt was curious about why Black Elk had *put aside his old religion*. According to Hilda (Petri), Black Elk merely replied, "My children had to live in this world," and Neihardt did not probe any further. (DeMallie, 1984, 47, italics added)

Although *Black Elk Speaks* met with critical acclaim, the Jesuits at Pine Ridge must have been shocked. There is no evidence that they even knew the Neihardt interviews were being conducted. To them, Black Elk was one of their prize catechists, even though they occasionally chided him for spending too much money on the conversion of new souls.[9] He was part of their showcase, and there was no reason for them to believe that he was anything but sincere. Although a claim has been made that there was a misunderstanding between Black Elk and Neihardt, the latter wanting simply to write a biography of the old man, and the former believing that Neihardt wanted to be instructed in the old religion, this claim is not supported empirically. Neihardt wanted to write a good book, one that would increase his own status as a poet and writer. It was not the money, he once told Black Elk, because he could make much more money writing other kinds of things. But later, when looking for a publisher for the work, he approached the publisher William Morrow, suggesting the chapter on the Horse dance might make a good movie and thus help promote book sales. Morrow published the book but died before any agreement with a motion picture producer could be arranged. The book, despite its critical acclaim, was not an immediate financial success.[10]

Countering the admonition Black Elk received from astonished clergy at Holy Rosary Mission, the old man issued a letter in 1934, two years after publication of *Black Elk Speaks.* The letter, witnessed by Reverend Joseph Zimmerman, S. J., at Holy Rosary was written by his daughter, Lucy (Looking Horse).[11] Its contents are instructive because it totally disclaimed Neihardt and the book that had made Black Elk famous, It stated:

> I shake hands with my white friends. Listen! I will speak words of truth. I told about the people's ways of long ago and some of this a white man put in a book but he did not tell about current ways. Therefore I will speak again, a final speech.
>
> Now I am an old man. I called my priest to pray for me and so he gave me Extreme Unction and Holy Eucharist. Therefore I will tell you the truth. Listen, my friends!
>
> For the last thirty years I have lived very differently from what the white man told about me. I am a believer. The Catholic priest Short Father baptized me thirty years ago. From then on they have called me Nick Black Elk. Very many of the Indians know me. Now I have converted and live in the true faith of God the Father, the Son, and the Holy Spirit. Accordingly, I say in my own Sioux Indian language, "Our Father, who art in heaven hallowed be thy name," as Christ taught us and instructed us to say. I say the Apostles' Creed and I believe it all.
>
> For very many years I went with several priests to fight for Christ among my people. For about twenty years I helped the priests and I was a catechist in several communities. So I think I know more about the Catholic religion than many white men.
>
> For eight years I participated in the retreat for Catechists and from this I learned a great deal about the faith. I am able to explain my faith. From my faith I know Who I believe in so my work is not in vain.
>
> All of my family is baptized. All my children and grandchildren belong to the Catholic Church and I am glad of that and I wish very much that they will always follow the holy road.
>
> I know what St. Peter has to say to those men who forsake the holy communities. My white friends should read carefully 2 Peter 2:20–22. I send my people on the straight road that Christ's church has taught us about. While I live I will never fall from faith in Christ.
>
> Thirty years ago I knew little about the one we call God. At that time I was a very good dancer. In England I danced before Our Grandmother, Queen Victoria. At that time I gave medicines to the sick. Perhaps I was proud, I considered myself brave and I considered myself to be a good Indian, but now I think I am better.

St. Paul also became better after his conversion. I know that the Catholic religion is good, better than the Sun dance or the Ghost dance. Long ago the Indians performed such dances only for glory. They cut themselves and caused the blood to flow. But for the sake of sin Christ was nailed on the cross to take our sins away. The Indian religion of long ago did not benefit mankind. The medicine men sought only glory and presents from their curing. Christ commanded us to be humble and He taught us to stop sin. The Indian medicine men did not stop sin. Now I despise sin. And I want to go straight in the righteous way that the Catholics teach us so my soul will reach heaven. This is the way I wish it to be. With a good heart I shake hands with all of you.

[signed]Nick Black Elk
Lucy Looks Twice
Joseph A. Zimmerman, S. J.
(Wanblee Wankatuya [High Eagle])

Despite all this empirical evidence for Black Elk's self-proclaimed allegiance to the Catholic Church, admittedly a Catholicism that could coexist with traditional Lakota religion, Neihardt returned a second time to record the "teachings" of Black Elk, this time hoping to write a more popular book on the Sioux. Disappointed that *Black Elk Speaks* was not a commercial success, he wanted to gather information for another book, *When the Tree Flowered,*[12] which he desperately wanted to become popular. Yet again we find no references to Black Elk the catechist even though by his own admission Neihardt knew that Black Elk was still a strong Catholic.

If this were not enough, just three years later, Joseph Epes Brown came to the Pine Ridge scene, actively looking for Black Elk, and ultimately wrote another popular book, *The Sacred Pipe.*[13] We know less about the methodology concerning the writing of this latter book, another which attempts to immortalize the "teachings" of Black Elk. Brown's foreword, presumably "told" by Black Elk, states quite unequivocally:

We have been told by the white man, or at least by those who are Christian, that God sent to men His son, who would restore order and peace upon the earth; and we have been told that Jesus the Christ was crucified, but that he shall come again at the Last Judgement, the end

of this world or cycle. This I understand and know that it is true. . . .
(Brown 1953, xix)

This statement was collected by Brown in 1947. On August 19, 1950,
Black Elk died and was buried in St. Agnes cemetery in Manderson, South
Dakota, with a full Christian burial. He never lived to see the publication
of Brown's book in 1953, and one wonders why and under what circumstances the Black Elk myth was repeated so few years after the old man
had refuted Neihardt's book.

Did Black Elk enjoy dictating his teachings to men who mysteriously
had been "sent" to him? Or were his "teachings carefully edited to conform to the white man's expectations of his life? In believing that Black
Elk was indeed an honorable man, one possessing the charisma that
attracted these authors, I opt for the latter.

Since *Black Elk Speaks* was written, countless numbers of articles and
references to it have proliferated in American literature. Interestingly, anthropologists, although keen on using the book in their classes on American
Indians have rarely entered into the controversy. One of the most critical
disciplines has ironically almost totally ignored the possibility that much
of what Black Elk had to say was manufactured by a white man. Those
least interested in Black Elk, either as a person or as a phenomenon, have
been the Oglalas at Pine Ridge themselves. Although Black Elk's "teachings"
still remain an important part of American literature and poetry, they
have not impressed the average Lakota, who today wonders why so many
people would be interested in the life of, what to them, was just another
Oglala.

According to traditional Lakota doctrine, medicine men do not rise
above each other. They practice their religion, they follow the way of the
pipe, and sooner or later they become old and impotent and are replaced
by other younger medicine men who take up the rituals of their predecessors. There is no room in Lakota religion or Lakota philosophy for
medicine men who place themselves above other medicine men and the
common people. It is a contradiction in terms. Lakota medicine men should
above all be humble, and to have a book written about them extolling
their virtues above others is unthinkable in Lakota terms. The idea of
focusing on one medicine man as some kind of paragon of Lakota virtue
is strictly a white man's idea. And this idea has been replicated over and
over now with the publication of other books that are epigonic of *Black*

Elk Speaks and whose authors also were mystically sent to write the teachings of their respective gurus.[14]

Despite the adulation of Black Elk by his white disciples, he is still remembered by Lakotas primarily as a Catholic catechist, but not greater than Silas Fills the Pipe, Ivan Star Comes Out, Peter Pourier, Joseph Horn Cloud, and others who were his contemporaries, but who have had no biographers to tell their deeds. They were all humble men, caught up in the period of time in which Christianity arrived upon the scene to compete with Lakota religion. In some cases, Lakota people were converted to orthodox Christianity, but perhaps in most cases, they compromised; they joined Christian denominations, but without totally forsaking their native religion.

Since the turn of the century, much of what passes today for Indian culture and religion has been fabricated by the white man, or Indians who have been trained in the white man's schools. If we were to focus only on the literature of the Lakota and Dakota, written by Indians or whites, pseudo-autobiographies[15] or biographies, we find an amazing, continuous list of titles, reissues, and translations appearing nearly every year. Chronologically, some of those include Charles Eastman's works, *Indian Boyhood* (1902), *The Soul of the Indian* (1911), and *From the Deep Woods to Civilization* (1916). These are characteristic of the Indian who has become educated and writes about his youth for a white audience. Next are Luther Standing Bear's "autobiographies," all obviously written by a New York editor, including *My People the Sioux* (1928) and *Land of the Spotted Eagle* (1933), among others. Between the publication of these is *Black Elk Speaks,* published in 1932, and Mari Sandoz's book, *Crazy Horse,* in 1942, which is also a romanticization of Lakota culture, written for whites, and refuted by some Indians who did not believe that Crazy Horse was a chief to be revered. *The Sacred Pipe* followed in 1953.

There was a German edition of Neihardt's *Black Elk Speaks* in 1955 prior to reissue in America in 1961, and in Germany in 1962. Neihardt's work appeared in Italian in 1968, and was again published in London in 1972 and reissued in 1974. *The Sacred Pipe* appeared in German in 1956, in Italian in 1970, and has been reissued in English in 1971, 1972, 1973, 1976, 1977, 1979, 1980, 1981, and 1982, at last count.

Then new medicine men happened upon the scene, all having in common the same as-told-to "autobiographies," and all written by white men sent for the purpose of recording Lakota religion. An example of this phenomenon is of course *Lame Deer: Seeker of Visions* with Richard Erdoes, published in 1972 and translated into German in West Germany in 1979 and in East Germany in 1982. *Lame Deer* is currently being translated into Hungarian.

Even without including the French translations, this incomplete publication record gives some indication of the popularity of the books under question, suggesting just how many *more* translations have stood between what Black Elk and others said and what the ultimate reader hears. Today, when Black Elk speaks, everybody listens, and everybody hears precisely what he or she feels inclined to hear with little regard for the meanings of the Lakota words.

Essentially, in *Black Elk Speaks* and other books written by white men for a white audience, the ideas, plots, persons, and situations of these books have been constructed to conform to the expectations of a white audience that generally knows little about what it means to be brought up as a Lakota over the past one hundred years. Of particular significance, I think, is that the only language to which *Black Elk Speaks* and other books have not been translated is Lakota, the native language of the people who presumably are the originators and benefactors of these religious ideas. *Black Elk Speaks,* although translated into many languages of the world with the belief that we can hear what Black Elk said through what has often been called the *authentic* voice of Neihardt, cannot be translated back into the original. *The Sacred Pipe* fares better, perhaps because there is no pretense in creating a voice, only a culture-history, whose contents include the seven sacred rites of the Oglala in which all Lakota medicine men believe.

But it is not only that the work cannot be translated back into the language of the people themselves. There is no interest in Black Elk on the reservation as a philosopher or spokesman for the traditional way of life, at least not by his living contemporaries. Hierarchical ranking of medicine men is, again, antithetical to Lakota thought. Furthermore, there are practical problems with Black Elk's interpretations of his life and vision. Some of his ideas, taken to be applicable to all Lakota by his various interpreters, are, in fact, idiosyncratic and mean very little to the uninitiated Lakota. The attempt to regard basic Judaeo-Christian tenets of Neihardt's culture as somehow characteristically Lakota makes the work unacceptable to the Indians on the reservation. They frankly do not need spiritual leaders like Black Elk. They have their own leaders, and their medicine men frequently disagree with Black Elk's philosophy.

There are, however, some Lakota today who do look to spiritual guidance from books. The new generation of Indians has moved to the cities away from their direct source of inspiration on the reservations. In many ways their needs are greater, for they must live in constant contact with the people who have attempted to destroy their culture and their religion. For these young Indians, *Black Elk Speaks* and other fabrications of the white man become not only increasingly acceptable but even desirable in the form of literature, given the Judaeo-Christian substructures introduced by contemporary white writers. To survive in the world today, a white man need only be a white man, but for an Indian to survive he must be both Indian and white. In many ways *Black Elk Speaks* is a form a literary imperialism as are so many other books on Indians. But it also represents literary compromise in that Indians are allowed to be Indians because the white man has dictated through clever prose and poetry the very parameters of being Indian. And through this process, the young Indian accepts a religion, one he calls Lakota religion, manifested in an acceptable form of literature and written by a white man who knows little or nothing of the real religion practiced by older and younger Lakotas today on the reservation. And this younger generation of Lakota does not even know the difference.

With each new translation and yet another subtitle, another translator's preface, another advertising copywriter's impression of the book that will make it sell, it is undeniable that the myth of Black Elk has captured the minds and emotions of white Americans and Europeans. Contemporary medicine men at Pine Ridge, however, would be surprised to know about this. This type of romantic culture has always appealed to the Euroamerican world. Not surprisingly, for example, the complete works of Karl May are recently undergoing a rejuvenation in Europe, as are the works of James Fennimore Cooper in the United States. But even from this Euroamerican background is it not immoral to witness the creation of an Indian religion by a romantic white man? The religious zeal of even more romanticists is overshadowed by their total ignorance of a Lakota religion learned first hand from those ritual specialists who are not the subjects of books, and who are therefore more nearly akin to the ideal type of Lakota medicine man accepted by Lakota culture.

When Nick Black Elk first spoke to Neihardt, only the old man's son and some of the other old timers who were present really heard what Black Elk had to say. But today when Black Elk speaks everybody listens – they listen in English, German, French, Italian, Russian, Hungarian,

Spanish, and in Portuguese, and each one hears and interprets Black Elk's meaning within the context of his or her own language and culture. And even the Indian who listens and others who are caught up in the old man's "teachings" are unaware that the true spiritual nature of the Lakota, or at least part of it, has been manufactured in the literary workshops of the white man. And that is precisely the way the white man wants it to be.

NOTES

1. This is an excerpt of a larger paper by the same title that was originally presented to a number of universities in Germany during May and June, 1985. I am particularly thankful to Drs. Christian and Johanna Feest for their hospitality and use of their library where I wrote the initial draft. I am also grateful for the hospitality provided by our German hosts, particularly Professor and Mrs. Helmbracht Breinig. Only publications relevant to this article will be cited. References to *Black Elk Speaks* and their works about Black Elk could themselves fill a not-so-modest volume.

2. DeMallie (1984).

3. See particularly Steinmetz (1980).

4. *Black Elk Speaks* and *The Sacred Pipe* lack any major criticisms. The major perpetuators of the Black Elk myth are found in Deloria (1984), which contains a comprehensive bibliography. For a critical evaluation of as-told-to autobiographies, the best work is by Krupat (1985). An interesting debate over the authenticity of Black Elk also appears in Swann (1983). For a critical evaluation of Neihardt's work in general see the infrequently-cited book by Whitney (1976).

5. There are a few other interpretations of the Horse dance which is still remembered by living Lakotas. It was a dramatic event in which persons who dreamed of the Thunderbeings wore masks and rode horses that danced to the songs. For references to the Horse dance see Feraca (1963) and Powers (1982).

6. For an analysis of dual participation in Lakota religion and Christianity, see Powers (1987).

7. The biographical material as well as his role in the Catholic church has been gleaned from archives at Holy Rosary Mission, Pine Ridge, South Dakota, *Liber Baptismorum*, 16 volumes, and *Registrum Confirmatorum*. Information related to marriages is contained on a special file index.

8. The claim was made in a review of DeMallie's book *The Sixth Grandfather* by Lueninghoener (1984).

9. Detailed records of expenditures and loans incurred by Lakota catechists were kept by the Jesuits and Holy Rosary Mission.

10. There are various references to Morrow and Neihardt in DeMallie (1984).

11. In the Jesuit Archives at Marquette University and published in DeMallie (1984).

12. Neihardt (1951).

13. For a discussion about the tension between Neihardt and Brown see McCluskey (1972).

14. In addition to Brown (1953), see also Lame Deer and Erdoes (1972) and Mails (1979).

15. See Krupat (1985).

BIBLIOGRAPHY

Brown, J. E. 1953. *The sacred pipe.* Norman: University of Oklahoma Press.

Deloria, Jr., Vine, ed. 1984. *A sender of words.* Salt Lake City: Howe Brothers.

DeMallie, Raymond J., ed. 1984. *The sixth grandfather.* Lincoln: University of Nebraska Press.

Feraca, Stephen E. 1963. Wakinyan: Contemporary Teton Dakota religion. Browning, Montana: Museum of the Plains Indian.

Krupat, Arnold. 1985. *For those who come after.* Berkeley: University of California Press.

Lame Deer, John (Fire), and Richard Erdoes. 1972. Lame Deer: Seeker of visions. New York: Simon and Schuster.

Lueninghoener, Florence Boring. 1984. Review of *The Sixth Grandfather, ed. Raymond J. DeMallie. Nebraska History* 65(4):545–56.

McCluskey, Sally. 1972. Black Elk speaks and so does John G. Neihardt. *Western American Literature* 6:231–42.

Mails, Thomas E. 1985. *Fools Crow.* Garden City: Doubleday and Company.

Neihardt, John G. 1932. *Black Elk speaks.* New York: William Morrow and Company.

1951. *When the tree flowered.* New York: MacMillan.

Powers, William K. 1982. *Yuwipi: Vision and experience in Oglala ritual.* Lincoln: University of Nebraska Press.

1987. *Beyond the vision: Essays on American Indian culture.* Norman: University of Oklahoma Press.

Steinmetz, S. J., Paul. 1980. *Pipe, bible and peyote among the Oglala Lakota: A study in religious identity.* Motala, Sweden: Borgstroms Tryckeri.

Swann, Brian, ed. 1983. *Smoothing the ground.* Berkeley: University of California Press.

Whitney, Blair. 1976. *John G. Neihardt.* Boston: Twayne Publishers.

American Indian Spirituality as a Countercultural Movement

Amanda Porterfield

American Indian spirituality is a countercultural movement whose proponents define themselves against the cultural system of American society. In contrast to the aggression against both the natural environment and American Indians that they perceive to be characteristic of American culture, proponents of American Indian spirituality regard both nature and Indians with religious respect. They regard Indians as exemplars of right attitudes to nature and as spiritual guides to the natural world whom all Americans should emulate.

Some of the most prominent spokespersons for this countercultural movement include Black Elk, the Oglala holy man whose life story is a classic text in American Indian spirituality studied in colleges and universities across North America (Neihardt 1932); John Fire Lame Deer, whose autobiography immortalizes the Sioux sit-in on the head of Teddy Roosevelt at Mt. Rushmore in 1970 and celebrates the Indian way of seeing religious meaning in ordinary phenomenon (1972); Vine Deloria, Jr., whose writings explain American Indian metaphysics and indict Americans for their sins against Indians and nature (1969, 1973); Oren Lyons, the Onondaga orator and chief who offers Iroquois political philosophy as a means to world peace and ecological renewal (1980); N. Scott Momaday, whose novels, poems, and essays emphasize the ethical dimensions of American Indian stories and story-telling (1975); and the controversial Hyemeyohsts Storm, whose book *Seven Arrows* (1972) offers a new-age rendering of

Cheyenne shields, ritual, and stories designed to promote American Indian spirituality among non-Indians.

Non-Indian spokespersons for American Indian spirituality are also influential, especially among non-Indians. They include the poet Gary Snyder, who calls on Americans to restructure their society in terms of the religious devotion to nature characteristic of American Indians and other tribal peoples (1957, 1974); the anthropologist Michael Harner, whose books and workshops instruct Americans in shamanic techniques (1980); and the popular but troublesome Jamake Highwater, alias Gregory Markapoulos, a son of Greek immigrants to America (Adams 1984), who argues that the "primal" consciousness manifest in Indian and African art inspired the pioneers of modern art (1981), and who represents himself in books and television appearances as having Blackfoot and Cherokee ancestry.

All of these spokespersons function independently of one another. The variety of tribal affiliations they represent helps explain the lack of unified institutional organization that permits such an array of independent representatives. These tribal affiliations also explain the persistent idea that some spokespersons are authentic while others are not. Although there is no single institutional supervising entry into and expulsion from the movement, tribal leaders have exercised a kind of *de facto* supervision over spokespersons for American Indian spirituality who claim tribal authenticity. For example, the activist Indian editor Rupert Costo questioned Hyemeyohsts Storm's ancestry and condemned his book as "blasphemous" (1972). Costo and Cheyenne tibal leaders found Storm's book offensive, not only because his rendering of Cheyenne colors and directions departed from their versions, but also because his published interpretation of Cheyenne religion occurred without tribal sanction.

Distinctions between authentic spokespersons and pretenders is a persistent theme in discussions about American Indian spirituality. Although the nature of these distinctions often seems to be racial, with critics of Storm and Highwater, for example, implying that these men are spiritually inauthentic because their parents were not full-blooded Indians, the real distinction behind this preoccupation with authenticity is a cultural one. Representatives of American Indian spirituality who actually participate in tribal culture speak with the authority of tribal rootedness. Their involvement in tribal culture sanctions their interpretation of American Indian spirituality.

Some direct connection with tribal cultures is essential to the religious movement of American Indian spirituality because its function is one of mediation between tribal and middle-class western cultures. This mediating function accounts for the role difference between religious leaders of tribal cultures and tribally sanctioned spokespersons for American Indian spirituality. For example, Oren Lyons represents the Haudenosaunee to the outside world, but this role is quite different from that of clan chiefs, whose primary responsibility is to represent the Haudenosaunee to themselves. Similarly, Black Elk's role as Oglala holy man was different from his role as representative of American Indian spirituality to non-Indian Americans. The function of American Indian spirituality as a bridge between tribal and middle-class western cultures explains both the importance of tribal representation in the movement and the difference between this representation and tribal leadership.

However divisive questions about authenticity and tribal sanction may be, advocates of American Indian spirituality are remarkably similar in their agreement on certain fundamental points of belief. The belief system of American Indian spirituality is not controversial, although representations of any particular tribe's relationship to that system may be, as in the case of Costo's criticism of Storm. The universally agreed-upon tenets of American Indian spirituality include condemnation of American exploitation of nature and mistreatment of Indians, regard to precolonial America as a sacred place where nature and humanity lived in plentiful harmony, certainty that American Indian attitudes are opposite to those of American culture and morally superior on every count, and an underlying belief that American Indian attitudes toward nature are a means of revitalizing American culture.

The common world view underlying the messages of various spokespersons for American Indian spirituality is both countercultural and religious: countercultural in its reversal of the dominant religious categories of Western culture,[1] and religious in its devotion to the Indian as a symbol of cosmic suffering and redemption as well as in its preoccupation with the immorality of Western culture and the moral superiority of native cultures. The appropriateness of characterizing American Indian spirituality as a countercultural religious movement emerges most clearly through discussion of its historical antecedents and evolution.

The American Indian spirituality movement is the historical successor of the Indian revitalization movements that began in the late eighteenth century with religious visionaries like the Delaware prophet, Neolin. It carries the beliefs and strategies of earlier revitalization movements into the present age by reaffirming the belief characteristic of those movements that American Indian lifeways are sacred and Euroamerican ways are profane and corrupt. Moveover, proponents of American Indian spirituality follow the same strategy as leaders of earlier revitalization movements in appealing to Christian ideas as a means of discrediting American culture and celebrating their own. But as they carry the beliefs and strategies of earlier movements into the present age, spokespersons for American Indian spirituality address a different and larger audience than did the prophets of earlier movements. While participation in those was largely confined to Indians whose tribal structures had been drastically altered by colonization, proponents of American Indian spirituality speak directly to non-Indian audiences disaffected by American government, capitalism, and technology. Moreover, while leaders of earlier movements worked to preserve Indian cultures against destruction and assimilation, proponents of American Indian spirituality work for the transformation of American culture in terms of Indian values. These differences reflect both the assimilation of Indians into American culture and their roles as spiritual authorities within it.

The Indian prophets of the late eighteenth and nineteenth centuries arose among tribes devastated by the process of colonization. They warned other Indians against succumbing to the vices of white men and depicted precolonial North America as a paradise that non-westernized Indians would return to after death. Among the first of these visionaries was the Delaware prophet, Neolin. His preaching played a role in Pontiac's attack on the British fort at Detroit in 1763 and in subsequent Indian attempts to drive the English back across the Allegheny Mountains (Wallace 1972, 117–21). His preaching also influenced other native prophets, notably the Seneca prophet Handsome Lake, whose visions at the turn of the nineteenth century led to the revitalization of Iroquois cultures, and the Shawnee prophet Tenskwatawa, whose visions sanctioned Tecumseh's efforts to establish a pan-Indian confederacy to drive Americans out of the Ohio River valley early in the nineteenth century (Wallace 1972; Drake 1856; Edmunds 1983, 1984). Later in the century, in the Pacific Northwest, a prophet dance eliciting visions of world destruction and renewal swept through many tribes. Its most well-known leaders were the Wanapum visionary Smohalla, whose Dreamer religion helped fuel the uprising against the U.S. Army led by the Nez Perce Chief Joseph in 1877, and the Paiute visionary Wovoka, whose reputation among Indians as a messiah alarmed the U.S. Army and led to a massacre of Sioux Indians in 1890 (Mooney 1896; Spier 1935; Howard, 1978).

Although the prophets of all these movements were hostile to Euroamerican culture, they were also influenced by its economic systems, technology, political and military agendas, and by the religious symbols that represented and sanctioned those forces. From the time of earliest contact, Indians attributed the military and technological powers of Western civilization to the god that Euroamericans worshipped. Both Catholic missionaries and Protestant colonists reinforced this idea with their own conviction that the biblical god enabled them to conquer and colonize the New World (Bowden 1981). Beginning with Neolin in the late eighteenth century, Indian prophets incorporated this god into their own visions. In Neolin's vision, the Master of Life introduced himself with a biblical phrase as "the Maker of Heaven and Earth" and told Neolin that Indians should pray to him and not to the Manito who led them to evil (Wallace 1972, 117–18). Handsome Lake received a similar vision, in which he was told that Indians should follow the Great Spirit, who "sees and knows all things and nothing is hid from Him" and not the Devil, who led them to evil (Wallace 1972, 246). Taking a slightly different tack, Tenskwatawa preached that the Master of Life had created the Indians, the British, and the French, but not the Americans, who were children of the evil serpent described in the Shawnee creation story (Edmunds 1984, 78-79). All three of these prophets had visions in which the supreme deity worshipped by Christians revealed his special interest in Indians. And they all appealed to this deity in their efforts to modify the religious lives of their people. Neolin identified the tribal Manito with the Christian devil and reported that the Master of Life wanted Indians to give up their medicine songs. Both Tenskwatawa and Handsome Lake hunted down shamans who continued to use their medicine bundles and who refused to substitute devotion to their messages for devotion to tribal deities (Wallace 1972, 118, 254-62; Drake 1856, 88; Goltz 1973, 68ff.).

As well as incorporating the Christian god into their new religions, the prophets incorporated biblical images and injunctions into their depictions of the spirit world. Neolin's visionary confrontation with the two impassible pillars of fire, and his scaling a glass mountain to see the Master of Life and be given his commandments, echoed the biblical story of Moses and the ten commandments (Wallace 1972, 117). Tenskwatawa and Handsome Lake incorporated Christian images of hell into their visions of terrible places in the spirit world where liquor-loving Indians were forced to drink molten lead and to submit to other fiery tortures (Edmunds 1983, 33; Wallace 1972, 244). Furthermore, all three prophets associated hell with a generic conception of sin that was Christian rather than Algonquian or Iroquois in origins. Pre-Christian Indian religions involved elaborate taboo systems in which persons avoided certain acts, such as the handling of weapons by menstruating women, because of the dire consequences such acts were believed to have. But the generic concept of sin, covering a variety of particular acts and implying an internal state of corruption out of which particular sins flowed, was a Christian idea. Neolin, Tenskwatawa, and Handsome Lake all preached the generic concept of sin and its corollary, redemption from sin (Wallace 1972, 117–21, 250–51; Mooney 1896, 672-73).

The new religions led by these prophets restructured tribal world views in ways that represented the colonizing influence of Western culture, serving as a means of criticizing colonial power and idealizing precolonial Indian life. Handsome Lake, for example, invoked the authority of Jesus in preaching that Indians should reject the vices of Western culture and return to traditional, tribal values. The Seneca prophet reported that on his journey to the spirit world he had encountered Jesus and seen his bleeding wounds. Jesus wished him greater success among Indians than he had enjoyed among whites and instructed Handsome Lake to tell his people not to follow white ways (Wallace 1972, 244). In thus pointing to the immorality of the whites, who had crucified their own prophet, Handsome Lake implied that Indians understood Jesus and his teachings better than Jesus' own people, and that the Indians were, in their own way, better Christians than those usually so called. This subversive strategy of invoking Christian imagery to condemn Christian culture and sanction tribal culture was typical of the religious movements led by Indian prophets in the late eighteenth and early nineteenth centuries.

As part of this subversive strategy, the prophets incorporated Christian ideas of paradise into their depictions of life in North America before colonization. Edenic images of precolonial North America were common among Europeans from the time of Columbus (O'Gorman 1961; Honour 1975), and Indians appropriated this imagery by picturing heaven as a natural paradise free of whites. In the Western prophet religions, participants received visions of this paradise as part of their ritual routine. Ghost dancers encountered deceased relatives who lived in a natural paradise in the spirit world that replicated the Edenic life believed to have existed in precolonial North America. Many dancers believed that Wovoka was the messiah, who would relieve their desperate existence, and that the present world would soon be rolled away and the earlier paradise return to replace it (Mooney 1896; Spier 1935).

In the Columbia River valley, the Wanapum prophet Smohalla reinforced the belief that America had once been a sacred paradise by preaching that the earth should be reverenced as a mother. In 1884, according to U.S. Army Major J.W. MacMurray, Smohalla spoke against a new law restricting Great Basin Indians to reservations and forcibly introducing agriculture by saying,

> You ask me to plow the ground! Shall I take a knife and tear my mother's bosom? You ask me to cut grass and make hay and sell it, and be rich like white men! But how dare I cut off my mother's hair?

Although it is possible that MacMurray's romantic perception of native Americans led him to put these words in Smohalla's mouth, it is also possible that MacMurray accurately recorded the words of the Wanapum chief. In this case, Smohalla's reference to the earth as mother is most reasonably interpreted not as a reference to an ancient deity but as a metaphor explaining his people's attachment to their lands (Gill 1987, 40-41, 51-53). The concept of the earth as a singular spiritual being is not present in the Shahaptian stories that predate Smohalla's religion (Phinney 1934), which describe the adventures of animal spirits in magic places, nor was it likely to have characterized the vision quests for animal spirits that were the ritual companions to these stories. Smohalla's concept of mother earth emerged in the context of colonization as a means of characterizing and defending an old way of life.

The concept of mother earth has become a hallmark of American Indian spirituality. It is the movement's primary symbol of respect for nature, and it figures prominently in claims that native attitudes toward life are antidotes to the abuses of nature that epitomize the corruptions of Western society. For example, while invoking native American lifeways to condemn Western rapacity, Gary Snyder preached that "mankind's mother is Nature, and Nature should be tenderly respected" (1957, 105). The Navajo tribal chairman Peterson Zah addressed the problems involved in mining Navajo lands by saying, "The earth is our Mother. When we talk about development of our land which involves mining, we ask ourselves: 'How can we take from her face?' " (Gill 1987, 144). At a symposium on American Indian environments, Oren Lyons asserted that

. . . there seems to be at this point very little consideration . . . for . . . the exploitations of wealth, blood, and guts of our mother, the earth. Without the earth, without your mother, you could not be sitting here . . . (1980).

These usages of the concept of mother earth reflect the general function of the American Indian spirituality movement as a bridge between tribal and Western cultures. On the one hand, the concept has its roots in the radical dependence on natural resources characteristic of tribal cultures, especially pre-reservation tribal cultures, as well as in the association between food and female fertility represented by female spirits in numerous tribes. Mother earth is a universalized distillation of these aspects of native life addressed to Americans and Europeans assumed to need education in moral attitudes toward land and its resources. On the other hand, the term "mother earth" has roots in classical mythology and Western roman- ticism. As a projection of Western idealism it functions both as a means of romanticizing native lifeways and as an indictment of Western culture from within.

Most important, mother earth represents an attitude toward nature that is essential to the belief system of American Indian spirituality. This atti- tude is prominent in the writings of spokespersons for American Indian spirituality, whether or not they invoke the term "mother earth." For exam- ple, Black Elk's conception of God involves the same mystical regard for the earth that Snyder, Zah, and Lyons represent by symbolizing the earth as mother. Thus, Black Elk's Great Spirit is not only a governing force "above all . . . things and people," but also a life force "within all things: the trees, the grasses, the rivers, the mountains, and all the fourlegged animals, and the winged people." Like the prophets of the nineteenth century, Black Elk identifies the Great Spirit with the god worshipped by Christians and asserts that Indians follow that god more righteously than Christians do. "There is much talk of peace among the Christians," reports Black Elk, "yet this is just talk." When Christians learn to appreciate the rituals that center on the sacred pipe of peace, "Then they will realize that we Indians know the One true God, and that we pray to Him continually" (Brown 1971, xx).[2]

In his development of a line of thought similar to Black Elk's, Vine Deloria, Jr. argues that the Indian view of god is a needed corrective to the Pauline conception of nature as fallen, corrupt, and awaiting redemption by a greater power. For Deloria, god is the spiritual force permeating the natural world, not a spiritual force set against nature. He offers an Indian version of the Fall as an alternative to the Pauline notion of nature. In his view, pre-Columbian America was a sacred cosmos once protected by nature-loving red men and now profaned by nature-hating white men. To explain his point, Deloria quotes Luther Standing Bear:

> We did not think of the great open plains, the beautiful rolling hills, and the winding streams with tangled growth as "wild". . . . To us it was tame. Earth was bountiful, and we were surrounded with the blessings of the Great Mystery. Not until the hairy man from the east came and with brutal frenzy heaped injustices upon us and the families that we loved was it "wild" for us. (1973, 105)

Deloria and other spokespersons for American Indian spirituality carry forward the beliefs and strategies of earlier prophets in their descriptions of pre-Columbian America as a kind of Eden, in their interpretation of the incoming of Western culture as a kind of fall from paradise, in their conception of the Indian's role in history as a suffering redeemer, and in their celebration of the Indian's understanding of God as superior to that of the whites. These latter-day preachers alter the message of earlier prophets by emphasizing a mystical view of nature that complements certain popular intellectual trends. Thus, Deloria titles his book *God is Red* as a rejoinder to Thomas J. Altizer's pronouncements in the late 1960s that "God is dead" and argues that the American Indian view of god is supported by the philosophy of Alfred North Whitehead and certain experimental theories in science, such as the theory that music stimulates plant growth (1969, 126; 1973, 91-109).

Deloria's view of god involves a mystical idealization of nature that is akin to supernaturalism in its attribution of cosmic existence to nature, but it is recognizably different from the frankly magical supernaturalism of earlier prophets. For example, Tenskwatawa preached that he could cause the sun to stand still and resurrect the dead and assured his followers that they would be aided by supernatural powers in their battles with U.S. soldiers (Drake 1856, 152-56). Deloria and other spokespersons for contemporary Indian spirituality have left such grandiose hopes for supernatural intervention behind.

Moreover, spokespersons for American Indian spirituality do not have the same status in the eyes of their followers as their predecessors did. Neolin, Tenskwatawa, Handsome Lake, Smohalla, and Wovoka were venerated by their followers as godlike agents inaugurating a transformation in world order. In contrast, recent spokespersons for American Indian spirituality are educators and artists, who define their religion in ethical and aesthetic terms. The Sioux holy men, Black Elk and Lame Deer, represent a transitional stage between these humanistic interpreters and the messianic prophets of the previous century. Black Elk and Lame Deer regarded themselves and were regarded by others as possessing supernatural power, but the writings by which they are widely known have been more appreciated as inspirational teachings about right attitudes toward nature than as testimonies of magical power. Lame Deer's discussion of the religious meaning that an Indian finds in an old cooking pot, rather than his assertions about supernatural power, is excerpted in a popular anthology of American Indian literature (Chapman 1975, 77-86). Similarly, Vine Deloria, Jr. praises *Black Elk Speaks* for its ethical teachings and political implications, not for its otherworldly visions (1973, 51).

Deloria, Lyons, and Momaday emphasize the ethical implications of Indian attitudes toward nature, with Deloria arguing that the Indians' god encourages ethical treatment of nature and people, while the anthropomorphic, historical god worshipped by many Christians encourages the exploitation of people and nature. Taking a similar tack, Oren Lyons argues that the Iroquois tree of peace symbolizes a political philosophy based on respect for the earth and that the roots of this tree can extend to all nations, making Iroquois philosophy the touchstone of world transformation. Lyons's views are not only influenced by the religion established by Handsome Lake, but also by the earlier revitalization movement centering on the legendary founder of the Iroquois confederacy, Dekanawidah, the Christlike prophet of peace, whose teachings have united the Iroquois at various times in their historical struggles for cultural survival (see Wallace 1958). Lyons is a modern spokesperson for the countercultural religion of the Iroquois confederacy, who reinterprets that long-standing religion to non-Indians as an ethic of third-world politics and ecological renewal (1980; Arden 1987, 380-82, 399-403).

In a different but equally didactic vein, the Kiowa writer N. Scott Momaday argues that American Indian storytelling is an ethical phenomenon, not only because Indian stories reflect moral respect for the natural environment and for human community, but also because men and women create themselves as moral beings through the process of telling stories. Only when persons invest themselves in stories, Momaday argues, do they "take possession" of themselves and realize their humanity.

Momaday points all readers interested in recovering moral self-understanding to the humanistic and self-possessed literature of the American Indians (1975).

Aesthetic interpretations of American Indian spirituality are closely related to these ethical interpretations. Lyons, Momaday, Snyder, and Highwater are all artists, whose aesthetic sensitivity to natural forms shapes their ethical appreciation for native attitudes toward nature. Thus, Snyder understands the image of America as Turtle Island both as poetry and as an ethical mandate for political and environmental reform (1974). And Highwater argues that the ethical astuteness of native peoples flows from their aesthetic sensitivity to the living essences of natural things (1981, 61-88).

Contemporary spokespersons for American Indian spirituality stand in a different relationship to American culture than their prophetic predecessors. As educated members of American society, they interpret Indian spirituality in ways that address tensions within American culture. These dual citizens preach the relevance of Indian spirituality for Western problems. While earlier prophets tried to revitalize Indian cultures and save them from destruction or assimilation, their successors look to the revitalization of Western culture.

In certain hidden but nevertheless important ways, American Indian spirituality is like a Christian reform movement within American society. As we have seen, the prophet religions that preceded American Indian spirituality appealed to Christian imagery and ethics as a means of criticizing Western culture and celebrating Indian culture. Spokespersons for American Indian spirituality build on this strategy in their representation of American Indian life to audiences that include persons of non-Indian descent. They call all Americans to a truer and purer understanding of God, to an ethic of peace and justice, and to an aesthetic of natural simplicity. In attributing these characteristics to Indians, proponents of Indian spirituality make Indians exemplars of the Christian values cherished by many members of American society.

NOTES

1. Sociologist J. Milton Yinger defines a counterculture as an "inversion" of "(historically) created designs for living" (1982, 40).

2. Black Elk's interpreters, John Neihardt and Joseph Epes Brown, have presented Black Elk's message as a religious lesson for all peoples. Brown especially has emphasized the relationship between American Indian spirituality and mys-

tical traditions in other religions, arguing that Black Elk's preaching carries special insight into the god of the great world religions (1971, 1982). For a more detached analysis of Black Elk's religiosity, see Holler (1984).

BIBIOGRAPHY

Adams, Hank. 1984. The golden Indian. *Akwesasne Notes*. (Late Summer): 10–12.

Arden, Harvey. 1987. From one sovereign people to another. *National Geographic* 172:3 (September): 370–403.

Bibliography of new religious movements in primal societies. North America: 2. Boston: G. K. Hall.

Bowden, Henry Warner. 1981. *American Indians and Christian missions: Studies in cultural conflict*. Chicago: University of Chicago Press.

Brown, Joseph Epes. [1953] 1971. *The sacred pipe: Black Elk's account of the seven rites of the Oglala Sioux*. New York: Penguin Books.

1982. *The spiritual legacy of the American Indian*. New York: Crossroad.

Costo, Rupert. 1972. *Seven Arrows* desecrates Cheyenne. *The Indian Historian* 5:2 (Summer).

Deloria, Vine, Jr. 1969. *Custer died for your sins: An Indian manifesto*. New York: Avon Books, 1969.

1973. *God is red*. New York: Dell Publishing Co.

Drake, Benjamin. 1856. *Life of Tecumseh, and of his brother the Prophet; with a historical sketch of the Shawanoe Indians*. Cincinnati and Philadelphia: Queen City and Quaker City Publishing Houses.

Edmunds, R. David. 1983. *The Shawnee Prophet*. Lincoln: University of Nebraska Press.

1984. *Tecumseh and the quest for Indian leadership*. Boston: Little, Brown and Company.

Gill, Sam D. 1987. *Mother earth: An American story*. Chicago: University of Chicago Press.

Goltz, Herbert Charles Walter, Jr. 1973. *Tecumseh, the Prophet and the rise of the northwest Indian confederation*. Ph.D Dissertation. University of Western Ontario.

Harner, Michael. 1980. *The way of the shaman: A guide to power and healing*. New York: Harper and Row.

Highwater, Jamake. 1981. *The primal mind: Vision and reality in Indian America*. New York: New American Library.

Holler, Clyde. 1984. Black Elk's relationship to Christianity. *American Indian Quarterly* 7:4 (April).

Honour, Hugh. 1975. *The new golden land: European images of America from the discoveries to the present time*. New York: Random House.

Howard, Helen Addison. [1941] 1978. *Saga of Chief Joseph*. Lincoln: University of Nebraska Press.

Lame Deer, John (Fire) and Richard Erdoes. 1972. *Lame Deer seeker of visions*. New York: Simon and Schuster.

Lyons, Oren. 1980. An Iroquois perspective. In *American Indian environments: Ecological issues in Native American history,* eds. Christopher Vecsey and Robert W. Venables. Syracuse: Syracuse University Press.

Momaday, N. Scott. 1975. The man made of words. In *Literature of the American Indians: Views and interpretations,* ed. Abraham Chapman. New York: New American Library.

Mooney, James. 1896. *The Ghost dance religion and the Sioux outbreak of 1890.* Fourteenth Annual Report 2. Washington: Bureau of American Ethnology.

Neihardt, John G. [1932] 1961. *Black Elk speaks: Being the life story of a holy man of the Oglala Sioux.* Lincoln: University of Nebraska Press.

O'Gorman, Edmund. 1961. *The invention of America: An inquiry into the historical nature of the New World and the meaning of its history.* Bloomington: Indiana University Press.

Phinney, Archie. 1934. *Nez Perce texts.* New York: Columbia University Press.

Synder, Gary. 1957. *Earth house hold.* New York: New Directions.

1974. *Turtle Island.* New York: New Directions.

Spier, Leslie. 1935. *The prophet dance of the northwest and its derivatives: The source of the ghost dance.* General Studies in Anthropology: 1. Menasha, Wisconsin: George Banta.

Storm, Hyemeyohsts. 1972. *Seven arrows.* New York: Ballantine Books.

Wallace, Anthony F. C. 1958. The Dekanawidah myth analyzed as the record of a revitalization movement. *Ethnohistory* V:118–130.

[1969] 1972. *The death and rebirth of the Seneca.* New York: Random House.

Yinger, Milton J. 1982. *Countercultures: The promise and the peril of a world turned upside down.* New York: The Free Press.

EPILOGUE

A Decade of Progress: Works on North American Indian Religions in the 1980s

Åke Hultkrantz

For a person like myself, who experienced the state of North American Indian studies in the 1940s, the present situation of research on native American religions is positively surprising.

Forty years ago the study of these religions was, it seemed, on the wane. Several of the great anthropologists of the Boasian generation were still active, but they were mainly busy with publishing their remaining manuscripts, for example Kroeber on the Mohave and Yurok, Radin on the Winnebago, Wallis on the Dakota, Reichard on the Navajo and Underhill on the Papago.[1] In Europe, publications of books and papers on American tribal religions were rather rare at this time. Joseph Haekel wrote occasional articles, Werner Müller prepared his book on Eastern Woodland religions, and I was occupied with work on my dissertation about the soul concepts. Otherwise, there was a feeling of a standstill in the North American Indian scene; old indigenous Indian culture was largely considered gone; Indians were becoming "civilized," and other than the recording of acculturative religions like the Peyote movement, there was not much more to investigate.

This was the general feeling; but it certainly did not correspond to facts. My own field work among the Western Shoshoni of Wyoming, which began in 1948, demonstrated clearly that the traditional religion lived on, although renewed and in part restructured to fit the demands of the day (cf. Hultkrantz 1987b, 37–84). Testimony from other places, in particular, of course, from the Southwest, pointed in the same direction. A few years afterwards groups of the Northwest Coast Indians revivified old Spirit dance ceremonies, and the Lakota left peyotism in favor of a reestablishment of their traditional religion. It became obvious that Indian culture and religion were not dying, but were changing. And this change often meant a revitalization of religious life.

Since then, new perspectives in anthropology, an expansion of the research scope in religious studies or history of religions, and a new subject, native American studies, have contributed to give new life to the research on American Indian religions. All this vigorous development has also been stimulated by political and theological trends among the Indians themselves, such as a new native American nationalism, both tribal and "pan-Indian" (cf. for instance McNickle 1973; Levine and Lurie 1968) and a debate on the relations between Christianity and traditional religions (cf. for instance Deloria 1973; Coffer 1978).

Not least has the renewed interest in American Indian religions, particularly noticeable after 1970, been provoked by the fact that nowadays Indians have become a contributing factor in the relations between whites and Indians. This began less promisingly with the spread of the drug culture in which Indians, though unwilling, were sought after by a young generation of whites who wanted to experiment with peyote and other hallucinogens. It continued more positively with the fascination of the American Indian ecological concern which was eagerly studied by representatives of the "green" movements, with its apex in the wave of interest in shamanism which is right now running its course through the white man's world, particularly in Europe.[2] Amerindian shamans appear as shamanic teachers at lectures and courses, and shamanic workshops based on American Indian shamanic experiences have been organized in many countries. The fashionable predilection for shamanism has fired studies in classic or ethnographical shamanism, alternative states of consciousness, such as trance and possession, and in alternative medicine. The negative outcome of the shamanic fervor is the publication of books on shamanism with pretentious, pseudo-shamanic contents.

However, all these trends have also awakened a new interest in the spiritual quality of American Indian religions. All over the world the old religions where they still exist have attracted the attention of seekers who feel the appeal of religions that put a strong emphasis on experiential religious emotions, whether they come from the East and Orient, which until now has been more common, or from the world of the American Indian. Also Indian cosmological symbolism has become attractive to many people. It is certainly no coincidence that spiritualism and symbolic interpretations are subjects of many books and articles on the Indians today.

This development has paved the way for an expansion of the literary output in the field of Native American religions, and an intensification and deepening of the studies. I have earlier described the history of this research up to about 1980 (Hultkrantz 1983d). It is now my intention to present some publications in the subject from the last ten years. It is, of course, impossible to give a full account, due to the quantity and dispersal of the literature. I hope, however, that the selection of books and articles offered in the following will give a reasonably fair picture of the range of themes.

Areal Surveys

For a long time an enormous number of reports on native American religions have been amassed in archival manuscripts and published works. Although the information contained in these sources is certainly uneven in quality and reliability, it is sufficient to supply us with material for general surveys of ethnic religions.

Two great encyclopedic works have recently appeared. One is the long awaited *Handbook of North American Indians,* a series of volumes edited by William Sturtevant. So far seven volumes have been issued of this magisterial work, covering Arctic, Subarctic, Northeastern, Southwestern, Californian, and Basin Indians. The tribal survey chapters, and separate sections in most of the volumes, contain information on religion. One may wonder about a heading such as "Expressive aspects of Subarctic Indian culture," which actually stands for a discussion of shamanism and hunting ceremonies among northern woodland tribes. The fact that the author was a psychoculturally engaged anthropologist might explain the caption (Honigmann 1981). The emphasis is everywhere in this work on more modern cults and movements, such as the Longhouse religion of the Iroquois, Pueblo culture-hero myths and Navajo and Great Basin peyotism. There will be volumes on particular topics, such as technology, art, and language, but none on religion. This is deplorable because to most Indians religion has been the ideological framework for their culture. An instructive comparison with the general work on North American Indians written by Franz Boas and his colleagues in 1915 shows that three out of nine of the papers in this work dealt with religion, ceremonies, and myths (Boas et al. 1915). Since that time the evaluation of religion in culture has sadly changed among anthropologists.

The other encyclopedic work is *The Encyclopedia of Religion*, edited by Mircea Eliade and published in 1987. Two large sections of the tenth volume are on the religions of the North American Indians, called "North American Indians" and "North American Religions," for a total of eighty pages. The former section consists of a series of articles on the culture areas of North America and their religious profiles. They are all written by area specialists, among them well-known names such as Werner Müller writing on the Subarctic, Charles Hudson on the Southeast Woodlands, and William K. Powers on the Plains. The second section has four articles referring to particular topics, a general interpretation of North American Indians, mythic themes, modern movements, and historiography. The last article, written by Raymond Fogelson, gives a very useful survey of the history of the study (Fogelson 1987). Although the disposition in two sections is a bit confusing, as they should have been parts of the same block, these articles convey good, concise insights into the religious world of North American aborigines. They are complemented by other articles in the encyclopedia treating particular subjects, such as iconography, the Ghost dance, the Sun dance, tricksters, potlatch, shamanism, as well as certain individual religions of the Apache, Blackfeet, Inuit, Iroquois, Lakota, Navajo and Pueblo. As far as North American religions are concerned, this encyclopedia marks a definite improvement over the older edition, *Encyclopedia of Religion and Ethics* (1908-1926).[3]

Attention should also be drawn to papers on the iconography of native American religions which are presently being published by the Institute of Religious Iconography at Groningen, Netherlands. These papers comprise together Volume X of the series *Iconography of Religions*. Hitherto six parts have been published, covering the Northeast, the Southeast, the Prairies and Plains, the Navajo, the Pueblo cultures, and the Hopi altar iconography. Some very competent scholars have collaborated in these works, including Charles Hudson, whose excellent book on the Southeast Indians reinforced the impression of a religious foundation of the Southeastern culture (Hudson 1976). Intricate religious structure, which anthropologists other than archaeologists have avoided for several decades, has now received an adequate account in Hudson's new paper (Hudson 1984). Sam Gill, prolific writer on American Indian religions and a Navajo specialist, gives us a good compendium of Navajo religion with, as could be expected, a particular emphasis on curing ceremonialism (Gill 1979). Barton Wright is the author of a general survey of the Pueblo religions, illustrated with pictures from the Hopi and Zuni (Wright 1986). Armin

Geertz, eminent Hopi connoisseur, focuses his account on the altars used at major Hopi ceremonials and reveals their calendrical contexts and iconography (Geertz 1987a). Christian Feest gives a well-rounded presentation of the main features of Northeastern religions, and includes both hunting and agricultural rituals (Feest 1986). All these fascicles are of course well illustrated, with photographs in black and white.

Another iconographic work, or almost so, is Peter and Jill Furst's beautiful book on the art of the North American Indians (Furst and Furst 1982). Here the whole range of expressive art is caught under a perspective that takes in mythology, world view, and religious rituals. Single artistic works, such as the cave paintings of the Chumash of central California, are interpreted according to this model, with the cave paintings seen as products of shamanic hallucinations. Certainly, iconographic analyses are important for the understanding of native American Indian religions, as Balaji Mundkur demonstrates in his paper on bicephalous zoomorphic religious art in the northern regions of Eurasia and North America (Mundkur 1984). Armin Geertz has written a good survey article on American Indian iconography in the new encyclopedia of religion (Geertz 1987c).

Several general books on Indian religions were published during the 1980s. Sam Gill provided us with an easily read survey of the typical features of native religions, with more attention given to rituals than to conceptions, that is, the religious ideas are placed in their contexts of world view and ritual (Gill 1982). A second book by Gill deals with North American traditions and their interpretations (Gill 1983). Also by the same author is a book on religious action among North American Indians (Gill 1987b). To Gill, Indian religions have their core in rituals and performances, making use of a fashionable folkloristic concept. Though there is much truth in that, we must not forget the import of their belief symbolism and the role of meditation. The latter aspects of Indian religions are treated in a thoughtful volume by Joseph Epes Brown containing a bouquet of previously published essays on Native American spirituality (Brown 1982). Brown writes with a fine feeling for the qualities inherent in aboriginal traditions and the mental attitude that carry them, while simultasneously offering their information as variations of a *philosophia perennis*. Myth and symbol also loom large in Werner Müller's book on North American Indians and their general spiritual culture, a collection of his best articles (Müller 1981). Müller emphasizes the spatial and temporal dimensions of American Indian myths. Myths are furthermore conceived of as metaphorical expressions of deep metaphysical truths.

Other general books covering different places, times, and themes in native American religions, and containing mostly earlier published articles, include my own collection of papers on beliefs, myths and ritual, and on scholars' ecological and historical interpretations of them (Hultkrantz 1981a). Christopher Vecsey's portfolio of myths and rituals from different American tribes (Vecsey 1988) will be discussed later. A missionary, Michael Steltenkamp, has also written a somewhat popular book on Indian religion from a Catholic perspective (1982), similar to Carl Starkloff's book on the same subject (Starkloff 1974). Of more scientific rigor are Henry Bowden's and John Webster Grant's historical surveys of the relations between Indians and Christian missions (Bowden 1981; Grant 1985), by far the best books so far on the subject. They are supplemented by a less analytical but very readable book on the history of missionary activities in North America by John Terrell (1979).

Several of the modern handbooks contain excellent brief surveys of North American religions, as exemplified by the accounts of Joseph Epes Brown (1985) and Guy Cooper (1988).

Two important area surveys should finally be noted. One is a major descriptive, partly analytical, volume on the characteristic features of the Eastern culture area by Elisabeth Tooker (1979). This competent scholar, best known for her Iroquoian research, has, first and foremost, given us a valid portrait of tribal and clan ceremonies.

The other book, a survey of Plains religion typified by four hunting tribes and written by Howard Harrod (1987), is more an interpretation of the Plains Indian religious ethos. This thoughtful volume is composed with great empathy and with some new insights into the little-discussed question of the relationship between morality and religion in this area.

Historical Research

In spite of the indifference to history in recent anthropological research and with the exception of the archaeological subdiscipline and the ethnohistorians grouped around the periodical *Ethnohistory* and the *Handbook of North American Indians*, several new papers and books both in anthropology and religious studies concentrate on the history of North American religions or religious features. To these works may also be counted publications on tribal religions, according to the model of the "ethnographical present." The latter model may seem to be a little outmoded, indeed, in some measures even antihistorical, but for almost a hundred years it has served some of the foremost scholars on American Indian religions, for example Boas, who investigated the Kwakiutl and Lowie, who wrote on the Crow. The republication of old works will be mentioned shortly, and attention given to the editing and publishing of manuscripts in American archives. This preoccupation with religious history may at least partly find its explanation in the fact that all religions are part of the heritage of the past.

Publication of old manuscripts

In my earlier bibliographical surveys, I stressed the importance of using the old manuscripts left by scholars, missionaries, travellers and Indian agents and preserved all over the United States, Canada, and Spain for a reconstruction of Indian religions in the past (cf. for instance Hultkrantz 1965, 96, 102; 1983d, 130 ff.). It is delightful to find that the publication of fine old manuscripts has become a pattern in modern Americanist research. Only a few examples of such publications will be given here.

The work of Raymond DeMallie and Douglas Parks stands in a particularly fine class. DeMallie has, together with Elaine Jahner, made Dr. James Walker's important manuscripts on the Lakota available to us in their entirety, thereby fulfilling an old wish among scholars. Two publications of particular interest to us are the compilation *Lakota Belief and Ritual* (Walker 1980) and a survey of mythological tales, *Lakota Myth* (Walker 1983). The former volume presents a rich trove of Lakota religious concepts and belief systems, and has already been widely used in different fields of research. However, the difficulty in separating the ideas of laymen from the ideas of medicine men, well-known from earlier work by Walker, remains. In *Lakota Myth,* Jahner has made an interesting comparison of tales retold by Walker (from his informants, George Sword and others) and tales found by the Dakota anthropologist, Ella Deloria. Surprisingly, Deloria disclaims the creation tales of the Lakota-Dakota.

DeMallie has reinterpreted the original documents that the writer John Neihardt used to compose his well-known biography of the holy man Black Elk (DeMallie 1984). DeMallie's work shows that Neihardt, for the most part, was faithful to the original text, as translated to and written down by his daughter. He suppressed, however, the fact that after 1904 Black Elk was a Catholic catechist.

Parks has been primarily interested in Caddoan tribes and has, in this connection, given us a useful account of Pawnee religion in James Murie's excellent manuscripts on Pawnee ceremonies (Murie 1981). The first part, which was originally worked over by Clark Wissler, contains calendar ceremonies and other rites of the Skiri Pawnee, whereas the second part conveys fine information on the ceremonies of the southern Pawnee bands, with particular emphasis on shamanic rites. Both DeMallie and Parks are good linguists and show remarkable care in their publications.

Reissue of important old works

Publishers have made ongoing attempts to reprint the classics of the field of American Indian religion. Here I restrict myself to mentioning Lafitau's classic work on North American Indian "customs", particularly religious observances, now for the first time translated into English from French (Lafitau 1974/77).

Accounts of largely obsolete religions in the "ethnographic present"

Monographs of this type were common in the days of Boasian scholars but are not as appreciated today. In those bygone days, Kroeber reminds us, the American "unhistorical-mindedness" had the result that the past was experienced "not as a receding stereoscopic continuum but as a uniform nonpresent" (Kroeber 1952, 151). Nevertheless, some books of this sort still occasionally come out, and in spite of their flat perspectives they should not be overlooked. Many good religio-ethnographical reports have been written in this style.

Two important scholars, who have recently died, may represent here the continuation of this tradition into our own time. W.W. Hill, whose book on the Santa Clara Pueblo (Hill 1982) was published after his death in 1974, collected fine material on a religion that cannot be found today. His lengthy chapter on ceremonial organization, for example, is outstanding. Another valuable publication of the same nature is James Howard's account of the religion, medicines, and other aspects of the Oklahoma Seminole Indians, research which has been largely forgotten in comparison with that of their Florida tribesmen (Howard 1984). James Howard, who died in 1982, produced many books of a similar type, for instance, his comprehensive survey of Shawnee ceremonialism (Howard 1981). The latter discloses material important to our understanding of Eastern Woodland religious forms.

In a similar vein, and with reference to historical changes, contemporary works include Christopher Vecsey's survey of traditional Ojibway religion. This superb compendium unites widely disjointed sources on this expansive tribe into a unified perspective (Vecsey 1983). We need many more works of this sort for comparative and historical purposes.

Some of Karl Luckert's publications on the Navajo also contain material lost in the historical process. For instance, his meticulous recording of a Navajo curing ceremonial came from probably the last person who knew it (Luckert 1979). A book on Navajo religion which was a *Festschrift* for the veteran specialist on this tribe, Leland Wyman, was published shortly before his death (Brugge and Frisbie 1982). Many well-known scholars have contributed here to illuminate Navajo religion in its many aspects, such as sandpainting symbolism, medicine and witchcraft, bear ceremonialism, sacred geography, and religious history.

Northwest Indian religions have been reinterpreted in several new ethnographic monographs. Stanley Walens, leaning exclusively on texts collected by Boas and his informant George Hunt, makes a skillful attempt to reveal the world view of the Kwakiutl (Walens 1981). As could be expected, his interpretation has been challenged by some; they consider it enigmatic, for instance, how hunger could be identified as a leading motif in this rich and well-adapted culture. World view is also a dominant theme in two recent books on Tsimshian culture and religion edited by Jay Miller and Carol Eastman (1984), and Margaret Seguin (1984), respectively. The former work contains articles discussing mythic and ritual images of the supernatural animal world, totemism, and shamanism, and also includes a paper on Salish concepts of power (by William Elmendorf). The second work has in particular two good articles by Marie-Francoise Guédon, one on world view and the other on shamanism. Both works carry the heavy stamp of structuralist analysis.

Ethnohistorical reconstructions of religion

The works considered here may be conveniently divided into two categories: those concerned with general, more intuitively based formulations of past processes, and those which have been guided solely by documentary and literary research. The latter are usually referred to as ethnohistorical in a stricter sense, and are more restricted in scope. Closely connected with them are historical deductions from archaeological materials.

Other than general introductions to different works, there is very little written based on the first type. With my own pen I have sketched the two roots of American Indian religious patterns and their mutual impact (Hultkrantz 1987a; 1987b, 9–19). I have also outlined the connections between American Indian and Circumpolar religions (Hultkrantz 1981b). Werner Müller (1982) has presented a very heterodox idea of the connections between cultures and religions in North America and ancient Europe. He theorizes an eastbound movement over the North Atlantic in ancient times, from Canada to Ireland and Scandinavia. Understandably, this thesis has met with strong opposition.

Another controversy, opened by the historian Calvin Martin, concerns the epidemics which reduced the number of Indians in post-Columbian days. The supernatural masters of the game caused these epidemics, according to Indian beliefs. These masters, it is argued, broke their agreements with the hunters when men ceased to pay attention to ritual and taboo rules of the hunt (Martin 1978). Specialists from different regions have protested this reconstruction, insisting that epidemics were not attributed to the masters of the game, but Martin perseveres (Krech 1981).

Richard Perry (1983) has tried to identify proto-Athapascan culture, reconstructing the salient religious traits of the first Athapascan immigrants. Karl Schlesier (1987) gives us a possible picture of the obsolete Massaum ceremony among the Cheyenne Indians. He finds a connection between Cheyenne ceremonies and Siberian shamanism as practiced by the Evenki (Tungus), thereby revivifying an old theory that Algonkian religions are closely related to Circumpolar religions. Schlesier's results remind us of John Grim's efforts to find a connection between Ojibway and Siberian shamanism, a less analytical undertaking, however (Grim 1984).

Schlesier refers to both archaeological and documentary sources which play such a great role in the ethnohistorical approaches. The new dependence on old archival manuscripts for historical reconstruction signals a fascinating new movement in the study of American Indian religious history. An excellent demonstration of what can be done in this way is contained in the work of William Simmons on the New England tribes. In a pioneering survey of the religious and folkloristic conceptions of these tribes since Puritan days, Simmons skillfully displays the developments of belief in shamans, ghosts, and spirits by recounting documentary evidence year by year (Simmons 1986). This well-researched and judicious book is written by a person who is both anthropologist and folklorist. His other recent publications include his articles on the Narragansett conversion to Christianity (Simmons 1983) and the Puritans' perception of Indian religion as Devil worship (Simmons 1981).

The ethnohistorical work of William Fenton is well known. About fifty years ago he wrote several interesting articles on the Iroquois False Face masks and the society making use of them. He has now published an impressive volume with exquisite illustrations on these masks (Fenton 1986). As we know, the masks are worn by Iroquois doctors in order to cure the sick. In his article Thomas McElwain concludes that the morphology of these masks is today more mythically oriented than was the case at the turn of the century (McElwain 1980). An important paper by the meticulous East German scholar Rolf Krusche on the origin of the mask compolex in the Eastern Highlands has been recently republished in English (Krusche 1986).

McElwain has also written a book on an isolated ethnic community of primarily Seneca Iroquois, whose Christian religion seems to be steeped in the structure of traditional native religion (McElwain 1981). In the author's belief, rather than seeing their religion today as Christian or non-Christian, we face a basically native religion persisting through the crises of culture contact (McElwain 1981, 6). Another article by the same author tries to prove that the remains of the prehistoric Adena culture give evidence of dual souls (McElwain 1985). This is one of the few extant papers which combine archaeological finds with definite religious ideas (cf. the Cheyenne, above, and the Pawnee, below).

Two works by William McLoughlin, both concerned with the Cherokee and their relations to the missionaries (McLoughlin 1984a, 1984b), emphasize the missionaries' ability to understand Cherokee psyche and religious thought.

Several recent historical works focus on the Plains Indians. The *berdache* complex, centering on Indians imitating the behavior and wearing the dress of the opposite sex, is also known in other culture areas, but was particularly intense on the northern Plains where it was integrated with religion (Thayer 1980). Callender and Kochems (1983) provide detailed discussion of this complex as found in North America. The Sun dance, the central religious ceremony on the Plains, still attracts scholarly attention. Its probable history, though historical evidence is lacking, has been more or less successfully traced by this author (Hultkrantz 1980). The transfer of the Shoshoni dance to the Crow Indians in the 1940s has been well described and analyzed in Fred Voget's comprehensive monograph,

which reveals the important role played by a charismatic Shoshoni medicine man (Voget 1984). Peter Bolz has investigated the continuity of the
Sun dance for the Oglala Lakota in recent time (Bolz 1986, 203–25).
Margot Liberty has done the same for the Plains Indians at large (Liberty
1980).

A third major area of interest in historical Plains research is the use of
the sacred pipe. The ritual of the sacred pipe has become a symbol of
unity among today's North American Indians, even in areas where no
such thing formerly existed. The scholarly debate intensified after Joseph
Brown's publication of Black Elk's exposition on the rites connected with
the Lakota sacred pipe (Brown 1953). The discussion took a new turn
after Paul Steinmetz's demonstration of the use of the pipe in the Indians'
Catholic service (Steinmetz 1970). Since then, several of the issues of the
American Indian Culture and Research Journal have been dedicated to the
subject, with contributions by Father Paul Steinmetz and Patricia Kaiser
(Steinmetz 1984, Kaiser 1984). Steinmetz gives an historical overview of
the sacred pipe complex and the literature around it, and describes its
religious significance. Kaiser limits her study to the Lakota and their different ways of handling the pipe. The variations in pipe rituals all over the
East have been noted by James Springer (1981), while Donald Blakeslee
(1981) and William Turnbough (1979) have dealt with the nature and
origin of the calumet dance. Jordan Paper (1989) has recently written a
comprehensive survey of the sacred pipe, its symbolism, ritual, and
mythology.

The interconnections between Lakota women's experiences and their
religiousness have been examined with fine insight by Marla Powers (1980;
1986). There should be many studies on native American women's religious lives in the decade to come, inspired by Powers' Lakota work.

The Lakota have on the whole been the center of much recent histori-
cal work. DeMallie's work on the Walker material has been mentioned.
Together with Parks, DeMallie has issued a collection of papers from a
symposium on Lakota religion, its tradition and innovation (DeMallie and
Parks 1987). The papers have been written by historians, anthropologists,
Church representatives, and Indians. A work with a similar purpose is
Steinmetz's presentation of contemporary native religious directions on
the Pine Ridge Reservation including a history of the cultic groups (Steinmetz
1980).

A little-used inroad to historical knowledge is the study of the picto-
graphs or "wintercounts" on the Lakota buffalo robes. Deciphering them

may make it possible to reach the years when certain events, such as important religious ceremonies, took place. Many such wintercounts have been published during recent years. William Wildhage (1988) has brought them together and analyzed them in a comprehensive and extensive volume. The author is particularly attentive to the sacred rituals. His careful, critical rendering of Lakota chronology are a great aid to the reconstruction of their religion and history.

Some ethnohistorical works on other Siouan groups include Robert Ridington's article on Omaha tribal religion after Fletcher and La Flesche (Ridington 1987; cf. below).

The Caddoan peoples are well known for their association of stars and cosmic divinities with earthly dimensions. Von del Chamberlain compares the Pawnee parallel between the structure of the heaven and the earth with the planning of their habitations in a cosmic light. He finds, not unexpectedly, that the lodge is a microcosm oriented in the cardinal directions with a quadripartition of space. This, he argues, makes an interesting counterpart to Mesoamerian cosmography (Chamberlain 1982). Patricia O'Brien extends this interpretation to prehistoric Pawnee structures. She suggests that priests' lodges were astronomical observatories used *inter-alia* for the time-bound openings of sacred bundles (O'Brien 1986).[4]

Other inroads into the past have been made in the Great Basin area through the ecological interpretations of Steward, Grant, and others. My study of Sheepeater Indian religious changes belongs to this group since it is based on religio-ecological methods inspired by Steward but modified to suit religion (Hultkrantz 1981c).

From the Southwest we have a truly religio-historical work in Guy Cooper's well-balanced study of the development of Navajo religion (Cooper 1984). He traces the different traditions in this religion, among them shamanism, and accounts for factors that have created stress in religious life.

Other good examples of what can be done with old manuscripts and ethnohistorical and comparative reconstructions are demonstrated in Travis Hudson's work on the Chumash of California. Under his experienced hands the intricate religion of the Chumash, originally thought to be lost, has slowly entered the light. Hudson worked with the enormous manuscripts left by the anthropologist John Peabody Harrington, an extraordinary linguist and field researcher. Hudson issued several important manuscripts on Chumash religion in the 1970s, among them an important paper on myth and ritual (Hudson 1978). Before his untimely death, Hudson managed to publish, together with Kathleen Conti, a paper on rock art caves as ritual shrines (Hudson and Conti 1984). A close colleague of Hudson's, Georgia Lee, wrote a book on cosmological effigies and stones from the Chumash area (Lee 1981).

On the Northwest Coast the potlatch feasts have for a long time been the subject of the most varied interpretations. These extreme gift-giving ceremonies have been regarded as validations of rank and status, as a means of redistributing wealth, as substitutes for warfare, and recently in a psychoanalytical interpretation as a means of displaying wealth or venting aggression (Dundes 1979). The potlatch may certainly, at least locally, fit all these explanations, but a more basic idea was launched by Irving Goldman (1975) and Stanley Walens (1981) who, referring to extant sources, postulated a religious origin for the potlatch. Two recent propositions apply this type of argument. Steven Vertovec considers that the rites to validate a "name" originally referred to mythic events in primeval times. Later, a process of secularization has veiled this motive (Vertovec 1983). Sergei Kan proceeds from the known fact that Tlingit potlatches were celebrated as commemorative ceremonies for the dead. He defines the Tlingit potlatch as a religious ritual in which the dead play the main role, and the mourners appear as hosts (Kan 1986). The author also hints that the same explanation could be preferably used for the potlatches among the other northern Pacific Indian tribes.

Another remarkable feature of the Northwest Coast Indians is the Coast Salish Spirit dance ceremony. The Salish are revivifying this ceremony, which for a long time has been eclipsed by such movements as Christian Methodism and Indian Shakerism. Pamela Amoss and Wolfgang Jilek (Amoss 1978; Jilek 1982) offer excellent reports of this new development in their eye-witness accounts. The return to old tribal religion is not unusual among tribes attempting to save their ethnicity in the last hundred tumultuous years. Among the Omaha and Lakota, for instance, are prime examples of the phenomena.

Documentations of Traditional Religions

The following review of modern books and articles on traditional religious life reports on work which has no particular historical bias. These works will be grouped into the studies of beliefs of rituals and ritual patterns, and of mythology. The precedence given here to beliefs mirrors the increasing understanding of the importance of beliefs, or "philosophical tenets," as symbols of religion and religious meaning.

Belief studies

Several authors have tried to examine the nature of religious beliefs. Thus, Robin Ridington emphasizes the highly individualized belief systems of the Subarctic Athapascan hunters who certainly have some basic religious conceptions in common but form them according to their own experiences, a natural phenomenon in a more or less atomistic society (Ridington 1988b). In the same article the author, following Jean-Guy Goulet, seems to discard the boundary between belief and knowledge. On this matter I have expressed a different opinion. Based on materials from different parts of North America, I have delineated a clear break between two experienced worlds, a natural world of daily experience and a supernatural or metaphysical reality (Hultkrantz 1983a, 1983b). This is, however, a vexing question.

Important religious conceptions have been discussed in some detail. There is a challenging study by Jordan Paper (1983) on the connection between the growth of the American high-god concept and the Christian suppression of woman's religion. Paper contends that "of all the aspects of Christian influence, it is probably the excision of the female from the aboriginal concept of creation that enabled the concept of a single high god to emerge" (p. 19). This provocative statement stands ironically in conflict with the thesis of another controversial work, Sam Gill's monograph on the North American Earth goddess (Gill 1987a). Gill's opinion is that this deity is a comparatively recent figure introduced by the whites. The whites supplied female metaphors, such as the goddess of liberty which in time the Indians transformed into a mythological and religious concept. This book has caused heated discussion. The present writer has ascribed a more positive role to the Mother goddess in American Indian religious history (Hultkrantz 1983c).

As pointed out earlier, Martin (1978) has accorded an important place to the masters of the animals in native religion. The masters of the fish in North America have been phenomenologically presented by this writer (Hultkrantz 1983e). Like many before him, Daniel Merkur has analyzed the Eskimo *inua* concepts. He finds that *inua* is no "master" concept but a designation for a kind of animistic "indweller"(Merkur 1985b). In this and another article (Merkur 1983), Merkur gives refreshingly new insights into the Eskimo soul-system and also defines the theistic nature of the mysterious Eskimo cosmic spirit, *Sila*.

Another northern conception that has been much debated is that of the Canadian Algonkian cannibal, *windigo* or *witigo,* which is by some researchers associated with psychotic ideas and behavior. This debate shows no signs of ending (Preston 1980; Marano 1982; Brightman 1988). The psychic states of the individual, however, are more at stake here than individually or socially held religious beliefs.

Some Navajo specialists have tried to penetrate the nature of this tribe's religious ideas. In his new book, James McNeley convincingly proves that it is possible to gain still deeper insights into traditional Navajo beliefs. The Navajo, as do the Eskimo, identify the wind with the basic life force. The author shows that there is a communication between the cosmic wind ruled over by the Holy People, or the gods, and the human wind. The latter endows the individual with life and character; its weakening may result in death (McNeley 1981). Another scholar, John Farella, points out that Navajo religious concepts are complex, sophisticated, and difficult to render into English. A single word may serve as a metaphor in distinct contexts (Farella 1984).

Studies of rituals and ritual patterns.

Three types of studies on ritual are distinguishable in the past ten years. The first group demonstrates an interest in ritual as such and a primarily social-anthropological concern for their mechanisms. The second group combines research on rituals with ideological interpretations. The final group of studies on ritual patterns focusses particularly on the northern part of the continent, where these rituals occur in an ecological framework. Studies of Ghost dance and Peyote rituals will be examined in a later section.

The articles collected by Charlotte Frisbie in an effort to show the variety and expressions of Indian ritual drama in the Southwest, though attractive, miss the definitions of what ritual is and only vaguely indicate their meaning (Frisbie 1980). Inéz Talamantez brings out the latter point in her discourse on religious dancing rituals (Talamantez 1982). Prayer is a particular form of ritual. Navajo prayer was analyzed by Gladys Reichard almost half a century ago. Sam Gill has returned to this subject and classified and analyzed more than three hundred Navajo prayers (Gill 1981).

He has concentrated on the performance aspect of prayer.[5] In another work, John Loftin demonstrates that Hopi prayers do not embody magical ideas but make use of instruments which have been wrongly interpreted, by Frazer and others, as magical devices (Loftin 1986).

Some recent works seemingly portray rituals as self-sufficient but, on closer perusal, testify to a lasting religious motivation. To this category belongs Rodney Frey's well-rounded display of present-day Crow religion (Frey 1987). Also to be mentioned are Robin Ridington's papers on the Omaha renewal rituals centered around the cosmic pole, which a hundred years ago was placed in a museum but today, at least temporarily, has been restored to the tribe (Ridington 1987, 1988a). This has resulted in a new tribal interest in old rituals. Barbara Tedlock, finally, has shown how present-day Zuni ceremonies stage a year-round theater in conformity with supernatural occurrences (Tedlock 1983).

In his typological survey of Hopi rituals, Armin Geertz (1986) gives a straightforward answer concerning the meaning of religious ritual. He emphasizes the utter dependence of ritual on religious ideology, only secondarily explainable by neurophysiology and psychiatry. The drama both symbolizes and realizes the presence of the gods. In an extensive monograph on Hopi puppet ceremonialism, Geertz sets forth an excellent analysis of the connection between religious faith and ritual drama (Geertz and Lomatuway'ma 1987).

Geertz has also demonstrated, in a separate article, the close integration between cosmographic mythology and ceremonialism in Hopi religion (Geertz 1984). This interest in cosmology and its ritual correlations is presently fashionable among scholars. General outlines of the Plains Indians' cosmic ideas of the circle and its ritual replicas have been produced by Enrico Comba (1987) and Kurt Almqvist (1987). Fred Miller has analyzed the symbolism of the Crow Sun dance, that is, the new, Shoshoni-inspired Sun dance from the 1940s (Miller 1980). In an original article, John Moore explains the reflection of Cheyenne cosmological structure in personal names. Names symbolizing the heavenly part of the world are believed to be more sacred than others (Moore 1984).

Sacred things, such as the Pueblo sacred dolls or *kachinas,* can be desacralized. In the same way, Navajo sand paintings today may become profane and commercialized in rigid form when they are fixed to plywood, as Nancy Parezo has demonstrated (Parezo 1983).

Rituals, more than beliefs, are part of sociocultural patterns and of ecological patterns. In works in the 1960s and 1970s, Richard Nelson described the game and the hunting techniques of Eskimo and Northern Athapascan hunters. In a more recent book he has described the ways in which Koyukon hunters understand and approach nature. Religious ideas and attitudes are important in this connection. They are, indeed, better accounted for here than in any comparable work since Frank Speck (Nelson 1983). A monograph by Ann Fierup-Riordan (1983) shows how Eskimo (Yupik) rituals are integrated into economic patterns. Adrian Tanner has written a superb book on Cree Indian hunting patterns and hunting ideology. The balance between hunting techniques and ideology is expressed in the formulation that divination is "not a substitute for environmental data gathering, but a parallel process which is of a symbolic order" (Tanner 1979, 134).

The American Indian's reaction to the environment in religious terms has been a recurrent theme since the publication of Calvin Martin's theory of the masters of the game and their supposed impact on native religions (cf. above). The complexity of the issue was delineated in Christopher Vecsey's assessments of the integration of religion into the environment by native cultures (Vecsey 1980). Some articles in *Environmental Review*, vol. 9, no. 2(1985) by Jeanne Kay, Stephanie Romeo, and Christopher Vecsey, for example, elaborate on this theme in detail, as do Baird Callicott (1982) and the present writer (Hultkrantz 1981a).

Douglas Parks and Waldo Wedel (1985) have demonstrated that the Pawnee perceived intimate bonds between geography and religion. Hultkrantz (1981c) has done the same for the Shoshonean Sheepeaters. I maintain, however, that there is little evidence that religious ideas and rituals were engendered by environmental stimulations (Hultkrantz 1982).

Mythological studies.

Since Claude Lévi-Strauss wrote his quaternion cycle *Mythologiques*, with materials from North and South America, mythological studies have appeared to come to a standstill. Some mythological interpreations in the structuralist manner followed, but they were few. It was as it the air had seeped out of the mythological balloon. The 1980s has seen, however, some slow regeneration of the genre.

First, Christopher Vecsey has completed a fascinating work on North American myths that displays his mastery of diverse tribal traditions (Vecsey 1988). In his introduction, he emphasizes their importance to the people who create them and believe them, and in particular he stresses their importance for the community. Vecsey believes that myths concern life-and-death matters. He rightly insists that the performance of a myth is a ritual in itself. Moreover, the student of myth should know that there is no one method applicable to all myths, following Percy Cohen's advice to use a multiperspective analysis in the study of myth. From this point of view, Vecsey, along with Carol Ann Lorenz, analyzed the Hopi emergence myth. With John Fisher, he wrote a structuralist analysis of the Ojibway creation myth. He has also examined the Navajo Chantway heroic myth, peyote origin myths, and other such narratives. In a separate article, he scrutinizes the Midewiwin origin myths among the Ojibway and concludes, as does Harold Hickerson, that the Midewiwin society and lodge are post-Columbian (Vecsey 1984).

Another important mythgraphic undertaking is the systematic geographical tabulation of North American myths by John Bierhorst (1985). This well-known folklorist distinguishes eleven myth areas in North America which do not exactly correspond to the culture areas designated by Wissler and Kroeber long ago. The constituents of these areas are characteristic myth types or myth themes, which also decide the subareas. This results in a list of the main themes of North American mythology, delimited according to areas. Bierhorst's book certainly fills a gap in the literature. More inventory accounts have not been published since the days of Alexander (1916) and Thompson (1929, republished 1966).[6]

The nature of myth is very much the object of Daniel Merkur's penetrating study of Eskimo myth symbolism (Merkur 1988). In this rich work, Merkur raises questions about the meaning of myth analysis and the meaning of myths, the truth of myths, the definitions of myth, and the relationship between myth and religious belief. In another article on the Eskimo, Merkur investigates the rapport between a cultic ceremony and a mythological tale, in which the symbolic release of a dead eagle's spirit that will become a spirit helper is accounted for in the tale of the eagle husband (Merkur 1987).

There are also other regional works of recent date. The myths and oral traditions of the Great Basin area have been dealt with by Hultkrantz (1986a) and Liljeblad (1986). Alaskan myths have been presented in a publication issued by Anna Birgitta Rooth (1980). Thomas Overholt and Baird Callicott have republished William Jones's *Ojibwa Texts* and illuminated them with world-view analyses (Overholt and Callicott 1982). Fine collections of Navajo and Hopi myths have been published in the series *American Tribal Religions* by its editor, Karl Luckert. During the 1980s the series has included several Navajo texts from Father Berard Haile's post-humous collection (he died in 1959), among them an origin myth of a major curing ceremony (Haile 1981) and a number of Coyote tales (Haile 1984). The latter book also contains a cogent interpretation of the Coyote figure by Luckert (Luckert 1984). In the same series, Ekkehart Malotki and Michael Lomatuway'ma have written books on Hopi myths centered around two personages of the trickster type, Coyote (Malotki and Lomatuway'ma 1984) and Maasaw (Malotki and Lomatuway'ma 1987).

The trickster is indeed the prominent character in most native American mythologies. Several new works try to analyze this enigmatic figure, whose essence and meaning scholars seem never to agree upon.[7] Some scholars like Michael Carroll prefer a structuralist analysis but abstain from Lévi-Strauss's arbitrary interpretations (Carroll 1981). Carroll, who mainly concentrates on the Eastern woodland trickster and culture hero Hare, opines that Lévi-Strauss has ignored the trickster's role as culture hero. On the other hand, Rémi Savard, who has carefully studied the Montagnais tales of the trickster, thinks that these stories have no real mythological value but express casual reflections on life (Savard 1985).

The Hopi trickster figure has been discussed by Geertz (1987b) and Malotki and Lomatuway'ma (1987c). According to Geertz, the trickster is Coyote or a whole family of coyotes, portrayed as the usual American trickster but with some clearly evil intentions. There is, however, he points out, a more successful trickster, Maasaw, dealt with by Malotki. It appears that Maasaw has become thoroughly integrated into Hopi agriculture and consequently also figures as a god of earth, crops, death, and even lately as a supreme being. This Hopi trickster indeed represents one of the exceptional cases in North America where the trickster has become associated with active religious functions and with a cult.

Most scholars agree that trickster tales span from obscene stories to sacred myths. Scrutinizing the Winnebago tale collected by Radin, Lawrence Sullivan speculates that even the obscene trickster tales have a symbolic, religious meaning (Sullivan 1982). Sullivan considers Radin's interpretation to represent a travesty of sacred texts. The ostentatious sexual passages or cases of distasteful voracity have, according to Sullivan, a religious meaning that we have to discern. On the other hand, Volney Gay contrasts the trickster to the culture hero, a different personage (Gay 1983). According to him, the two figures represent the contrasting systems of chaos and order. This survey shows how difficult it is to reach agreement in mythological matters, particularly when the trickster is the subject.

There are, as we know, quite a few popular publications of American Indian myths. Some are designed for the general public yet retain a value for scholars needing quick references. The selection of myths and legends published by Erdoes and Ortiz (1984) is a good compilation with occasional explanatory notes.

The ancient Greek concept of myth also allows for the interpretation of myth as a falsehood. One is reminded of this when reading the reports on the Saskuatch from a Vancouver conference (Markotić and Krantz 1984). Although there are many Indian legends about this mysterious ogre of the Northwest, here it is presented simply as a possible but unknown hominoid.

Shamanism and Medicine Men

Because of the recent interest in shamanic studies, a few words need to be said about the last decade's research on North American shamanism and related subjects. Presentations of North American shamans figure largely in recent books on the topic edited by Shirley Nicholson (1987) and Gary Doore(1988), and particularly in one edited by Amelie Schenk and Holger Kalweit (1987). Although intended for a general readership, these books contain important information for specialists, as does Amanda Porterfield's article defining shamanism from a "psychosocial" perspective (Porterfield 1987). Shamanism has been especially concentrated in the Eskimo area, and from this northern region we now have two excellent surveys, both founded on thorough reading of extant source material. Daniel Merkur has written a detailed psychological analysis of the Eskimo shaman, introducing valuable new ideas and concepts (Merkur 1985a). Evelin Haase's monograph on Eskimo shamanism complements Merkur's book, containing ethnographical and ritual details Merkur bypasses (Haase 1987). Although not based upon primary field research, both books order our understanding of Eskimo shamanism, so varied from east to west and so rich in its phenomenology.

There are no other inclusive shamanic books from the North American field, but there are important special investigations. We have already discussed the research on the *berdache* system. The connections between this and shamanism have already been commented upon. James Thayer's (1980) discussion of the mediating role of the *berdache* has also been taken up by Jay Miller (1982). As does the shaman, the *berdache* assumes his role usually as a consequence of instructions from a supernatural vision.

Whether *berdaches* were from the outset shamanic persons remains an enigma.

The types of vision quest and their import, once discussed by Ruth Benedict, are the object of an article of mine (Hultkrantz 1986b). The tension between voluntary and involuntary visions among the Shoshoni constitutes the theme of another of my articles (Hultkrantz 1986c).

As hinted above, Ojibway shamanism has received a general treatment in a book by John Grim (1984). The author has drawn together various sources to reconstruct a complex whole. In what he calls a "speculative study," Jordan Paper, sinologist and Americanist, has followed the development of an Ojibway shaman to mystic (Paper 1980). He defines a mystic as a person who in ecstasy experiences a complete loss of self-identity. The Ojibway shaman becomes a mystic when his outwardly directed activities, shamanic healing, for example fall away, and he unites in ecstasy with the ultimate object of mystic experience.

Oglala Lakota medicine men and shamans figure in two fine studies by William Powers. One concerns the two types of sacred language used by these "holy men." One language is used between medicine men when they come together; the other serves as an individual means of communication between a medicine man and his guardian spirit (Powers 1986). Other themes in this book concern the concept of the sacred and the identity of the medicine man and priest. The second book is slightly more popular, concentrating on the shamanic show, the *yuwipi* medicine ceremony (Powers 1982). This is the most circumstantial description and discussion of this variation of the old shaking tent ceremony.

The most famous of Oglala medicine men, Black Elk, appeared in the foregoing. His dependence on Christianity has been heatedly debated by, for instance, Steinmetz (1980), DeMallie (1984), and Holler (1984). We can no longer exclude the fact that Christian attitudes of faith had an impact on Black Elk's traditional theological system, even though he tried to keep the two religions apart and was generally successful in doing so.

The curative aspects of shamanism come to the fore in articles on southwestern and northwestern data. These include a sketch on Hopi healing rites by Richard Grant (1982) and a book on Piman diseases and their cures by a team consisting of an anthropoligist, linguist, interpreter, and the shaman they consulted (Bahr et al. 1981). The theme of this book is the "staying disease," a noncontagious disease caused by moral transgression. Finally, Aldona Jonaitis's discourse on Tlingit shamanism (Jonaitis 1983) compares symbolically the shaman's absence in the trance during curing to Victor Turner's and Arnold van Gennep's concepts of the liminal situation.

Religious Revitalization Movements

All books and other publications on present-day native American religions deal, at least in part, with the new forms of religion introduced by creative religious leaders or prophets. The following selection of works are more directly concerned with the "new religions," some of which, like the Peyote religion, are now of considerable age. Finally, we shall pay attention to the blend of Christianity and traditional religion within a tribal frame, and discuss new ideas of religious freedom.

With Clifford Trafzer as guest editor, *The American Indian Quarterly* has dedicated an entire issue (9:3, 1985) to the subject of prophetic and other revitalization movements. Included are articles about Smohalla by Trafzer and M.A. Beach, the Feather religion by M.A. Beach, Wovoka by L.G. Moses, and the northern California Shakers by A.L. Slagle. Duane Champagne illuminates the impact of the Delaware revitalization movement on their national and religious ideology (Champagne 1988), and Paul Lenhoff's sketch of the Shaker religion is a plea for Indians to write its history (Lenhoff 1982). A separate monograph by Christopher Miller discusses the leaders, both Indian prophets and whites, in the aftermath of the Prophet dance on the Plateau (Miller 1985).

The Ghost Dance remains a topic that attracts scholarly attention. Raymond DeMallie has traced the history of the Lakota dance (DeMallie 1982). Garold Barney tries to show that the idea of the invulnerability of those wearing a ghost shirt or other items was inspired by Mormonism (Barney 1986). Russell Thornton's effort to prove that Indians joined the Ghost dance in order to strengthen their numbers through the return of the dead is rather exceptional, proceeding from an argument that religious explanations are inadequate (Thornton 1986). Judith Vander's investigation of Ghost dance songs among the Wind River Shoshoni reveals the peaceful attitude of this people (Vander 1986). Omer Stewart generalizes about the Ghost dance attitude holding true as well for the reputedly warlike Sioux (Stewart 1980).[8]

The other great revitalization movement, the Peyote religion, has been treated in a few larger works. Omer Stewart's recent book, *Peyote Religion: A History*, will be in many respects the definitive document on the devel-

opment of this religion. His particular interests in the leaders of the movement and in the late historical diffusion, rather than in the phases of its
history, give a characteristically individual stamp to this account. Together
with David Aberle, Stewart has produced another book which brings
together several important papers on peyotism that the two authors published between 1944 and 1982 (Steward and Aberle 1984). The new
introduction to the second edition of Aberle's classic book on Navajo
peyotism brings his ideas into sharper relief (Aberle 1982).

Stewart's early studies in Washo shamanism can now be supplemented
by Edgar Siskin's monograph on the enduring rivalry between indigenous
shamanism and intruding peyotism (Siskin 1983). Siskin has followed
this drama since 1939, a few years after the introduction of peyote, and
until the time when shamanism was ousted.

On all the reservations, Christianity in one form or another has a grip
on at least a fraction of the population. The relations between Christianity
and aboriginal religion have been analyzed in many works (cf above,
McElwain 1981; DeMallie and Parks 1987). We select here two examples.
Catherine Albanese points out that among the Eastern Cherokee, traditional religion or "Cherokee Christianity" adapted to the old native patterns, and a blend of both religions presently characterizes reservation life
(Albanese 1984). She states, somewhat like McElwain for the Allegheny
Indians, that "running through all the expressions of Cherokee religion
was the regionalism that marked it with its distinctive identity" (p. 365).
Kenneth Morrison, writing about the Abnaki, defines their religion as a
syncretic blend of Catholicism and traditional religion (Morrison 1981).
In his interpretation there is, thus, no compartmentalization but a unitary
faith, wherein the mythic example of the culture hero decides the core of
ethical values. Catholicism is selectively used to express ancient Abnaki
ideas.

During this decade, the American Indian Religious Freedom Act of 1978
has meant much juridically, politically, and religiously. In a careful and
judicious paper, Robert Michaelsen has illuminated those implications (Michaelsen 1983). In another paper he discusses the various difficulties of the sacred land claims. He underlines the legal obstacles that
native litigants encounter, particularly the fact that sacred sites do not
play a prominent role in white American religion and culture (Michaelsen
1986). We may conclude that the move toward religious freedom and
the protection of sacred sites are forceful parts of the new religious
revitalization.

Looking Ahead

The number and quality of the papers on North American Indian religions during the last ten years is astounding. In all probability, this scholarly interest will grow still stronger. More data will be found in archaeological work, archives, and older literature that will bear further upon the history. More collections of field data illustrating current conditions will be published. New theories and interpretations will create new insights and provide new syntheses of native religions. And certainly, new opportunities for research will appear when native religions change and steer themselves in new directions, whether in collaboration or conflict with Christianity.

The task of recording and analyzing these religions will thus continue. University disciplines, including anthropology, native studies, the history, sociology, and psychology of religion, and folklore as well will all, each with its own presuppositions, contribute to the task in a positive and constructive interaction.

NOTES

1. Concerning the decline of interest in American Indian studies generally and Indian religious studies at that time, see Stocking (1976, 23) and Hultkrantz (1965, 93ff.; 1983d, 59ff.).

2. Amusing pictures of the meetings of such shamans or so-called shamans and the European public have been given by Mandl (1987) and Feest (1987) under the common heading "Medicine Men Department," in the new *European Review of Native American Studies*, edited by Feest.

3. A detailed review of the new encyclopedia fills the entire issue of *Religious Studies* 24/1(1988), with contributions from seven scholars.

4. The study of American Indian ethnoastronomy or archaeoastronomy, introduced by Anthony Aveni, has considerably enriched our knowledge of American Indian ceremonies and myths. Included among these works are the general survey on American archaeoastronomy edited by Aveni (1982), and the study of North American Indian astronomy with its connections to indigenous religions by Ray Williamson (1984).

5. See also Gill 1977.

6. There is a valuable article on the study of North American myths in Gill, *Mythic Themes* (1987).

7. Cf. Hultkrantz (1984).

8. It could be added that Brad Logan has gone through the early documents on the origin of the Paiute Ghost dance and can state that the charismatic leadership of Wovoka (Jack Wilson) was the primary factor in the adoption of this religion by the Paiute (Logan 1980).

BIBLIOGRAPHY

Aberle, D. F. 1982. *The peyote religion among the Navajo.* 2nd ed. Chicago and London: University of Chicago Press.

Albanese, C.L. 1984. Exploring regional religion: A case study of the Eastern Cherokee. *History of Religions* 23:344–71.

Alexander, H.B. 1919. *North American mythology.* Boston: Marshall Jones Company.

Almqvist, K. 1987. The three circles of existence. *Studies in Comparative Religion* 17:24–29.

Amoss, P. 1978. *Coast Salish spirit dancing: The survival of an ancestral religion.* Seattle: University of Washington Press.

Aveni, A.F., ed. 1982. *Archaeoastronomy in the New World.* Cambridge: Cambridge University Press.

Bahr, D.M. et al. 1981. *Piman shamanism and staying disease.* Tucson: University of Arizona Press.

Barney, G.D. 1986. *Mormons, Indians, and the ghost dance religion of 1890.* Lanham, Maryland: University Press of America.

Bierhorst, J. 1985. *The mythology of North America.* New York: William Morrow.

Blakeslee, D.J. 1981. The origin and spread of the Calumet ceremony. *American Antiquity* 46:759–68.

Boas, F. et al. 1915. *Anthropology in North America.* New York: Stechert.

Bolz, P. 1986. *Ethnische identität und kultureller Widerstand: Die Oglala-Sioux der Pine Ridge-Reservation in South Dakota.* Frankfurt and New York: Campus Verlag.

Bowden, H.W. 1981. *American Indians and Christian missions: Studies in cultural conflict.* Chicago and London: University of Chicago Press.

Brightman, R.A. 1988. The Windigo in the material world. *Ethnohistory* 35:337–79.

Brown, J.E. 1953. *The sacred pipe.* Norman: University of Oklahoma Press.

1982. *The spiritual legacy of the American Indian.* New York: Crossroad.

1985. Religions in primal societies: North American Indian religions. In *A handbook of living religions,* ed. J.R. Hinnells, 392–411. New York: Penguin Books.

Brugge, D.M. and C.J. Frisbie, eds. 1982. *Navajo religion and culture: Selected views.* Papers in honor of Leland C. Wyman. Santa Fe: Museum of New Mexico Press.

Callender, C. and L. M. Kochems. 1983. The North American berdache. *Current Anthropology* 24:443–70.

Callicott, J.B. 1982. Traditional American Indian and Western European attitudes toward nature: An overview. *Environmental Ethics* 4:293–318.

Carroll, M.P. 1981. Lévi-Strauss, Freud, and the trickster: A new perspective upon an old problem. *American Ethnologist* 8:301–13.

Chamberlain, V.D. 1982. *When stars came down to earth: Cosmology of the Skidi Pawnee Indians of North America.* Los Altos, California: Ballena Press.

Champagne, D. 1988. The Delaware revitalization movement of the early 1760s: A suggested reinterpretation. *American Indian Quarterly* 12:107–26.

Coffer, W.E. (Koi Hosh). 1978. *Spirits of the sacred mountains: Creation stories of the American Indian.* New York: Van Nostrand Reinhold.

Comba, E. 1987. Inside a circle: The structure of the cosmos among the Plains Indians. *Temenos* 23:9–34.

Cooper, G.H. 1984. *Development and stress in Navajo religion.* Stockholm Studies in Comparative Religion 23. Stockholm: Almqvist & Wiksell.

1988. North American traditional religion. In *The World's Religions,* eds. Stewart Sutherland et al., 873–82. London: Routledge.

Deloria, V. 1973. *God is red.* New York: Grosset and Dunlap.

DeMallie, R.J. 1982. The Lakota ghost dance: An ethnohistorical account. *Pacific Historical Review* 51:385–405.

1984. *The sixth grandfather: Black Elk's teachings given to John G. Neihardt.* Lincoln: University of Nebraska Press.

DeMallie, R.J. and D.R. Parks, eds. 1987 Sioux Indian religion: *Traditional and Innovation.* Norman: University of Oklahoma Press.

Doore, G., ed. 1988. *Shaman's path: Healing, personal growth, and empowerment.* Boston: Shambhala,

Dundes, A. 1979. Heads or tails: A psychoanalytic study of potlatch. *The Journal of Psychological Anthropology* 2:395–424.

Encyclopaedia of religion and ethics. 1908–1926. 13 vols. Ed. J. Hastings. Edinburgh and New York: Macmillan.

Erdoes, R. and A. Ortiz, eds. 1984. *American Indian myths and legends.* New York: Pantheon Books.

Farella, J.R. 1984. *The main stalk: A synthesis of Navajo philosophy.* Tucson: University of Arizona Press.

Feest, C.F. 1986. Indians of northeastern North America. *Iconography of Religions* 10/7. Leiden: E.J. Brill.

1987. Medicine men department. *European Review of Native American Studies.* 1:53ff.

Fenton, W.N. 1986. *The false faces of the Iroquois.* Norman: University of Oklahoma Press.

Fienup-Riordan, A. 1983. *The Nelson Island Eskimo.* Anchorage: University of Alaska Press.

Fogelson, R. 1987. North American religions: History of study. In *The Encyclopedia of Religion,* ed. M. Eliade. 10/545–50. New York: Macmillan.

Frey, R. 1987. *The world of the Crow Indians: As driftwood lodges.* Norman: University of Oklahoma Press.

Frisbie, C., ed. 1980. *Southwestern Indian ritual drama.* Albuquerque: University of New Mexico Press.

Furst, P.T. and J.L. Furst. 1982. *North American Indian art.* New York: Rizzoli International Publications.

Gay, V. 1983. Winnicott's contribution to religious studies: The resurrection of the culture hero. *Journal of the American Academy of Religion* 51:371–95.

Geertz, A.W. 1984. A reed pierced the sky: Hopi Indian cosmography on Third Mesa, Arizona. *Numen* 31:216–41.

1986. A typology of Hopi Indian ritual. *Temenos* 22:41–56.

1987a. Hopi Indian altar iconography. *Iconography of Religions* 10/5. Leiden: E.J. Brill.

1987b. Hopi Coyote: Trickster, corpse, or god? *History of Religions* 27:89–92.

1987c. Native American iconography. In *The Encyclopedia of Religion*, ed. M. Eliade. 7, 17–21. New York: Macmillan.

Geertz, A.W. and M. Lomatuway'ma. 1987. *Children of the cottonwood: Piety and ceremonialism in Hopi Indian puppetry*. American Traditional Religions 12. Lincoln: University of Nebraska Press.

Gill, S.D. 1977. Prayer as person: The performative force in Navajo prayer acts. *History of Religions* 17:143–57.

1979. Songs of life: An introduction to Navajo religious culture. *Iconography of Religions* 10/3. Leiden: E.J. Brill.

1981. *Sacred words: A study of Navajo religion and prayer*. Westport, Connecticut: Greenwood Press.

1982. *Native American religions: An introduction*. Belmont, California: Wadsworth Publishing Co.

1983. *Native American traditions: Sources and interpretations*. Belmont, California: Wadsworth Publishing Co.

1987a. *Mother earth: An American story*. Chicago: University of Chicago Press.

1987b. *Native American religious action: A performance approach to religion*. Columbia: University of South Carolina Press.

1987c. North American religions: Mythic themes. In *The Encyclopedia of Religion*, ed. M. Eliade, 10, 535–41. New York: Macmillan.

Goldman, I. 1975. *The mouth of heaven: An introduction to Kwakiutl religious thought*. New York: Wiley.

Grant, J.W. 1985. *Moon of wintertime. Missionaries and the Indians of Canada since 1534*. Toronto: University of Toronto Press.

Grant, R.E. 1982. Tuuhikya: The Hopi healer. *The American Indian Quarterly* 6:291–304.

Grim, J.A. 1984. *The shaman: Patterns of Siberian and Ojibway healing*. Norman: University of Oklahoma Press.

Haase. E. 1987. *Der Schamanismus der Eskimos*. Acta Culturologica 3. Aachen: Rader Verlag.

Haile, B. 1981. *Upward moving and emergence way*. American Tribal Religions 7. Lincoln: University of Nebraska Press.

1984. *Navajo Coyote tales: The Curly to Aheedliinii version*. American Tribal Religions 8. Lincoln: University of Nebraska Press.

1987. *Stories of Maasaw, a Hopi god*. American Tribal Religions 10. Lincoln: University of Nebraska Press.

Harrod, H.L. 1987. *Renewing the world: Plains Indian religion and morality*. Tucson: University of Arizona Press.

Hill, W.W. 1982. *An ethnography of Santa Clara pueblo, New Mexico*, ed. Charles H. Lange. Albuquerque: University of New Mexico Press.

Holler, C. 1984. Black Elk's relationship to Christianity. *The American Indian Quarterly* 8:37–49.

Honigmann, J.J. 1981. Expressive aspects of subarctic Indian culture. In *Handbook of North American Indians*, ed. W.C. Sturtevant. 6, 718–38. Washington: Smithsonian Institution.

Howard, J.H. 1981. *Shawnee! The ceremonialism of a Native American tribe and its cultural background.* Athens: Ohio University Press.

1984. *Oklahoma Seminole medicines, magic, and religion.* Norman: University of Oklahoma Press.

Hudson, C. 1976. *The Southeastern Indians.* Knoxville: University of Tennessee Press.

1984. Elements of southeastern Indian religion. *Iconography of Religions* 10/1. Leiden: E.J. Brill.

Hudson, T. 1978. The integration of myth and ritual in South- Central California: The "northern complex." *The Journal of California Anthropology* 5:25–250.

Hudson, T. and K. Conti. 1984. The rock art of Indian Creek: Ritual sanctuary of the gifted Chumash. *San Luis Obispo County Archaeological Society: Occasional Papers* 12:49–88.

Hultkrantz, Å. 1965. The study of North American Indian religion: Retrospect, present trends and future tasks. *Temenos* 1:87–121.

1980. The development of the Plains Indian sun dance. In *Perennitas, studi in onore di Angelo Brelich*, ed. G. Piccaluga, 225–43. Rome: Edizioni dell'Ateneo.

1981a. *Belief and worship in native North America*, ed. C. Vecsey. Syracuse: Syracuse University Press.

1981b. North American Indian religions in a circumpolar perspective. In *North American Indian studies: European contributions*, ed. P. Hovens. 11–28. Göttingen: Edition Herodot.

1981c. Accommodation and persistence: Ecological analysis of the religion of the Sheepeater Indians in Wyoming, U.S.A. *Temenos* 17:35–44.

1982. Religion and experience of nature among North American hunting Indians. In *The Hunters: Their culture and way of life*, ed. Å. Hultkrantz and Ø. Vorren. 163–86. Tromsø, Oslo, and Bergen: Universitetsforlaget.

1983a. Das Wirklichkeitsbild eines Medizinmannes. In *Der gläserne Zaun*, eds. R. Gehlen and B. Wolf. 169–75. Frankfurt: Syndikat.

1983b. The concept of the supernatural in primal religion. *History of Religions* 22:231–53.

1983c. The religion of the goddess in North America. In *The book of the goddess, Past and present*, ed. C. Olsen. 202–16. New York: Crossroad.

1983d. *The study of American Indian religions*, ed. C. Vecsey. New York and Chico: Crossroad and Scholars Press.

1983e. Water sprites: The elders of the fish in aboriginal North America. *The American Indian Quarterly* 7:1–22.

1984. The myths of the trickster and culture hero.. In *Anthropology as a historical science: Essays in honour of Stephen Fuchs,* eds. M. Bhuriy and S.M. Michael. 113–26. Indore: San Prakashan Sanchar Kendra.

1986a. Mythology and religious concepts. In *Handbook of North American Indians,* ed. W.C. Sturtevant. 11, 630–40.

1986b. The American Indian vision quest: A transition ritual or a device for spiritual aid? In *Transition Rites: Cosmic, Social, and Individual Order,* ed. U. Bianchi. 29–43. Roma: "L'Erma" di Bretschneider.

1986c. The peril of visions: Changes of vision patterns among the Wind River Shoshoni. *History of Religions* 26:34–46.

1987a. De två stora traditionerna i de nordamerikanska indianernas religioner. In *Uppsala North American Studies Reports* 2: Perspektiv på Nordamerika, ed. E. Åsard. 57–81.

1987b. *Native religions of North America.* San Francisco: Harper & Row.

Jilek. W.G. 1982. *Indian healing: Shamanic ceremonialism in the Pacific Northwest today.* Blaine, Washington: Hancock House.

Jonaitis, A. 1983. Liminality and incorporation in the art of the Tlingit shaman. *The American Indian Quarterly* 7:41–68.

Kaiser, P.L. 1984. The Lakota sacred pipe: Its tribal use and religious philosophy. *American Indian Culture and Research Journal* 8:1–26.

Kan, S. 1986. The 19th-century Tlingit potlatch: A new perspective. *American Ethnologist* 13:191–212.

Krech, S., ed. 1981. *Indians, animals, and the fur trade: A critique of Keepers of the game.* Athens: University of Georgia Press.

Kroeber, A.L. 1952. *The nature of culture.* Chicago: University of Chicago Press.

Krusche, R. 1986. The origin of the mask concept in the eastern woodlands of North America. *Man in the Northeast.* 31:1–47.

Lafitau, J.F. 1974–77. *Customs of the American Indians compared with the customs of primitive times,* eds. W.N. Fenton and E.L. Moore. 2 vols. Toronto: Champlain Society.

Lee, G. 1981. *The portable cosmos: Effigies, ornaments, and incised stone from the Chumash area.* Socorro: Ballena Press Anthropological Papers 21.

Lenhodd, P. 1982. Indian Shaker religion. *American Indian Quarterly* 6:283–90.

Levine, S. and N.O. Lurie, eds. 1968. *The American Indian today.* Deland, Florida: Everett/Edwards.

Liberty, M. 1980. The sun dance. In *Anthropology on the Great Plains,* eds. W.R. Wood and M. Liberty. 164–78. Lincoln: University of Nebraska Press.

Liljeblad, S. 1986. Oral tradition: Content and style of verbal arts. In *Handbook of North American Indians,* ed. W.C. Sturtevant. 11, 641–59. Washington: Smithsonian Institution.

Loftin, J.D. 1986. Supplication and participation: The distance and relation of the sacred in Hopi prayer rites. *Anthropos* 81:177–201.

Logan, B. 1980. The ghost dance among the Paiute: An ethnohistorical view of the documentary evidence 1889–1893. *Ethnohistory* 27:267–88.

Luckert, K.W. 1979. *Coyoteway: A Navaho holyway healing ceremonial*. Tucson: University of Arizona Press.

Malotki, E. and M. Lomatuway'ma. 1984. *Hopi Coyote tales: Istutuwutsi*. American Tribal Religions 9. Lincoln: University of Nebraska Press.

1987a. *Maasaw: Profile of a Hopi god*. American Tribal Religions 11. Lincoln: University of Nebraska Press.

1987b. *Stories of Maasaw, a Hopi god*. American Tribal Religions 10. Lincoln: University of Nebraska Press.

Marano, L. 1982. Windigo psychosis: The anatomy of an emic-etic confusion. *Current Anthropology* 23:385–412.

Markotić, V. and G. Krantz, eds. 1934. *The sasquatch and other unknown hominoids*. Calgary, Alberta: Western Publishers.

Martin, C. 1978. *Keepers of the game: Indian-animal relationships and the fur trade*. Berkeley and London: University of California Press.

Maudl, R. 1987. Medicine men department. *European Review of Native American Studies*. 1:54.

McElwain, T. 1980. Methods in mask morphology: Iroquoian false faces in the Ethnographical Museum, Stockholm. *Temenos* 16:68–83.

1981. *Our kind of people: Identity, community and religion on Chestnut Ridge*. Stockholm Studies in Comparative Religion 20. Stockholm: Almqvist & Wiksell.

1985. The archaic roots of eastern woodland eschatology: A soul-dualism explanation of Adena mortuary. In *Duality*, ed. E. Lyle. *Cosmos* 1:37–43. Edinburgh.

McLoughlin, W.G. 1984a. *Cherokees and missionaries, 1789–1839*. New Haven: Yale University Press.

1984b. *The Cherokee ghost dance: Essays on the southeastern Indians, 1789–1861*. Macon, George: Mercer University Press.

McNeley, J.K. 1981. *Holy wind in Navajo philosophy*. Tucson: University of Arizona Press.

McNickle, D. 1973. *Native American tribalism: Indian survivals and renewals*. London: Oxford University Press.

Merkur, D. 1983. Breath-soul and wind owner: The many and the one in Inuit religion. *American Indian Quarterly* 7:23–39.

1985a. *Becoming half hidden: Shamanism and initiation among the Inuit*. Stockholm Studies in Comparative Religion 24. Stockholm: Almqvist & Wiksell.

1985b. Souls, spirits, and indwellers in nature: Metaphysical dualism in Inuit religion. *Temenos* 21:91–126.

1987. Eagle, the hunter's helper: The cultic significance of Inuit mythological tales. *History of Religions* 27:171–88.

1988. Adaptive symbolism and the theory of myth: The symbolic understanding of myths in Inuit religion. In *The Psychoanalytic Study of Society*, eds. S.A. Grolnick and L.B. Boyer. 63–94. Hillsdale, N.J.: The Analytic Press.

Michaelsen, R.S. 1983. "We also have a religion." The free exercise of religion among native Americans. *American Indian Quarterly* 7:111–42.

1986. Sacred land in America: What is it? How can it be protected? *Religion* 16:249–68.

Miller, C.L. 1985. *Prophetic worlds: Indians and whites on the Columbia Plateau.* New Brunswick, N.J.: Rutgers University Press.

Miller, F. 1980. The Crow sun dance lodge: Form, process, and geometry in the creation of sacred space. *Temenos* 16:92–102.

Miller, J. 1982. People, berdaches, and left-handed bears: Human variation in native America. *Journal of Anthropological Research* 38:274–87.

1983. Numic religion: An overview of power in the great basin of native North America. *Anthropos* 78: 337–54.

1985. Great Basin religion and theology: A comparative study of power (puha). *Journal of California and Great Basin Anthropology* 5: 66–86.

1988. *Shamanic odyssey: The Lushootseed Salish jouney to the land of the dead..* Menlo Park, California: Ballena Press.

Miller, J. and C.M. Eastman, eds. 1984. *The Tsimshian and their neighbors of the north Pacific coast.* Seattle: University of Washington Press.

Moore, J.H. 1984. Cheyenne names and cosmology. *American Ethnologist* 11:291–312.

Morrison, K.M. 1981. The mythological sources of Abenaki Catholicism: A case study of the social history of power. *Religion* 11:235–63.

Müller, W. 1981. *Neue Sonne—Neues Licht: Aufsätze zu Geschichte, Kultur und Sprache der Indianer Nordamerikas,* eds. R. Gehlen and B. Wolf. Berlin: Dietrich Reimer Verlag.

1982. *Amerika—die Neue oder die Alte Welt?* Berlin: Dietrich Reimer Verlag.

Mundkur, B. 1984. The bicephalous "animal style" in northern Eurasian religious art and its western hemispheric analogues. *Current Anthropology* 25: 451–82.

Murie, J.R. 1981. *Ceremonies of the Pawnee: Part I, the Skiri; Part II, the south bands,* ed. D.R. Parks. Smithsonian Contributions to Anthropology 27. Washington.

Nelson, R.K. 1983. *Make prayers to the raven: A Koyukon view of the northern forest.* Chicago: University of Chicago Press.

Nicholson, S., ed. 1987. *Shamanism: An expanded view of reality.* Wheaton, Illinois: The Theosophical Publishing House.

O'Brien, P.J. 1986. Prehistoric evidence for Pawnee cosmology. *American Anthropologist* 88:939–46.

Overholt, T.W. and J.B. Callicott. 1982. *Clothed-in-fur and other tales: An introduction to an Ojibwa world.* Washington, D.C.: University Press of America.

Paper, J. 1980. From shaman to mystic in Ojibwa religion. *Studies in Religion* 9:185–99.

1983. The post-contact origin of an American Indian high god: The suppression of feminine spirituality. *American Indian Quarterly* 7:1–24.

1989. *Offering smoke: The sacred pipe and native American religion.* Moscow, Idaho: University of Idaho Press.

Parezo, N.J. 1983. *Navajo sandpainting: From religious act to commercial art.* Tucson: University of Arizona Press.

Parks, D.R. and W.R. Wedel. 1985. Pawnee geography, historical and sacred. *Great Plains Quarterly* 5:143–76.

Perry, R.J. 1983. Proto-Athapascan culture: The use of ethnographic reconstruction. *American Ethnologist* 10:715–33.

Porterfield, A. 1987. Shamanism: A pscychosocial definition. *Journal of the American Academy of Religion* 55:721–39.

Powers, M.N. 1980. Menstruation and reproduction: An Oglala case. *Signs* 6:54–63.

1986. *Oglala women.* Chicago: University of Chicago Press.

Powers, W.K. 1982. *Yuwipi: Vision and experience in Oglala ritual.* Lincoln: University of Nebraska Press.

1986. *Sacred language: The nature of supernatural discourse in Lakota.* Norman: University of Oklahoma Press.

Preston, R.J. 1980. The witiko: Algonkian knowledge and whiteman knowledge. In *Manlike Monsters on Trials,* eds. M. Halpin and M. Ames. 111–31. Vancouver: University of British Columbia Press.

Ridington, R. 1987. Omaha survival: A vanishing Indian tribe that would not vanish. *American Indian Quarterly* 11:37–51.

1988a. Images of cosmic union: Omaha ceremonies of renewal. *History of Religions* 28:135–50.

1988b. Knowledge, power, and the individual in subarctic hunting societies. *American Anthropologist* 90:98–110.

Rooth, A.B., ed. 1980. The Alaska seminar. *Studia Ethnologia Upsaliensia* 6. Uppsala.

Savard, R. 1985. *La voix des autres.* Montréal: Éditions de l'Hexagone.

Schenk, A. and H. Kalweit, eds. 1987. *Heilung des Wissens.* Munich: Wilhelm Goldmann Verlag.

Schlesier, K.H. 1987. *The wolves of heaven: Cheyenne shamanism, ceremonies, and prehistoric origins.* Norman: University of Oklahoma Press.

Seguin, M., ed. 1984. *The Tsimshian: Images of the past, views for the present.* Vancouver: University of British Columbia Press.

Simmons, W.S. 1981. Cultural bias in the New England Puritans' perception of Indians. *The William and Mary Quarterly.* 38:56–72.

1983. Red yankees: Narragansett conversion in the Great Awakening. *American Ethnologist* 10:253–71.

1986. *Spirit of the New England tribes: Indian history and folklore, 1620–1984.* Hanover: University Press of New England.

Siskin, E.E. 1983. *Washo shamans and peyotists: Religious conflict in an American Indian tribe.* Salt Lake City: University of Utah Press.

Springer, J.W. 1981. An ethnohistoric study of the smoking complex in eastern North America. *Ethnohistory* 28:217–35.

Starkloff, C. 1974. *The people of the center: American Indian religion and Christianity.* New York: Seabury Press.

Steinmetz, P.B. 1970. The relationship between Plains Indian religion and Christianity: A priest's viewpoint. *Plains Anthropologist* 15:83–86.

1980. *Pipe, bible and peyote among the Oglala Lakota.* Stockholm Studies in Comparative Religion 19. Stockholm: Almqvist & Wiksell.

1984. The sacred pipe in American Indian religions. *American Indian Culture and Research Journal* 8:27–80.

Steltenkamp, M.F. 1982. *The sacred vision: Native American religion and its practice today.* New York: Paulist Press.

Stewart, O.C. 1980. The ghost dance. In *Anthropology on the Great Plains,* eds. W.R. Wood and M. Liberty. 179–87. Lincoln: University of Nebraska Press.

1987. *Peyote religion: A history.* Norman: University of Oklahoma Press.

Stewart, O.C. and D.F. Aberle. 1984. *Peyotism in the West.* Salt Lake City: University of Utah Press.

Stocking, G.W., Jr. 1976. Ideas and institutions in American anthropology: Thoughts toward a history of the interwar years. In *Selected Papers from the American Anthropologist 1921–1945,* ed. G.W. Stocking. 1–53. Washington: American Anthropological Association.

Sullivan, L.E. 1982. Multiple levels of religious meaning in culture: A new look at Winnebago sacred texts. *The Canadian Journal of Native Studies* 2:221–47.

Talamantez, I.M. 1982. Dance and ritual in the study of native American religious traditions. *New Scholar* 8:535–49.

Tanner, A. 1979. *Bringing home animals: Religious ideology and mode of production of the Mistassini Cree hunters.* New York: St. Martin's Press.

Tedlock, B. 1983. Zuni sacred theater. *American Indian Quarterly* 7:93–110.

Terrell, J.U. 1979. *The arrow and the cross: A history of the American Indian and the missionaries.* Santa Barbara: Capra Press.

Thayer, J.S. 1980. The berdache of the northern plains: A socioreligious perspective. *Journal of Anthropological Research* 36:287–93.

The Encyclopedia of Religion. 1987. 16 vols. Ed. M. Eliade. New York: Macmillan.

Thompson, S. 1966. *Tales of the North American Indians.* 2nd. edition. Bloomington: Indiana University Press.

Thornton, R. 1986. *We shall live again: The 1870 and 1890 ghost dance movements as demographic revitalization.* Cambridge: Cambridge University Press.

Tooker, E. 1979. *Native North American spirituality of the eastern woodlands: Sacred myths, dreams, visions, speeches, healing formulas, rituals and ceremonials.* New York: Paulist Press.

Turnbough, W. 1979. Calumet ceremonialism as a nativisitic response. *American Antiquity* 44:685–91.

Vander, J. 1986. *Ghost dance songs and religion of a Wind River Shoshone woman.* Monograph Series in Ethnomusicology 4. Los Angeles.

Vecsey, C. 1980. American Indian environmental religions. In *American Indian Environments: Ecological Issues in Native American History,* eds. C. Vecsey and R.W. Venables. 1–37. Syracuse: Syracuse University Press.

1983. *Traditional Ojibwa religion and its historical changes.* Philadelphia: The American Philosophical Society.

1984. Midewiwin myths of origin. In *Papers of the Fifteenth Algonquian Conference,* ed. W. Cowan. 445–67. Carleton University, Ottawa,

1988. *Imagine ourselves richly: Mythic narratives of North American Indians.* New York: Crossroad.

Vertovec, St. 1983. Potlatching and the mythic past: A reevaluation of the traditional northwest coast American Indian complex. *Religion* 13:323–44.

Voget, F.W. 1984. *The Shoshoni-Crow sun dance.* Norman: University of Oklahoma Press.

Walens, S. 1981. *Feasting with cannibals: An essay in Kwakiutl cosmology.* Princeton: Princeton University Press.

Walker, J.R. 1980. *Lakota belief and ritual,* eds. R.J. DeMallie and E.A. Jahner. Lincoln: University of Nebraska Press.

1983. *Lakota myth,* ed. E.A. Jahner. Lincoln: University of Nebraska Press.

Wildhage, W. 1988. *Die Winterzählunger der Oglala.* Wyk: Verlag für Amerikanistik.

Williamson, R.A. 1984. *Living the sky: The cosmos of the American Indian.* Boston: Houghton Mifflin Co.

Wright, B. 1986. Pueblo cultures. *Iconography of Religions* 10/4. Leiden: E.J. Brill.